MW00807485

LEADING LIKE THE SWAMP FOX

LEADING LIKE THE SWAMP FOX

The Leadership Lessons of Francis Marion

KEVIN DOUGHERTY AND STEVEN D. SMITH

CASEMATE

Philadelphia & Oxford

Published in the United States of America and Great Britain in 2022 by
CASEMATE PUBLISHERS
1950 Lawrence Road, Havertown, PA 19083, USA
and
The Old Music Hall, 106–108 Cowley Road, Oxford OX4 1JE, UK

© 2022 Kevin Dougherty and Steven D. Smith

Hardcover Edition: ISBN 978-1-63624-115-9
Digital Edition: ISBN 978-1-63624-116-6

A CIP record for this book is available from the British Library

Printed and bound in the United Kingdom by TJ Books

For a complete list of Casemate titles, please contact:

CASEMATE PUBLISHERS (US)
Telephone (610) 853-9131
Fax (610) 853-9146
Email: casemate@casematepublishers.com
www.casematepublishers.com

CASEMATE PUBLISHERS (UK)
Telephone (01865) 241249
Email: casemate-uk@casematepublishers.co.uk
www.casematepublishers.co.uk

Cover Credit: The Ride of General Marion's Men (Artist Alonzo Chappel, *c.* 1850, courtesy
Minneapolis Institute of Art, Wikimedia commons)

Contents

Foreword   viii
Introduction   xv

Part One: Understanding Francis Marion's Revolutionary War   1
Leadership During the American Revolution   3
The Key Players   26
Campaign Overview   54

Part Two: Leadership Lessons and Vignettes   83
Francis Marion and a Leader's Frame of Reference   85
Francis Marion and the Responsibility of Leadership   97
Francis Marion and the Interpersonal Component of
Leadership   106
Francis Marion and Communicating as a Leader   125
Francis Marion and a Leader's Need to Solve Problems   137
Francis Marion and a Leader's Use of Resources   150
Francis Marion and Leadership's Demand for Stamina and
Resiliency   160
Francis Marion and Growth as a Leader   171

Part Three: Summary   185
Conclusions about Leadership During the Lowcountry
Campaign   187

Epilogue   190
Appendix: Some Reminders of the Lowcountry Campaign   193
Bibliography   202
Notes   210
Index   235

To Francis Marion and the other patriots who gave America its freedom and to those who safeguard it today.

Acknowledgements

The authors would like to thank the following individuals for their assistance in completing this project. First and foremost, the talented production team at Casemate, including Ruth Sheppard, Felicity Goldsack, Megan Yates, and Declan Ingram. What an accommodating and helpful group! Vally M. Sharpe of United Writers Press, Inc. drafted the maps and assisted in image production. James B. Legg assisted in editing and commenting on portions of the manuscript. John Oller allowed us to modify his maps from his excellent biography of Francis Marion. The maps were originally drafted by James B. Legg.

As noted in the Foreword, Samuel K. Fore, Curator of the Harlan Crow Library, was instrumental in getting us together to write this book. Sam is a great friend of ours and quite an expert on the American Revolution himself.

The authors would also like to especially acknowledge the support of their wives and families who went above and beyond their usual significant contributions in order to allow the authors to devote time to this project.

Despite the outstanding editorial assistance of Casemate, any errors or omissions in this book remain the responsibility of the authors.

Foreword

From Kevin Dougherty:
Like most of us, I have had a lifetime of experience being either a leader or a follower or both. I've been a son and a father. A cadet and an army officer. A student and a teacher. A player and a coach. It wasn't until 2014 when I became the assistant commandant for Leadership Programs at The Citadel: The Military College of South Carolina, however, that I began a much more deliberate and systematic study of leadership and, perhaps more significantly, leader development.

The mission of The Citadel is "to educate and develop our students to become principled leaders in all walks of life by instilling the core values of The Citadel in a disciplined and intellectually challenging environment."[1] I contribute to that mission as a member of the Leader Development Council (LDC) by helping design and promulgate the college's Cadet Leader Development Program (LDP) and as the assistant commandant for Leadership Programs by developing, implementing, and integrating many of those aspects of the LDP that fall under the auspices of the commandant of cadets. These include proponency for The Citadel Training Manual which builds on work started by Michael Rosebush at the United States Air Force Academy to provide a practical guide to the exercise of principled leadership, and responsibility for designing and overseeing the Leadership Training Program (LTP) which comprises weekly non–academic credit classes that train specific aspects of leadership tailored to each stage in The Citadel's four-year development model.

In the pursuit of these duties, I would regularly come across anecdotes, observations, articles, and other odds and ends of leadership information that at first seemed rather random. I initially filed them as individual items, but soon various themes began to emerge. An explanation of that evolution follows.

My colleagues at The Citadel come from all the military services and a variety of locations in the civilian sector. They bring with them certain understandings based on these formative experiences. Even our cadets do not report to us as completely blank slates. They too have been shaped by the influences of where they grew up, their families, their extracurricular activities, their socio-economic situations, and their high schools. Then a course I took in social psychology broadened my understanding of bias. I was reminded that there are all types of bias; not just the motivated, fundamental attribution, and self-serving varieties that are often prejudicial, but also the unmotivated biases and bounded rationality that are the result of the inherent simplifications necessary to process ambiguity and the human limitations of gaining and then processing information. In many cases, individuals draw on past experiences to help them deal with these present realities. The importance of these "frames of reference" and the impact they have on how a leader views people, situations, and organizations struck me as something that profoundly affects leader development.

The Citadel has adopted a five-step Citadel Training Model (CTM) of setting expectations, building necessary skills, giving and receiving feedback, following through with consequences, and growing.[2] The second step of CTM is compatible with the skills approach to the study of leadership. The skills approach is a "leader-centered model that stresses the importance of developing particular leadership skills."[3] It "frames leadership as the capabilities (knowledge and skills) that make effective leadership possible."[4] Viewing leadership as a definable set of skills and abilities is very useful to an organization like The Citadel with a mission of leader development, because it means that leadership, like any skill, can be learned, strengthened, honed, improved, and enhanced.[5]

The challenge then becomes identifying the exact traits that distinguish a good leader; a subject I found has generated much discussion, but no clear consensus. One list developed by John Gardner resonated with me; particularly his identification of a "willingness (eagerness) to accept responsibilities" and "skill in dealing with people."[6] Both of these attributes embraced a broad skill set, but because leadership is inherently relational, my efforts to quantify "skill in dealing with people" quickly became unwieldy. To help better get my arms around this skill, I subdivided it into interpersonal relations and communicating.

Then COVID-19 descended upon us. The Citadel faced all the same issues every other college did about delivering education, rescheduling athletic programs, and managing finances, but we had a unique set of challenges when it came to the military part of our program. Drill and ceremony, physical training, inspections, close quarters life in the barracks, formations, the fourthclass (freshman) system, and countless other heretofore routine aspects of The Citadel experience quickly were no longer routine. The organizational process model and the highly refined standard operating procedures that had served us so well in the past became largely irrelevant overnight. In their place emerged an almost unprecedented and seemingly relentless demand for solving one problem after another which convinced me of the criticality of this aspect of leadership.

In addition to being the assistant commandant for Leadership Programs, I often have the privilege of teaching classes as an adjunct professor in our Department of Political Science. My favorite definition of politics is "the process by which decisions are made about the distribution of finite resources." Again, the COVID-19 crisis impacted my thinking as I read stories of how ventilators, government funds, toilet paper, test kits, vaccines, and other finite resources were being distributed. I was particularly struck by the responsibility of executive leaders to make these decisions from a holistic perspective in the wake of demands from various interest groups to make them instead reflect their more narrowly focused priorities. I had learned in the army that the leader's responsibility to accomplish the mission also "includes making the best use of available resources,"[7] and the current environment reminded me of this mandate.

The Citadel is not for everyone and a certain amount of attrition, especially among freshmen faced with the challenges of the fourthclass system, is to be expected. Nonetheless, for both the sake of the school, and the cadet and his or her family, we try to retain every cadet who is willing and able to be successful. When cadets resign, we carefully scrutinize the reason why. There is a standard set of proximate causes that we use to explain withdrawals—financial, medical, inability to adapt, injury, and the like—but the overarching reason in most cases seems to have something to do with a lack of resiliency. My unscientific findings were confirmed by the research done by Dr. Angela Duckworth at the United States Military Academy that found that the combination of passion and perseverance—what she called "grit"—was a much better predictor of cadet success than the traditional yardsticks such as SAT or ACT scores, high-school class rank, and objective measures of physical fitness.[8] I added stamina and resiliency as an organizational category.

Whenever I hear the phrase "leadership development," I am reminded of my doctoral studies in International Development at the University of Southern Mississippi. One of the first concepts we had to come to grips with was what exactly was meant by "development." We were exposed to a variety of definitions and descriptions, but the one that stuck with me was the rather colloquial one that development is "good change."[9] This idea of "good change" is represented in the fifth step of The Citadel Training Model which is growth. Leaders must grow personally, but also ensure growth in the organization and in those under their care.

Frame of reference, responsibility, interpersonal skills, communication, problem-solving, use of resources, stamina and resiliency, and growth. It seemed to me that I now had a pretty good framework for organizing the bits and pieces of leadership information that I had been collecting. The question now was what to do with them?

I have had a long interest in what military history can teach us about leadership and have used the Civil War campaigns of Vicksburg and Charleston as sources for two such studies. One of these is *Military Leadership Lessons of the Charleston Campaign, 1861–1865* (McFarland, 2014). While Charleston's importance during the Civil War was well known to me, I was a latecomer to realizing the pivotal role played by the South Carolina lowcountry in the American Revolution. As I worked to correct this personal deficiency, I was particularly drawn to the contribution of Francis Marion. Reminders of his legacy are readily visible in the Charleston area. Marion Square is a popular downtown greenspace. The Francis Marion National Forest is just north of the city. A copy of the John Blake White painting "General Marion Inviting a British Officer to Share His Meal" for years hung in the building where I work at The Citadel. Intrigued by these and other references, I began to study more about Marion, to include reading Scott Aiken's *The Swamp Fox: Lessons in Leadership from the Partisan Campaigns of Francis Marion.*

While Aiken's excellent book focuses much of its attention on Marion's military tactical decision making, it suggested to me that Marion might also provide the vehicle to illustrate the components of the framework I had developed to organize my own broader thoughts on leadership. Using the structure of *Military Leadership Lessons of the Charleston Campaign, 1861–1865* to get me started, I began work on *Leading like the Swamp Fox: The Leadership Lessons of Francis Marion.*

As I trudged along in fits and starts, I came across a brief article on the subject by Samuel Fore, an old army friend of mine. One thing led to another, and Sam soon connected me with a friend of his, Steven Smith. That was a good day for me.

From Steven D. Smith:
When Sam let me know about Kevin's project, I was immediately interested and intrigued. Although I had been the director of the South Carolina Institute of Archaeology and Anthropology, a research professor and teacher, and principal investigator of numerous archaeological projects, my only formal training in leadership was in Basic Officers' School at Fort Benning, Georgia, back in 1974. Other than that, for me, learning leadership always has been a matter of on-the-job training. After exchanging emails, I was excited about the opportunity to work with Kevin. I figured I might even learn something along the way.

I did know a little about Francis Marion. I have conducted historical and archaeological research on Francis Marion since the early 1990s, published various articles on that research, and eventually wrote my Ph.D. dissertation in 2010 on Marion's partisans. During that time, I have often found myself wondering what made Marion a successful leader. Marion is widely recognized as the consummate partisan-guerrilla tactician by military historians. Literally hundreds of books and articles, both academic and popular, have been published describing his partisan career. I understand that the Department of Defense still studies his tactics. These writings *describe* Marion's tactics and leadership; however, they rarely probe the question, what leadership characteristics made him so successful? Scott Aiken's book, as Kevin noted, is that rare exception.

We can probably rule out his military bearing or appearance. Marion certainly did not fit the Hollywood "John Wayne" image. One of his lieutenants described him as "an ugly, cross, knock-kneed, hook-nosed, son of a b-t-h!"[10] Colonel Henry Lee, a one-time friend of Marion whom we will meet in this book, described Marion thusly:

> General Marion was in stature of the smallest size, thin as well as low. His visage was not pleasing, and his manners not captivating. He was reserved and silent, entering into conversation only when necessary, and then with modesty and good sense.[11]

Another early biographer, William Dobein James, had a similar impression of Marion:

> He was rather below the middle stature of men, lean and swarthy. His body was well set, but his knees and ancles [sic] were badly formed; and he still limped on one leg. He had a contenance [sic] remarkably steady; his nose aquiline, his chin projecting; his forehead was large and high, and his eyes black and piercing.[12]

So, to find an answer we must look beyond Marion's command presence. Perhaps it was his personality. The lieutenant noted above had been AWOL and had just been embarrassed in front of other officers when Marion cut him down with a snide remark. It was, according to biographers Mason Locke Weems and Peter Horry, quite effective in turning the lieutenant into an excellent officer. Still, it shows Marion was not one to suffer fools.

As Lee noted, Marion was reserved and silent; in other words, an introvert. He shared few decisions with his men. According to James, they watched Marion's cook, and if he became busy preparing a meal, they did too, knowing they were likely about to make a long march.[13] Horry also said Marion never "made a speech anywhere, or thanked any Officer for his Services but to Col. Horry once …."[14] So, maybe he was not the inspirational speaker-type either.

Horry did say Marion was "very humane & Merciful"[15] and that fits with his cautious approach to battle, where he rarely risked his men's lives if the odds were against him. As far as we know, he rarely led from the front either, and it is said he never drew his sword. Yet he could be a harsh disciplinarian. His orderly book during the early part of the war indicates he was quite liberal with the whip.[16] He brooked no nonsense in the ranks.

So, what was it about this short, ugly, cautious man that made him perhaps America's finest guerrilla fighter? A man who was loved by his contemporaries and lauded by generations of Americans? We hope this book provides at least a partial answer.

Introduction

Henry St. John, 1st Viscount Bolingbroke, is among those who have repeated the assertion first stated perhaps by Thucydides that "history is philosophy teaching by examples." *Leading like the Swamp Fox: The Leadership Lessons of Francis Marion* is based on this wisdom and is designed to teach leadership by the historical example of Francis Marion.

The book has three parts. Part One is "Understanding Francis Marion's Revolutionary War." The purpose of this section is to establish the historical background and context necessary to appreciate Marion's situation. It begins with a general discussion of the variables that influenced leadership during the American Revolution and then provides an overview of the Southern Campaign with particular emphasis on the lowcountry of South Carolina where Marion was most active. As a convenient reference, it also includes brief biographic sketches of the *dramatis personae* the reader will encounter. The section is written to be a review for those familiar with the history and as a foundation for newcomers. Its goal is to establish a common base of knowledge as a prelude to the book's next section.

Part Two is "Leadership Lessons and Vignettes." Eight different broad leadership categories are addressed, each with a brief explanation of the leadership competency at hand and then an example of that competency as demonstrated by Marion. Each subsection has between four and six such vignettes.

Part Three is a "Summary." It captures some conclusions about how leadership impacted the American Revolution in the Southern Campaign and the South Carolina lowcountry. The Appendix provides some information about how the reader might explore those physical reminders of Marion and his exploits that exist today.

At this point must be noted the difficulty that any author faces in distinguishing between the historic Marion and the mythological Marion. Marion became almost an instant folk-hero to a young country starving for national identity after the American Revolution. America needed heroes to forge an American identity, and Marion's exploits, like those of George Washington, exemplified the leadership qualities valued by the nascent nation. Like Washington, Marion's leadership gained national recognition as a result of early 19th-century iconic biographies authored by Mason Locke Weems, a clergyman and bookseller. In Marion's case, Weems took a memoir of one of Marion's officers, Peter Horry, and turned it into a hagiography full of dramatic scenes, many with obvious embellishment and some of dubious veracity. The resulting *The Life of General Francis Marion* remains in print today and serves as the baseline of much of what has since been written about Marion. When appropriate, we have tried to identify which elements of Marion's conventional story are less credible than others, but we have also allowed ourselves the luxury of using the full litany of primary sources, secondary sources, and folklore associated with Marion to illustrate leadership lessons of Marion and those around him.

Leading like the Swamp Fox: The Leadership Lessons of Francis Marion is designed to appeal to those interested in the American Revolution and to those interested in leadership. It offers Francis Marion as the intersection between those two subjects. If the objective military resources available to the British and the Patriots in South Carolina in 1780 were compared side by side, most observers would have predicted a British victory. Such an analysis, however, fails to account for subjective variables, and one of those, the leadership of Francis Marion, did much to tip the balance in the Patriots' favor.

PART ONE

Understanding Francis Marion's Revolutionary War

Leadership During the American Revolution

Current U.S. Army doctrine describes combat power as "the total means of destructive, constructive, and information capabilities that a military unit or formation can apply at a given time." Combat power has eight elements: leadership, information, mission command, movement and maneuver, intelligence, fires, sustainment, and protection.[1] The first two elements encompass all aspects of military operations and affect all the other elements, while the remaining six are considered "warfighting functions." Key to describing combat power in the 18th century is to understand exactly what capabilities were available to the combatants in North America given the limitations of 18th-century technology, the primeval landscape and distances involved, the level of knowledge, and the political and cultural environment in which they operated. While the modern construct of combat power is asynchronous to the American Revolution, it still provides a useful means of describing the battlefield on which the British and Patriots fought and how that affected leaders like Francis Marion.

Leadership

The U.S. Army defines leadership as "the process of influencing people by providing purpose, direction, and motivation, while operating to accomplish the mission and improve the organization."[2] It is the force multiplier and unifying element to maximize combat power. It is only through leadership that the warfighting functions are executed.

Many historians, perhaps most notably British ones, have been highly critical of British leadership during the American Revolution. They commonly point to the patronage system, whereby men of wealth could purchase a commission, and their rank would be determined by the amount they were able to finance. This is often seen as a reason that British leaders appeared incompetent; a reason given additional credence by both political and military leaders who blamed each other for the loss of the colonies after the war.[3] As noted in the Key Players chapter of this book, it is true that many of the British officers in the Southern Campaign began their career through either purchasing a commission or having a patron do so on their behalf. Charles Cornwallis is an example of an officer who purchased his colonelcy. This system could certainly produce incompetent leadership; however, looking at the British leaders in America overall, many rose through the ranks before the Revolution, and some even had experience in North America before the conflict. As Andrew Jackson O'Shaughnessey notes, British generals in America "had much in common with modern-day career professionals in their dedication and commitment." He explains that "George III and his Cabinet ignored seniority to select the ablest generals …. The men they chose went to great lengths to improve their military skills and knowledge of warfare … they were seasoned veterans who had served in junior commands in Europe and America." By 1780, many who would fight the Southern Campaign had already gained hard-won experience fighting in the northern colonies. It must also be remembered that "the men who lost America were also the men who saved Canada, India, Gibraltar, and the British Caribbean." The widespread purchase of commissions was not, in fact, the cause of British leadership failure.[4]

True, the British leadership made many blunders, but they did not have a monopoly on blunders; the Americans also made poor decisions. Furthermore, the British won many battles, suggesting their leadership had some level of competency. Indeed, most of the classic 18th-century conventional, stand-up battles in the Southern Campaign were won by the British, or they at least held the field after the battle. The British were tactically competent on the battlefield, even if their main tactic was a straight-ahead full-on frontal attack. O'Shaughnessey argues that British strategies "failed not as a result of incompetence and blundering, but because of insufficient resources, unanticipated lack of loyalist support, and the popularity of the Revolution."[5] Where the British did suffer was from a "fractured system of command."[6] Time and distance, and political infighting among the leadership, tore at an efficient, top-down command system.

Perhaps the key difference between the British leadership and the Patriot leadership was that among the Americans there was no professional military corps at the beginning of the conflict. Horatio Gates was one of the few leaders in the Southern Campaign that had come up through the ranks of the British military system. The Americans in the Southern Campaign did, however, have practical military experience, gained by participating in various mid-18th-century conflicts like the French and Indian War before the Revolution. Francis Marion, Thomas Sumter, and Andrew Pickens are examples. At the opening of the conflict, however, the vast majority of what became the American officer corps were civilians, not soldiers.[7] British contempt for the American officer corps can be illustrated in a letter by Sir Guy Carleton describing American prisoners: "You can have no conception what kind of men composed their officers. Of those we took, one major was a blacksmith, another a hatter. Of their captains there was a butcher … a tanner, a shoemaker, a tavernkeeper etc. Yet they all pretended to be gentlemen."[8]

George Washington worked diligently to form a professional officer corps out of what he considered "utterly unprofessional, ill-trained, and above all ill-bred" men.[9] His efforts to purge the army of unqualified officers were made more difficult by the fact that Congress had the right to appoint general officers, while field grade officers were selected by each colony. Nevertheless, by 1780, a professional officer corps in the American Continental Army had been established. As for the American militia, the officer corps was more egalitarian, yet, like the British and American regulars, officers usually came from the wealthier members of civilian society. For instance, in South Carolina, military leadership came from middle class and wealthy citizens who had been elected local officials and militia officers prior to the war and joined provincial congresses when the colonies were debating revolution.

Information

Leaders base their strategic and tactical decisions on information. They must not only obtain, but also manage information. Although British leaders in America were given broad latitude to prosecute war strategy, the British were hindered by the distance between those who made strategic and policy decisions in England and the field officers who were supposed to execute those decisions in North America. Real-time information exchange was impossible. On average, it took a month to travel from North America to England and two months for the return trip. Likewise, the distance between the northern and southern theaters of war was equally time-consuming for both sides. It took a month for a letter to go from Georgia to New Hampshire.[10] By default, British field officers had wide latitude to carry out general policies, which sometimes negatively impacted synchronization. The problem was exacerbated by the fact that there was disagreement in strategy not only between field officers in America, but also within the British Crown in England. Unity of command and objective, two traditional principles of war, were further strained when the British commander in the Southern Campaign, Lord Charles Cornwallis, sought advice from not only the commander of British forces, General Henry Clinton, but also from England.

During the war the Americans held an advantage in the general knowledge of the countryside. In the Southern Campaign this advantage was particularly significant. Although American Colonel Henry Lee lamented "the ignorance of the topography of the country in which we fought,"[11] partisans like Marion, Sumter, and Pickens were fighting on their home ground. Marion especially took advantage of his knowledge of the roads, trails, and river crossings in the northeastern part of South Carolina to both harass and evade the British. The British certainly turned to their Loyalist friends for such knowledge which, for example, led to their ability to find and destroy Marion's camp on Snow's Island.[12] Nevertheless, British leaders generally distrusted Loyalists and often operated in the dark. This distrust was ironic because the British Crown's information provided by Loyalist leaders suggested that there were large enclaves of Loyal citizens in the South who would rise up and join the British regulars once they showed the flag. This information turned out to be false.

Mission Command

Mission command is "related to tasks and systems that develop and integrate those activities enabling a commander to balance the art of command and the science of control in order to integrate the other warfighting functions."[13] It calls for a successful leader to dictate and control the action in any situation, coordinating efforts across the command structure, while delegating decision making to trusted subordinates. It also calls for the leader to influence those beyond the direct command structure to accomplish their goals and objectives.

It was not only the British command structure that was fragmented by the large distances involved in communicating command decisions and by disagreements among the military and political leaders about overall strategy. The Americans too suffered from a lack of top-down mission command structure. Congress lacked the direct control of the colonial governments needed to dictate an overall strategic plan of action. Furthermore, it was simply impossible for either side's top commanders to exercise direct control of the local tactical situation. This situation arguably gave the Americans an advantage since they were on the strategic defensive. The Patriots simply had to survive, while the British had to take coordinated offensive action to destroy the rebellion's formal organization and occupy territory.

Some British commanders and historians have noted that the key to British victory was to find and destroy the Continental Army. They believed this would cause the rebellion to lose confidence and return to the Crown. Indeed, both General Washington in the Northern Theater and General Nathanael Greene in the Southern Theater took great pains to preserve their armies and never commit all their forces to a decisive battle. Nevertheless, because of the lack of overall command control among the Americans, a defeat in a single battle, even a disaster like the battle of Camden, did not dissuade the various colonial governments or militias from continuing the fight. The history of the Southern Campaign strongly suggests that backcountry militias would have carried on the fight regardless of the outcome of any single military disaster on the part of the Continental command.

At the force level—that is at the campaign level, not the overall command level—the British may have held an advantage. The British command structure in the Southern Campaign was clearly known and top-down. Leaders exercised direct and strong control over subordinate actions and detachments. There may have been disagreement within the command structure as to how to carry out orders, but there were clear objectives and no rogue officers. Meanwhile, the Patriots were by necessity more egalitarian in command structure, to the determent of coordinated action. Greene had to deal with insubordination by militia commanders like Sumter, who would not always cooperate with Greene's desires. At the small unit level, idiosyncratic behavior of militiamen thwarted Marion's plans and actions, as they often would not rally when called or stay when needed.

Movement and Maneuver

Movement and maneuver are obviously critical elements in combat power and include the "tasks associated with force projection related to gaining a position of advantage over the enemy."[14] Both sides applied generally the same basic movement and maneuver methods and battlefield tactics because of the limited technology of the fire systems of the 18th century. Broadly speaking, a set-piece open battle would begin with artillery firing at ranges of around 1,000 yards. Both sides would then maneuver units of men in long columns for speed of maneuver and then quickly form lines parallel to the enemy for exchanging fire. Cavalry protected the infantry flanks and looked for an opening to exploit. After one or two volleys of musket fire, one side would charge with the bayonet. In the Southern Campaign, it was usually the British who would charge, such as at the battles of Camden, Cowpens, Guilford Court House, and Hobkirk's Hill. When one side gave way, cavalry exploited the weakness and followed up with swords and handguns.

Learning from the French and Indian War, British leadership modified their battle tactics, breaking away from the rigid linear battle lines typical on European battlefields. In North America, the British opened their ranks and changed from three lines to two. They also adjusted their engagement techniques. The British infantry would often fire only a single general volley and then rush the enemy with their three-sided, 15-inch bayonets fixed to the muzzles of their guns.[15] The battle of Camden is a perfect example of the effectiveness of this tactic. One difference between Patriot and British tactics was that, generally speaking, the British soldier from Europe had been taught to fire at a mass of the enemy, while Americans, having fought against the Native Americans, emphasized aimed fire. British provincials and Loyalist troops, having experienced Indian fighting, would have also been accustomed to aimed fire.

With only a few exceptions, the Americans tended to avoid a slug-fest or decisive battle. Washington and Greene were especially careful not to over-extend their armies, choosing to fall back if the battle situation became unfavorable. They understood the importance of preserving their armies while attritting the British who had difficulties replacing casualties.

In the backcountry forests, the maneuvering of large masses of men was obviously restricted, as was the use of cavalry and artillery. In battle, men preferred to hide behind trees and fire at individual targets. At the battle of King's Mountain, the British formed in lines at the top of King's Mountain, while the Patriots who had surrounded them, charged up the hill firing behind trees. When the British massed and charged, the Patriots retreated down the hill, only to return again and again until the British ranks were thinned and eventually overrun. There, and in partisan skirmishes like those of Marion, the militia was often mounted and rode to battle but fought on foot. This mobility made Marion's partisans difficult to find and engage.

Intelligence

Intelligence involves collecting and analyzing information about the enemy's location, size, and capabilities. It involves reconnaissance, surveillance, and security, and includes any information that might affect operations, such as weather and terrain. Both sides employed spies and gathered information about the enemy using local informants. Operating in their own territory, the Patriots had the intelligence advantage.

The British were usually woefully ignorant of the local terrain and had to rely on local informants.[16] If the local population was not loyal to the Crown, the information was not freely given or trustworthy. Escaped slaves, though, did provide information and were often employed as guides. A notable example was the British capture of Savannah, Georgia, aided by a slave who showed the British a route around the American defenses. The British also employed some Loyalists, like the South Carolina Rangers, who scouted and foraged for them.[17]

Overall, though, in the Southern Campaign, the Patriots were much more efficient in their gathering of information and use of spies. Marion had an extensive network of mounted scouts and spies, and private citizens also provided him with intelligence.[18] Marion was specifically tasked by Greene to "fix some plan for procuring such information and for conveying it to me with all possible dispatch."[19] Marion responded that he needed real money (gold or silver, not paper) to employ spies. He apparently got it, because private citizens in Charleston sympathetic to the Patriot cause plagued the British throughout the war by slipping in and out of the town with intelligence to be passed on to Marion and Greene, including women smuggling messages under their petticoats.[20]

Fires

Current army doctrine uses the word "fires" primarily in the context of indirect fire such as artillery. Such fires can be offensive and defensive in nature.[21] For the purposes of this discussion, "fires" will be considered to include direct as well as indirect weapons systems.

The basic arm of the infantry and cavalry consisted of some variety of a shoulder or hand-fired, muzzle-loading, black powder, smooth-bored, flintlock firearm. The standard arm of the British regular in 1775 was the land pattern, .75-caliber musket, later referred to as the "Brown Bess." It fired a .69-inch, spherical lead ball and had a 42- or 46-inch barrel. Cavalry and mounted infantry were issued even shorter barreled carbines.[22] The only real competition for the British musket was the French "Charleville" musket, a lighter weapon that became the standard arm of the Continental Army when the French entered the war in 1778. It was a .69-caliber weapon that fired a .64-inch spherical lead ball. The French supplied the Americans with over 100,000 stand of arms during the course of the war.

For these muskets, both sides made paper cartridges, consisting of a measure of black powder and a ball wrapped in paper, and carried in a cartridge box. The American Continental cartridge also held three small lead balls called buckshot in addition to the larger ball.[23] Muskets were loaded by opening the tail of the cartridge and using a small amount of powder to prime a pan on the side of the musket, which led to a vent at the breech of the barrel. The rest of the cartridge was rammed down the barrel. When the trigger was pulled, the flintlock hammer, with a flint in its jaws, would fall against an iron frizzen, causing a spark which ignited the powder in the pan and then in the barrel.

The technology had several limitations. Black powder burned inefficiently, and flames and smoke shot out of the barrel and the vent. In battle, it took only a few volleys before the enemy would become hidden behind a screen of smoke. In high humidity or rain, black powder could become moist and useless. Furthermore, after four or five rounds were fired, gun barrels became hot, and black powder residue would become built up in the bore, causing misfires. The solution was to use a ball smaller than the gun bore, but this increased the inaccuracy of the weapon.[24] To make matters worse, the flints used in the flintlock became dull after several fires and had to be adjusted or changed. All this worked against combatants trying to keep up a sustained fire for a long period.

At ranges within 100 yards, muskets were quite lethal, but beyond that, smoothbore weapons rapidly lost velocity and were highly inaccurate. For this reason, linear tactics were usually employed in open battle. Soldiers stood side by side in ranks and fired in volleys at the mass of an enemy who also was standing in close order ranks.

Beyond the standard muskets, there were a variety of shoulder-fired weapons in America prior to the Revolution that were used throughout the war by militia, light infantry, and Native Americans. The most important of these was the rifle. Backcountry settlers and Native Americans found the rifle a superior weapon for hunting and naturally also used it in battle. The grooves, or rifling, in the barrels imparted a spin to the ball, providing stability in flight and making it extremely accurate at 200 to 300 yards. Unfortunately, rifles required a tight fit in the barrel so that the ball was gripped by the grooves, making it more difficult to ram down the barrel as compared to a smoothbore musket. This greatly increased the loading time. Nevertheless, Mathew Spring suggests that historians have downplayed the combat effectiveness of American riflemen, who "were undeniably able to do horrifying execution when employed as auxiliaries to smoothbore-armed troops."[25] Rifles were not mass produced but instead were built individually, and therefore, bore calibers varied, generally from .40 to .65.[26] Each rifleman was required to have a mold to make his own lead shot to fit his rifle's bore size. Within many British, American, and French light infantry units, rifled guns were used to harass their enemy from long distances, prior to engaging the regular forces.

From the late 17th-century, both the English and French mass produced cheaply made, light muskets to sell to the Native Americans. These "trade guns" were ubiquitous on the frontier and no doubt made it to the battlefields of the Revolution. They were generally smooth-bored. These guns varied widely in bore diameter, but usually were between .55- and .62-caliber.[27] Likewise throughout the colonies there were a number of civilian guns called fowlers (shotguns) and fusils (short barreled, light muskets used by officers and non-commissioned officers) which were also smooth-bored muskets. These weapons could fire several sizes of lead balls or small shot called buckshot, swan shot, and bird shot for hunting. Many of Marion's men fired buckshot or swan shot, and because of the shortage of lead, sometimes mixed pewter with the lead. Dutch, German, and even Spanish muskets and rifles added to the variety of weapons seen on the battlefield. There were also flintlock pistols of a variety of sizes and calibers, all smoothbore and with short barrels, that were wildly inaccurate.

There were three types of land-based iron or brass artillery at the time of the American Revolution: guns, howitzers, and mortars.[28] Guns, or cannon, fired their projectiles horizontally or at very low angles and were the most portable. Howitzers were short barreled and able to fire at higher angles than guns. Mortars, the shortest barreled of the four, were used for firing at steep angles but were very heavy and not very portable. Their high angle fire made mortars useful in sieges to fire over walls.

There was a variety of calibers of artillery that could fire iron shot weighing as much as 42 pounds. Cannon were named for the weight of the spherical round shot fired; such as "one-pounder" or "two-pounder."[29] They usually fired either a solid iron ball or case shot, the latter consisting of a can filled with either small iron balls or lead shot (this round later was called canister).

Iron shot was most effective against fortifications and against ships. Because each shot was a single ball, iron shot was not particularly useful against a line of infantry, but its noise and damage to a human body certainly played on an enemy soldier's morale. Lethal at ranges out to 1,000 yards, iron shot was often fired in open battle at long range and in enfilade. Case shot, on the other hand, was quite effective against an infantry line, acting like a large shotgun and causing multiple casualties at a longer distance than a shoulder-fired weapon. For instance, a can of case shot for a six-pounder cannon fired 56 one-and-a-half-ounce iron balls and was extremely effective out to 300 yards.[30] Cannon could also fire iron scrap, called langrage, or even nails in a pinch. Howitzers and mortars usually fired shells, which were hollow iron balls filled with black powder and equipped with a time fuse. When the fuse burned down, the shell exploded into fragments. Although guns of all type were very lethal at long range, these weapons were heavy, and thus were usually mounted on a wheeled carriage. For this reason, mobile units like Marion's partisans usually did not employ cannon in the offense.

The most common gun in the Southern Campaign was the six-pounder field cannon. Both sides used these weapons effectively. Another common gun was the three-pounder "grasshopper" cannon.[31] These small cannon were light and could be packed on horses, or even carried on the shoulders. A cartridge of case shot for a grasshopper had as many as 36 iron balls.[32] Both six- and three-pounder cannon were usually deployed with a battalion of infantry in pairs. An even lighter cannon was the swivel gun which usually fired a one- or two-pound iron shot. These pieces typically did not have a carriage, but instead had a spike, which allowed them to be mounted onto a fixed base such as a tree stump for firing.

Since 18th-century combat was so often close-in and face-to-face, soldiers carried bladed weapons like swords and knives. The most lethal bladed weapon was the socket bayonet, which was attached to the muzzle of the flintlock musket and used with great effectiveness as a thrusting weapon. It was especially common for the British to employ the tactic of closing with the enemy to about 70 yards, firing their muskets, and then charging with fixed bayonets. Other bladed weapons occasionally used included long-handled, iron-tipped weapons such as spears, halberds, and spontoons. These were used by officers and non-commissioned officers in open, classic battle, but were not very useful in frontier battles and skirmishes.

Sustainment

Sustainment is the ability to provide for the army in the field so that it can perform its mission. It is "the tasks and systems that provide support and services to ensure freedom of action, extend operational reach, and prolong endurance."[33] There are three components to sustainment: logistics, personnel services, and health support.

Logistics

In military operations, logistics means planning and executing the process of obtaining and distributing food, forage, ammunition, and other supplies to troops in the field. Although both sides had extreme difficulties providing for their soldiers, perhaps the British had the disadvantage based on three problems. The first was compartmentalized and inefficient organization. At the beginning of the war, there were a dozen different departments that provided administration to the total British army, and three different government departments that were responsible for the transportation and supply of that part of the army in America and the Caribbean.[34] Second, the logistical problems of fighting a war across the Atlantic Ocean compounded all other shortcomings. The government's initial assumption that the army would become relatively self-sufficient proved unrealistic, and the army and navy had to rely on provisions, supplies, and munitions shipped from Britain. This was no small task considering that the army was larger than most cities in America. With an average size of 34,000 men and 4,000 horses, the British army in America consumed 37 tons of food and 38 tons of hay and oats daily.[35] Rum was considered essential and had to be transported from the Caribbean to supply an army that consumed 360,000 gallons per year.[36] As the war went on, increasing numbers of women and children that accompanied the British army also had to be fed, along with slaves, prisoners, and sometimes Native American allies.

The third and most significant problem for the British was that the Americans were very good at harassing and keeping British foraging detachments from obtaining food and forage locally. American partisans in both the northern and southern colonies kept the British from freely foraging beyond their camps and occupied towns. Indeed, the British were largely confined to the major occupied coastal towns. In the Southern Campaign these were Savannah, Georgia; Charleston, South Carolina; and Wilmington, North Carolina. The Americans encouraged privateers to prey on British supply ships. When France and Spain entered the war, it became a global war, increasing the pressure on supply lines and reducing the number of soldiers available for the war in North America as the British attempted to also maintain their colonies elsewhere.

Meanwhile, the Americans had multiple problems of their own. First of all, they had to create a logistical system largely from scratch. Congress was the only government agency that could do the job, but it had no teeth to force the individual colonies to comply. At the beginning of the war, individual colonies competed for food, forage, guns, and ammunition to supply their militias. The colonies also rejected a national tax to fund the new nation's war machine. With no credit, Congress had to turn to private business to finance the war in the first months. Naturally these private companies found ways to skim from the procurements.[37]

Although a Board of War was established in January 1776, it was simply a subcommittee of Congress and not particularly effective. A quartermaster general, in charge of planning marches, selecting campsites, and conducting surveys, and a commissary general, in charge of feeding the army, were established that same month. Before Nathanael Greene took command of the Southern Theater, he was the second quartermaster general from 1778 to 1780 and did much to develop an efficient quartermaster corps. Although as quartermaster he was complicit in making side deals for profit, the war left Greene bankrupt because the loan he guaranteed for John Banks and Company, which supplied the southern army, was never repaid during his lifetime.[38]

Both sides established a standard food ration for their soldiers, but how often the soldiers actually got a full ration is unknown. The daily ration for the British soldier was one pound of beef, one pound of bread or flour, a third of a pint of peas, an ounce of butter or cheese, an ounce of oatmeal, and one and a half gills of rum. The daily ration for the American soldier was either one pound of beef, three quarters of a pound of pork, or one pound of salted fish; one pound of bread or flour; a pint of milk; a quart of spruce beer or cider, and three quarters of a pint of molasses.[39] These rations were low on Vitamins C and A, and the troops suffered the consequences.

In lean times and on the march, men ate what they could forage from the countryside or obtain from the farms they passed. Foraging for food quite likely provided greater variety in soldiers' diets and improved their health. A credit system was developed during the war in which Patriot officers on foraging expeditions would give a certificate to citizens who provided provisions, which were to be honored by the government after the war. These certificates were basically an IOU and were indeed honored by the state governments. The extant stub indents from South Carolina, which summarize the provisions provided and the date, are invaluable for understanding how Marion fed his militia. The most common items recorded were hogs, corn, and corn stalks (to feed cattle and hogs).[40]

Salt was critical for both flavor and as a meat preservative, and also aided in digestion. Before the Revolution, America obtained its salt from the Bahamas. When the war started, these shipments were blocked, and there were shortages throughout the war. In South Carolina, Marion's men produced salt from sea water, and Marion distributed it to his friends and allies.[41] The lack of sufficient salt for meat preservation necessitated that cattle and hogs traveled on the hoof with the army until it was time for them to be slaughtered.

Both armies had to deal with transportation issues. In the 18th century, the main transportation routes were by water. Roads up and down the continent were mere trails, which usually became impassable in bad weather. Bridges were rare, so knowledge of fords and ferries became vital intelligence, and their locations were strategically critical. Because the density of population was greater in the northern colonies, there were more roads in the north than in the south, but neither road system was in any way comparable to those in Europe.

Wagons were in short supply also. The starvation suffered by men of Washington's army at Valley Forge was in large part due to the lack of wagons and wagon masters to get food and forage to them. Congress attempted to establish a wagon department, which failed, and the transport of supplies was left to the merchants who sold the supplies. Wagon masters might get drunk, lighten their loads, or dump their loads for a better offer from another merchant.[42] Wagons required horses and mules, and horses needed as much as 50 pounds of green forage and half as much dry each day. Most of this requirement had to be found locally, and for the British, this meant going beyond their camps where they were harassed by partisans.[43]

Personnel Services

The personnel services component includes functions associated with soldier welfare such as finances, legal, and religious support. Neither side did much in the way of personnel services for their troops. In terms of pay, the British soldier was induced to join for a bounty of £3 and the "King's shilling" (a crown) which often was spent on the first day of enlistment.[44] Once enlisted, the British soldier of the American Revolution was paid eight pence per day (about £2.87 in 21st-century money); however, he had to pay for food, clothing, and for the services of the paymaster and surgeon. In other words, he basically broke even. To actually make any money, a soldier had to hire himself out for odd jobs. There were no barracks, and the soldiers were billeted in private homes and inns. In spite of these difficulties, with high rates of unemployment in the civilian population, soldiering was better than starvation for some young men.[45]

American Continentals were also recruited with bounties that varied throughout the war and among colonies. At the beginning of the war, bounties were only $10.00, but, by 1779, there were increased to as much as $200.00 plus a clothing provision if one served for the duration of the war.[46] Because recruitment did not fill out the ranks, eventually, like the British, the Americans impressed criminals and indentured servants into the ranks, and drafted militia based on state quotas.

Pay also varied, and the American soldier, like his British counterpart, was charged for uniforms and equipment. Out of an annual salary of about $75.00, it was not unusual for a Continental private to receive just $12 after deductions.[47] There were also times when there was no pay whatsoever, which sparked mutinies in the ranks. On the other hand, the government did offer and honor land grants, which spurred the great migration westward after the war. Pensions were also allotted to veterans and their families.

Although both sides had chaplains, religious support was limited. American chaplains were colonels attached to a brigade, and they often addressed the troops during special days, like the entry of the French into the war. The British chaplains were attached to regiments, and a chaplaincy was purchased. American chaplains strove to instill the men with patriotism, discipline, and godliness, while the British chaplains emphasized submission to authorities. Generally, Americans were more religious, or appealed to God more, than their British counterparts, but the German Hessians were especially vocal in their religious zeal, singing psalms in the evening and before battle.[48]

Health Service

Compared to today, 18th-century medical practices were rudimentary. Congress attempted to develop a "Hospital Department," but it was not successful. Doctors and medical facilities were scarce on both sides. Death from a lead ball was not always quick, and the victim could suffer slowly on the battlefield by bleeding out or weeks later from infection. Strokes from bladed weapons like swords created horrific wounds, cutting off limbs or heads. Disease ravaged the ranks.

Both sides relied mainly on regimental surgeons and surgeon mates, men often with little experience.[49] Of the 1,200 physicians who served in the American military, perhaps 100 were qualified doctors with medical degrees.[50] The doctors had few medicines to help their patients. Alcohol and opium were two of the few pain relievers available, and Jesuit's bark, camphor, castor oil, ipecac, sulfur hog's lard, jalap, senna, potassium nitrate, mercuric oxide, and mercurial ointment were common items in the medicine chest. Probes, ball extractors, lancets, splints, saws, tourniquets, suturing needles, and bandages were among the tools of the physician.[51]

Men died on the battlefield of their wounds because those who survived were often too tired after a battle to bring the wounded to a hospital, assuming there was one. Wounded men got to a hospital only if they had friends that would help them. Obviously, the victors assisted their own first, and if the losers left the field, their wounded had less of a chance of making it to a hospital. Officers had a better chance of being carried from the battlefield. Where there was a hospital, it was often just a house or church where the wounded were gathered in the open until they could be looked after by a physician.

Many wounded died waiting their turn or much later of gangrene. Amputation was often the only solution for wounded limbs that might otherwise become infected. The dead were buried by the victors or left on the battlefield to be ravaged by animals and birds. In battles with many casualties, ditches were dug, and the dead thrown in mass graves.

In spite of these horrors, both sides suffered more casualties from disease than in battle. While musket fire accounted for some 60% of battlefield casualties, disease caused perhaps 80 to 90% of the total deaths in the American Revolution.[52] Dysentery, typhus, scurvy, malaria, and smallpox were common causes of non-combat deaths, and their ravages were especially pronounced where soldiers lived in close proximity in unsanitary camps.

From 1775 to 1782, smallpox raged through the North American continent, killing or maiming thousands of Americans, British, and Native Americans. Both sides were susceptible to the epidemic, although British regulars were better off as smallpox was endemic in Europe, and many had been exposed at a young age and by adulthood were immune. Furthermore, the British standard procedure when an outbreak threatened was to inoculate those soldiers who had not had the disease. In America, with a less dense population, and greater distances between dense populations, once the disease entered a localized population the results were devastating.[53] This meant that the majority of American, Loyalist, and Provincial soldiers were not immune. Americans even feared that the British would use smallpox as a biological weapon.

The solution to the smallpox problem for the Americans was either isolation or inoculation. Both were risky and left an army vulnerable. Nevertheless, Washington inoculated his Continental Army in secrecy in 1777. This involved introducing the live virus into an incision and awaiting the results. Patients generally got a mild case of the pox, survived, and were forever immune.

In the Southern Campaign, smallpox was greatly feared among the Patriot militia, who were largely not immune. Many Patriot prisoners of war contracted the disease on prison ships and in the Camden jail. When Greene took charge of the small Continental Army in the Southern Campaign, he had to rely on the militia to fill out the ranks. Most of these men were not immune, but Greene decided against inoculation for the militia because it would take too many resources and weaken the army in the face of the British threat.[54] Marion never had the smallpox, so while he and his men may have been insulted by not being invited into Charleston upon the British abandonment in 1782, he was perfectly happy to miss the festivities. Concerned about an outbreak in the town, he dismissed his men and went home.

While the Americans feared smallpox, the British in the Southern Campaign had to deal with other diseases, especially yellow fever and malaria. American-born Patriots were somewhat inured to these infections, having survived many hot, mosquito-filled summers throughout their lives. The British regular, however, lacked that exposure, and many became sick and died. Cornwallis's army in the Southern Campaign was reduced in size and effectiveness as much by malaria as by combat.[55] The British faced additional health problems as slaves saw the British as a means of obtaining freedom and flocked to the British lines. The British mustered some escaped slaves into the army, but, most were not well-provided for, and smallpox spread throughout the ranks of these new soldiers.

Protection

The protection warfighting function is "the related tasks and systems that preserve the force so the commander can apply maximum combat power to accomplish the mission."[56] It involves securing the leader's forces from disruption and destruction. Such elements as the security of camps and strategic locations, and the construction of defensive positions fall under the protection warfighting function.

Both sides employed similar security methods. These included using scouts to conduct reconnaissance patrols, guards and picket posts beyond the perimeter when encamped, and the use of passwords. On the march, the cavalry scouted ahead, provided early warning, and screened armies from being seen by the enemy's reconnaissance patrols.

Communication security occasionally included the encryption of letters through a system of numbers corresponding to letters or a series of numbers corresponding to the names of commanders.[57] However, there are surprisingly few examples of encryption, and most correspondence between leaders was not coded. Duplicate messages were carried by couriers to ensure that the message made it to the recipient, but this technique also increased the possibility of capture. There are numerous examples of captured correspondence being forwarded to the proper recipient after being read, especially personal letters. Such treatment was considered a point of honor.

Both sides fortified according to European models based largely on the defensive theories made popular by French military engineer Sebastien Le Prestre de Vauban in the 17th century. Vauban was commissioner general of fortification for the French and developed scientific methods and principles for sieging strongholds. He also constructed some of Europe's most formidable defensive works. Although Vauban was not the sole inventor of these methods, he was largely the one who documented them, and his name became synonymous with them. Vauban's fundamentals remained relevant up to World War I.[58] Formal sieges in the Southern Campaign following the principles of Vauban included the sieges of Savannah, Charleston, Ninety Six, and Fort Motte.

American fortification efforts improved as a result of the French entrance into the war, which brought with it access to French and other European engineers. Greene's military engineer in the Southern Campaign was Thaddeus Kosciuszko, who had been quite successful in stopping the British General John Burgoyne's army at Saratoga during their invasion from Canada.[59] An excellent example of a British defensive structure that still stands in South Carolina is the star fort at the Ninety Six National Historic site. The park also has replicated the American siege trenches that followed Vauban's principles.

The star fort, however, is a rare example. More often, American and British field fortifications consisted of digging a trench and using the dirt from the trench to construct a dirt wall, reinforced with logs, which was effective against musket and iron shot. Shapes included triangular, square, and rectangular forts. A notable example is Fort Sullivan, which was built with soft palmetto logs that absorbed iron shot fired against it by the British navy in 1776.

The British often fortified houses as their outposts by digging a ditch and throwing the dirt against a palisade of logs around a house. Beyond the ditch, soldiers cut down trees and placed the tree limbs outward towards the enemy as abatis. Remains of such redoubts are still visible at Camden.

The Americans applied what they had learned about fortifications from the French, the British, and Native Americans during earlier warfare. The most common defensive structure was a palisaded fort, consisting of a wall of adjacent log poles. Blockhouses of logs were also common. Both were effective against musket and rifle fire.

Organizing Combat Power

Leaders organize combat power by force tailoring, task organizing, and mutual support. Force tailoring means determining the best mix of forces and the sequence of their deployment. Task organizing means mixing the correct numbers and composition of the force to be used in a campaign. Mutual support means that units within the force are interconnected so that they are able to assist each other and not be isolated.[60]

Leaders in the American Revolution had limited resources for tailoring their forces. As noted in the "Fires" section, units primarily consisted of infantry, artillery, and cavalry. All three were essential in a set-piece battle, and the usual order of deployment was artillery at long range, infantry during the heart of the battle, and cavalry to either cover a retreat or disperse the enemy infantry that broke. There were also dragoons who rode to battle but fought on foot, and light infantry, who carried short-barreled muskets or rifles.

The concept of tailoring forces can also be viewed through the lens of organization. For the Americans, there were regular forces or Continentals, militia units (citizen soldiers) at the county level, and state troops at the state level. Continentals were the backbone of the American army and were essential to stand up to the British regular forces in full scale battle. The militias were unreliable, often refusing to serve outside of their colony and reluctant to even serve beyond their region. Their terms of enlistment were limited to months, and they came and went without regard to the immediate strategic situation. They were also without standard arms.

In spite of these shortcomings, the militia played an important, perhaps critical, role in the defeat of the British army. As Andrew O'Shaughnessey points out: "the British army was gradually eroded in small-scale skirmishes and expeditions, a process known in the 18th century as *la petite guerre*, that turned the American war into one of attrition, in which the British army was worn down in unconventional warfare against citizen soldiers."[61] The Patriot militia also tied up British regulars that could have been used elsewhere. In a December 1780 letter to Cornwallis, Colonel Nesbit Balfour lamented this reality, writing that "Marion is too formidable to trust so near the boats [at Nelson's Ferry] and stores without something better than militia …."[62] Importantly, Greene, despite not fully trusting the militia, was able to effectively mix regulars and militia to defeat the British. Learning from Daniel Morgan's experience of placing the militia in the front ranks to blunt the British aggressive attacks, the Americans in the Southern Campaign were able to severely damage the British in stand-up battle.

British forces consisted of regulars, Loyalist militias, and provincial units. The British regulars were considered the best in Europe at the time, even though at the continental level they were one of the smallest standing armies in Europe. The provincial units were regularized units of Loyalists formed in and serving in North America, while the Loyalist militias were the same as Patriot militias, organized at the county level. Loyalist militias, however, had much less impact in the Southern Campaign than the Patriot militias did. The Loyalists were good at harassing Patriot militias, raiding Patriot strongholds, and mutually supporting the regulars in battle, but they rarely acted on their own against Continental forces. David Fanning in North Carolina and William Cunningham did cause great trouble for the Patriots.

The Balance

Certainly, in the scientific aspects of combat power, the British seemed to have many advantages. Their leaders tended to have more experience and more formal training. Their technology, equipment, and weaponry were superior, especially early in the war. They had more resources. They were a global power.

Each of those advantages came with a flip side, however. Their leaders often had a frame of reference that did not match perfectly with the current situation. Their technology was designed to support a different tactical situation than what confronted them in the South Carolina backcountry. All their abundant resources required transportation to a distant theater. What was going on in America was just one of their many global obligations.

The Patriots benefited greatly from the "home court advantage." They had access to vast amounts of intelligence. They could gain both sustainment and protection at the local level.

The Patriots also seemed often to excel in the art of combat power. Their leadership was able to tap into the fledgling concept of nationalism that Napoleon would later exploit to even greater effect in the French

Revolution. They used the terrain to tactical advantage in a way that mitigated many technological disadvantages. They learned to endure hardship and do without. They exhibited great flexibility and adaptability.

Perhaps the greatest Patriot advantage lay in the war's objective. The Patriots wanted independence. They did not need to defeat the British. They merely wanted to be left alone, and to accomplish that objective, they only had to convince their enemy that continuing the war was not worth the effort. To that end, Patriot leaders employed the elements of combat power in a way designed more to wear down British will than to defeat British field forces. Among those who exemplified this approach was Francis Marion.

The Key Players

British

Henry Clinton (1730–1795)

It is believed Henry Clinton was born in 1730 to Admiral George Clinton, who was the governor of New York at that time. His cousin and patron was the Duke of Newcastle, Thomas Pelham, who assisted in Henry's career through most of his life. Clinton lived in Manhattan until 1749 when the family returned to England. During the Seven Years' War, he served with gallantry in Germany as an aide-de-camp to Prince Charles of Brunswick and was promoted to colonel. In 1772, Newcastle assisted Clinton in obtaining a seat in Parliament.[1] That same year, Harriet Carter, Clinton's wife of five years, died. The death affected him the rest of his life.

Clinton returned to America in support of General Thomas Gage in 1775 as a major general, but with no command experience. With him were William Howe and John Burgoyne, who together made up a threesome of commanders who would unsuccessfully prosecute the war on behalf of the British. When Clinton arrived in Boston, the Patriots had fortified Breed's Hill on Charlestown Neck. Clinton suggested to Gage that the Americans could be cut off if attacked from the front while he flanked the Americans and landed behind them on the narrow isthmus to the neck. Gage refused Clinton's advice and ordered a frontal attack against the Americans' fortified line, losing about 40 percent of his command.

That fall Clinton became second-in-command to Howe, and in 1776 Clinton was detached in joint command of an expedition to the southern colonies with Admiral Peter Parker. Their objective was to rally the Loyalists in North Carolina, but the campaign proved unsuccessful. Both men returned north, blaming each other for the campaign's failure.

Back north, Clinton resumed his position as second-in-command, and when the New York campaign of 1776 began, he convinced Howe to allow him to land on Long Island and make a long march around Washington's open left flank. It was one of the most successful maneuvers of the British army during the war. Clinton then proposed this same tactic to attack the Americans in New York, but Howe turned him down. Clinton was made garrison commander in New York and continued to bicker with Howe about strategy. Against Clinton's advice, Howe decided to capture Philadelphia, instead of supporting John Burgoyne's on-going invasion from Canada. In October, Clinton moved north on his own to try to support Burgoyne, but Burgoyne surrendered before the two could rendezvous.[2]

After the loss of Burgoyne's army, Howe was relieved of command, and Clinton was given command of the British forces in America in February 1778. The timing was not optimal. With the entry of France into the war, British authorities were much more concerned about preserving the West Indies than defending the colonies. Clinton was ordered to abandon Philadelphia and to detach a third of his command to the Caribbean. It was then that the idea that there were thousands of Loyalists in the south just waiting for support was rekindled in the British government. With that in mind, Clinton sailed south in December 1779.

Clinton arrived off Tybee Island, Georgia at the end of January 1780 and by May had captured Charleston. Leaving Lord Cornwallis in charge of the southern command, Clinton returned north to a host of problems. First, there was the strategic problem of commanding two armies, separated by hundreds of miles, and with France now in the war, Britain no longer had the control of the seas necessary to unite the two theaters. Second, before Clinton left for the northern colonies, he issued his infamous proclamation in South Carolina requiring all paroled rebels to take up arms against their recalcitrant neighbors, a demand which only served to rally the Patriots.

The largest problem, though, was one of achieving some strategic consensus with Lord Cornwallis and Admiral Marriot Arbuthnot. Clinton's strategy to win the war was one of slow, gradual control of the southern colonies one at a time while marching up the coast. Cornwallis was supposed to move northward from South Carolina along the coast, keeping in touch with Clinton and consolidating gains before continuing northward. Clinton planned to send troops into the Chesapeake and establish control there at the same time. Once North Carolina was in hand, Cornwallis could move into Virginia, and then Clinton and Cornwallis would attack Philadelphia. It would be a war of attrition, using Loyalists to assist in holding gains made while the regulars moved on. Unfortunately, Clinton did not trust Arbuthnot or Cornwallis to carry out the plan, and his suspicions would prove well warranted.[3]

Before Clinton could act, a French fleet landed a French army at Newport, Rhode Island, in July 1780. Clinton seemed paralyzed to act, but eventually Arbuthnot bottled up the French fleet in Narragansett Bay. In December, Clinton sent Benedict Arnold to Virginia but replaced him with Major General William Phillips in March 1781. Meanwhile, Cornwallis began a campaign on his own, marching into the interior to root out the rebellion. He kept Clinton largely in the dark throughout the "Race to the Dan" campaign into North Carolina to capture American General Nathanael Greene. After being stunned at Guilford Court House and forced to retreat to Wilmington, Cornwallis informed the surprised Clinton where he was. A month later, before Clinton could tell him otherwise, Cornwallis was marching into Virginia.

Clinton's plans were now destroyed, and the disposition of his troops was a strategic mess, with more troops in the south than in the northern colonies. Throughout the summer, Clinton tried to get Cornwallis to find a suitable naval base in the Chesapeake but at the same time send some of the Virginia detachment back to New York where Clinton felt threatened by Washington and the possibility of a French fleet showing up. Cornwallis decided Yorktown was the best location for such a base and in late summer began to dig in. However, he did not send any troops back to New York. As the situation unfolded, the Americans, with the aid of the French fleet, were able to trap Cornwallis at Yorktown. In October Cornwallis surrendered, effectively ending the American Revolution.

Immediately, Clinton and Cornwallis began a war of words over who was responsible for the failure. The British government largely supported Cornwallis because they favored Cornwallis's offensive war over Clinton's slow war of attrition. As a result, Cornwallis went on to fame in India as Governor General, while Clinton resigned in May 1782. Returning to England, Clinton found that the country held him responsible for Cornwallis's surrender and Clinton lost his seat in Parliament in 1784. At the very end of his life, he was able to recover somewhat, returning to Parliament in 1790. He was promoted to full general in 1793 and appointed governor of Gibraltar in 1794. He died in 1795.[4]

Charles, Earl Cornwallis (1738–1805)

Charles Cornwallis was born in London on December 31, 1738, to a well-connected and established family. His education began at Eton and he matriculated at Clare College, Cambridge, but changed course and took a commission as an ensign in 1756. Desiring a military career, he went to Europe and enrolled in the Turin Military Academy. Like Henry Clinton, Cornwallis gained real military experience in the Seven Years' War, serving first as a volunteer with the Prussians and then as an aide-de-camp to the Marquis of Granby. In May 1761, Cornwallis became a lieutenant colonel of the 12th Regiment of Foot.[5]

At 24, Cornwallis's father died. Cornwallis then became the 2nd Earl Cornwallis and inherited his father's seat in the House of Lords. He married and had two children, and while his wife preferred him to remain home, he purchased a colonelcy in 1766 and took command of the 33rd Regiment of Foot.[6]

Cornwallis's career in the American Revolution began when he volunteered for service in the Americas and became a lieutenant general in the British army in North America in 1776. He came to America commanding 10 regiments as part of the reinforcements sent from Ireland under Sir Peter Parker. He was thus part of the failed attack against Fort Sullivan in Charleston Harbor.

The expedition returned to New York, and Cornwallis commanded the reserves as part of Clinton's masterful flanking of Washington's army on Long Island. Washington got his revenge at Trenton on January 2, 1777, when Cornwallis arrived late with exhausted troops. With Washington across the river, Cornwallis allowed his troops to rest. Washington, however, did not, and with diversionary campfires blazing, he slipped away that evening and attacked the British post at Princeton.[7]

In the Philadelphia campaign, Cornwallis served under General Howe and performed well at Brandywine and Germantown, demonstrating his talent as a battlefield commander. After a short leave back home, he returned to America in 1778, serving under Clinton and commanding the British counterattack at Monmouth. At the end of December, Cornwallis returned home to find his wife dying. When she died, he felt he had to leave England. Returning to America at the end of 1779, he became second-in-command of British forces in North America under Clinton. The pair soon sailed south and began the campaign to subdue the southern colonies. After Charleston fell in May 1780, Clinton returned north, leaving Cornwallis in charge.[8]

This mission started out brilliantly for Cornwallis, and with a pool of talented subordinates like Banastre Tarleton, Nesbit Balfour, and Francis Lord Rawdon, the British soon captured the backcountry villages. On August 16, 1780, Cornwallis destroyed General Horatio Gates's Continental Army at the battle of Camden. Despite a series of Patriot partisan victories through the summer and fall, Cornwallis began to feel that he had secured South Carolina. Though Clinton wanted him to stay close to the coast for support, Cornwallis moved to the interior with plans to move into North Carolina.

In December, General Nathanael Greene arrived to take charge of the Continental forces in the south and would turn out to be Cornwallis's able nemesis. A major blow to the British occurred in January 1781 when Tarleton was soundly defeated by Daniel Morgan at the battle of Cowpens. This defeat thoroughly upset Cornwallis's plans for subduing the southern colonies. From this point on, Cornwallis, who was clearly a superb battle commander, showed he was much less talented at strategic thinking. His anger got the best of him, and he vowed revenge.

Leaving Lord Francis Rawdon in command of the British forces in South Carolina, Cornwallis marched back into North Carolina on a vendetta to find and destroy Morgan and Greene. To move as fast as possible, Cornwallis burned his baggage. For the next month, he chased Greene's army across North Carolina, always one step behind. Greene made it to the safety of the Dan River, and Cornwallis was left with an exhausted army at Hillsborough, North Carolina.

In March, Greene returned to North Carolina, and the two forces met at Guilford Court House in a standup fight, the kind Cornwallis had wanted all along. It was a slug-fest with Greene using a similar deployment to Morgan's at Cowpens, and the British meeting successive lines of militia and then regulars. Cornwallis was technically the winner, but his army suffered heavily, and he was forced to withdraw to British-occupied Wilmington, North Carolina, where he had access to the sea and resupply.

By the time he reached Wilmington, Cornwallis's attitude about his chances of subduing the southern states had radically changed. Still seeking a decisive victory against the Patriots, he began to believe that such an opportunity lay to the north in Virginia. Still, he also knew South Carolina was in peril with Greene's army threatening Rawdon at Camden. Cornwallis's correspondence at this time suggests an internal debate with himself about whether the best course of action lay in Virginia or South Carolina. He prepared for both, writing the garrison commander in Charleston to be ready to send transport vessels to Wilmington in case Cornwallis decided to return to South Carolina. According to historian John Buchanan, however, Cornwallis's mind was always toward Virginia. Indeed, Cornwallis began to march there at the end of April.[9]

Once Cornwallis was in Virginia, Clinton, who had heard little from his subordinate, reluctantly accepted Cornwallis's presence in the Chesapeake as a *fait accompli*. After all, Clinton too wanted a presence and a naval base in the Chesapeake and back in December 1780 had dispatched an army there under Benedict Arnold, replacing him with Major General William Phillips in March 1781.

Although Clinton and Cornwallis had long been friends, their relationship by this time had become quite rocky. Earlier in the war, Cornwallis had relayed to Howe an indiscreet comment Clinton had made about Howe. Before leaving for England after being relieved of command, Howe confronted a deeply embarrassed Clinton. Although Clinton and Cornwallis reconciled, the incident undoubtedly contributed to Clinton's mistrust of Cornwallis when he left Cornwallis behind in South Carolina. Indeed, Clinton had every right to mistrust Cornwallis, as he ignored Clinton's orders and had also been corresponding with government authorities in London over Clinton's head. Now with Cornwallis in Virginia and taking command of the late General Phillips's detachment, Clinton requested that Cornwallis send him reinforcements and find a suitable harbor for the British fleet. The former request Clinton later retracted. Meanwhile, Cornwallis, more conflicted than ever, wanted to return to South Carolina. Through the summer the two exchanged letters, bickering about what to do, while Cornwallis sought an appropriate harbor. Eventually, he settled on Yorktown.[10]

By that time though, it was August and constructing defensive works in the hot summer sun proved difficult. In early September, the British learned that Washington was marching south, and a French fleet soon appeared. A sea battle off-shore between the British and French sent the British fleet back to New York as the combined land forces of Americans and French closed in and began a formal siege of Yorktown. Trapped, Cornwallis surrendered on October 19, 1781.[11]

Ultimately, it was Cornwallis who came out of the American rebellion untarnished. Returning to England on parole, Cornwallis was greeted as a hero, and the blame for the surrender was placed on Clinton. Rancor and debate between them continued until Clinton's death, and while Clinton's reputation was ruined, Cornwallis went on to greater fame as Governor General of India in 1786 and then Lord Lieutenant of Ireland in 1797. He returned to India in 1805 as Governor General and died that same year.[12]

Robert McLeroth (dates of birth and death unknown)

Robert McLeroth was from Argyll, Scotland, and became a captain in the 64th Regiment in 1766. He arrived in America in 1768, well before the American Revolution. He was promoted to major in 1776 and commanded the regiment. He was at the battle of Brandywine, where he was wounded. He participated in the capture of Charleston in 1780 and was part of the garrison afterward. In late 1780, he was placed in command of a detachment to occupy Kingstree, South Carolina, which was in the heart of the region where Marion operated. Fearing Marion might attack, McLeroth remained in the area only briefly before retreating to the Santee River and camping at Thomas Sumter's plantation where McLeroth was reinforced.[13]

Now stronger, McLeroth and his 64th were ordered to escort 200 raw recruits to Camden, South Carolina. On the march, Marion ambushed McLeroth at Halfway Swamp. McLeroth fell back to a strong position, preparing the scene for a classic legend that surrounds Marion. McLeroth reportedly challenged Marion to a fair fight in an open field. Marion countered by offering to fight a duel of 20 men each. The challenge was accepted but after the lines formed up and moved forward, the British fell back when the two sides were around 100 yards apart. That night McLeroth left his fires burning and slipped away. Historian John Oller notes that the story of the duel may well be a fabrication, as it makes little sense that Marion would have accepted such a deal.[14]

Both the Americans and British recognized McLeroth's benevolence toward the enemy. Marion biographer William Dobein James called McLeroth "the most humane of all the officers in the British army." Cornwallis, on the other hand, was quite concerned about McLeroth's ability to act in the best interests of the British army, probably because of that benevolence. Although McLeroth was promoted to lieutenant colonel, he sold his commission in 1782.[15]

Francis Rawdon-Hastings (1754–1826)

Francis Rawdon was born on December 9, 1754, attended Harrow, and matriculated but did not attend Oxford. He was the oldest son of John, Baron Rawdon by his second wife, Lady Elizabeth Hastings. Rawdon's military career began as an ensign in the 15th Regiment of Foot in 1771 and as a result of the opportunities posed by the American Revolution, he rose rapidly through the ranks.

Rawdon was appointed lieutenant of the 5th Foot in 1773 and came to America. He was recognized for gallantry at the battle of Bunker Hill and also participated in the battles of Brooklyn, White Plains, and Forts Washington and Clinton. On June 15, 1778, he was made a lieutenant colonel.[16]

In 1778 Rawdon took command of the Volunteers of Ireland, a provincial unit, in Philadelphia. When Clinton moved south in 1780, Rawdon came with him and participated in the siege of Charleston. Rawdon was detached to Camden immediately after Charleston fell, and in the battle of Camden, he commanded the British left, which included his Volunteers of Ireland.

Rawdon was left in command of British field forces in South Carolina when Cornwallis marched north into North Carolina in late January 1781 in an attempt to catch the American army under General Nathanael Greene. Rawdon had a daunting challenge in holding onto the South Carolina interior against numerous partisan militias including Francis Marion, Thomas Sumter, and Andrew Pickens. Then in April, Greene and his Continental Army returned to South Carolina, and Rawdon lost the colony. While Greene kept Rawdon busy at Camden, Marion and Sumter struck the British posts between Camden and Charleston. Rawdon fought well at the battle of Hobkirk's Hill, just north of Camden, but it was really a last desperate attempt to hold on before abandoning the village on May 10, 1781, and falling back to Moncks Corner. His last hurrah came when, after obtaining reinforcements, Rawdon marched to the relief of Ninety Six in the hot summer of 1781. Although he was able to save the garrison from Greene's siege, Rawdon gave orders for the town to be burned and the post abandoned, and then he returned to the coast.

Rawdon had been ill on several occasions during the Southern Campaign and eventually was forced to resign and return to England late that summer. He went on to a long and sterling career, continuing to rise in the ranks until he eventually reached general. In 1790, honoring his uncle's will, Rawdon added the surname Hastings and in 1793 became the second Earl of Moira. He served some 32 years as a politician, being elected to the Irish House of Commons and the

British House of Lords. He married Flora, Countess of Loudoun, in 1804 and they had six children. He was invested with the Order of the Garter in 1812 and later that year was appointed Governor General of Bengal and commander of all British forces in India. He successfully carried out three separate wars while in India and was created the Marquess of Hastings in 1817. Rawdon ended his career as governor of Malta in 1824, dying two years later.[17]

Banastre Tarleton (1754–1833)

Sir Banastre Tarleton was born on August 21, 1754, in Liverpool and was educated there and at Oxford. On April 20, 1775, a commission as a cornet was purchased for him in the King's Dragoons. He volunteered for service in North America and was among the reinforcements who joined General Henry Clinton off Cape Fear, North Carolina under Cornwallis in 1776. Tarleton participated in the failed attack on Fort Sullivan and followed Clinton to New York afterward.

In the New York campaign, Tarleton served in the cavalry and participated in the battle of White Plains and the captures of Forts Washington and Lee. In a daring raid, he captured General Charles Henry Lee. Tarleton also participated in the battles of Brandywine and Germantown in 1777. He was promoted to captain in January 1778. His service soon caught the eye of Clinton, and he was given command of the British Legion with the title of commandant lieutenant colonel and promoted to brevet major in the British service in August of 1779. Tarleton was one of the few British officers that rose through the ranks due largely to his military accomplishments rather than through the purchase of commissions.[18]

Tarleton returned to the south as part of Clinton's 1780 campaign to capture Charleston. His legion lost most of its horses on the voyage south due to Atlantic storms, but he quickly remounted by capturing Patriot horses at skirmishes outside of Charleston at Moncks Corner, Biggin Bridge, and Lenud's Ferry.

After the fall of Charleston, the British quickly marched into the interior to capture backcountry villages. It was at this time that Tarleton gained his reputation as a bloody butcher. As Cornwallis drove to overtake a detachment of continental soldiers under Colonel Abraham Buford that Cornwallis thought included South Carolina Governor John Rutledge, he detached Tarleton with some 40 men of the 17th Dragoons, 130 horsemen, and 100 mounted infantry with an artillery piece to dash ahead. Tarleton began a forced march and through relentless pursuit caught up to Buford on May 29, 1780, at the Waxhaws near the South Carolina-North Carolina line.

When his demand for surrender was refused, Tarleton divided his force into three detachments and attacked Buford's front and flanks. In the course of the battle, Tarleton's horse was shot, and although he was unhurt, Tarleton's men thought he had been killed. In their anger, they began hacking at the Americans who were trying to surrender. Many claimed afterwards it was a massacre, and certainly the casualties were decidedly one-sided; the Americans losing 316, most of those wounded or killed, while Tarleton admits to 17 men killed and wounded. Whether it was a massacre or not, it was perceived as such by the Patriots. "Tarleton's quarter," and "Bloody Ban" became Patriot rallying cries.[19]

One thing is clear: Tarleton was an aggressive battle commander who believed in seeking the enemy and immediately attacking like a bulldog. This worked well when he commanded at the battle of Camden in August 1780. There, Cornwallis let loose the legion when the Patriots' left flank gave way. Tarleton's men cut up the fleeing militia, turning and attacking the rear of the right flank of the Continental line. Then they charged up the road and chased the American baggage and fleeing soldiers for some 22 miles to Hanging Rock, hacking men all the way. The legion also did its work well at Fishing Creek two days later, surprising Thomas Sumter. However, it was less effective at the battle of Blackstock's on September 20, 1780, and Tarleton's failure to do any reconnaissance before attacking cost him dearly at the battle of Cowpens in January 1781 when he was soundly defeated by General Daniel Morgan. In the Race to the Dan, Tarleton performed well at Torrence's Tavern and at Guilford Court House. He was with Cornwallis when Cornwallis marched to Virginia and was among those who surrendered at Yorktown in October 1781.

Returning to England in January 1782, Tarleton was welcomed as a hero. He was created a baronet in 1815 and was active in politics and a member of Parliament for Liverpool. He married Susan Priscilla Bertie in 1798, but the couple had no children.[20] He died in 1833.

John Watson (1748–1826)

John Watson was born in London and became a captain in the 3rd Regiment of Foot Guards (Scots Guards), which "carried with it a lt colonelcy." He came to America in 1777 and commanded the light company of the Brigade of Guards. He was an aide-de-camp to General Henry Clinton in the siege of Charleston in 1780 but returned to New York after the town was captured. Returning to South Carolina in 1781 with General Alexander Leslie's reinforcement of General Charles Cornwallis, Watson was placed in command of a corps of provincial light infantry. He was not liked by the British command, including Cornwallis, who considered him a "plague."[21]

Watson was given command of the region encompassing the northeastern part of South Carolina, with around 500 men. As a result, his main nemesis would be Francis Marion. To help control his territory, Watson constructed a palisaded fort on top of an Indian mound near the Santee River and named it Fort Watson.

In March, Lord Francis Rawdon ordered Watson to get at Marion and his depot on Snow's Island. For the next few weeks, Watson marched toward Snow's Island but was continually harassed by Marion in what has become known as the "Bridges Campaign." Eventually, Watson was forced to retreat to Georgetown to rest and refit after Marion's battering. Watson later emerged from Georgetown to attack Marion on the Pee Dee above Snow's Island but had to retreat again upon learning that General Nathanael Greene had reentered the state.[22]

Lord Rawdon then ordered Watson to join him to help defend Camden. Watson was able to elude Marion and Henry Lee and make his way to Camden, but missed the battle of Hobkirk's Hill. He was recalled to New York in June 1781. After the war, he rose to the rank of general but never saw active service.[23]

Patriot

Horatio Gates (1727 or 1728–1806)

His disastrous defeat at the battle of Camden on August 16, 1781, has rendered General Horatio Gates a tarnished figure in the history of the American Revolution. Born in England of relatively modest parents, he gained a commission as an ensign in the 20th Regiment in 1745 from Charles Powlett, third Duke of Bolton. That same year Gates was appointed a lieutenant in a regiment that the Duke was forming. Gates did well and in 1749 came to Halifax as an aide-de-camp to Colonel Edward Cornwallis, uncle of Lord Charles Cornwallis. Gates returned to England in 1754, but finding few promising prospects there, he went back to Halifax.[24]

Gates's opportunity for fame came with the Seven Years' War. A commission as captain came open in the 4th Regiment of Foot, and Gates was recommended by Edward Cornwallis. Gates was able to negotiate a down payment and pay the rest on credit and was able to marry Elizabeth Phillips. He joined Major General Edward Braddock and was in the front of Braddock's column on the 1755 expedition to Fort Duquesne. When Braddock was ambushed, Gates took a ball to the chest and was thought to be dead. However, Private Francis Penfold rescued him.

The years between the wars were frustrating and full of sorrow for Gates. His father died, his expected appointment to major in New York was filled by another, and he got into a spat with Edward Cornwallis's wife, which ended the patronage of Cornwallis. Back in England, Gates sold his commission in 1769 and looked to possibilities in India.

Things did not get better, however, and Gates decided to return to America in 1772. He settled in western Virginia, purchasing 659 acres on the Potomac River. When he heard about the battle of Lexington and Concord in 1775, he quickly rode to Mount Vernon to offer his services to George Washington, who he had first met in Braddock's army. Once Washington was appointed commander in chief, he recommended Gates for a commission.

On June 21, 1775, Gates was commissioned a brigadier general and ordered to organize the Continental Army. The Americans were no doubt pleased to have a trained British officer among their officer corps. In 1776, he became a major general and at Fort Ticonderoga reorganized the defeated American army that had failed in its attempt to capture Quebec.

Gates was given command of the northern army in August 1777. By that time, British General John Burgoyne's invasion force was driving south from Canada and threatening Albany, New York. As historian John Buchanan noted, Gates was at the right place at the right time. With two excellent battle commanders under him, Daniel Morgan and Benedict Arnold, Gates wisely stayed in camp, patiently waiting for Burgoyne to come to him and then letting Morgan and Arnold handle the battle. The surrender of the British at Saratoga was the highlight of Gates's career and is widely acknowledged as the turning point of the Revolution.[25]

With this victory, whispers began circulating that Gates, the "Hero of Saratoga," should replace George Washington as commander-in-chief. There developed a pro-Gates faction and a pro-Washington faction among the officer corps and Congress. General Thomas Conway led the pro-Gates faction, and despite the efforts of what historians have grandly styled the "Conway Cabal," Washington remained in command.[26]

Congress, then appointed Gates President of the Board of War, and in 1778 he was ordered to mount an expedition against the Iroquois. Gates procrastinated until 1779, when he asked Washington permission to return home. His leave granted, Gates began to lobby for the command of the Southern Theater. On June 13, 1780, Congress, over the protests of Washington, gave Gates that command. General Charles Lee warned him to "beware of exchanging his Northern laurels for Southern willows."[27]

On July 25, 1780, Gates arrived at Cox's Mill (Buffalo Ford) where the remnants of the southern command were encamped after the fall of Charleston. Just two days later, the Patriots were on the march to Camden, South Carolina to face the British detachment there. The march route was through land without forage or food, and the army suffered greatly. Francis Marion and about 20 Patriots joined Gates on the march.

Gates's strung-out army eventually arrived at Rugeley's Mill, 13 miles north of Camden on August 15. Most were militia from North Carolina and Virginia. Meanwhile Gates found a camp closer to Camden, and the next evening, his army marched for Saunders Creek. Marion and his men were detached southward to command the Williamsburg militia. Unfortunately, British General Lord Charles Cornwallis had been alerted to Gates's arrival and at that same time marched for Gates's camp at Rugeley's along the same road that Gates was on. The two armies crashed into each other around 2:00am on August 16.

The battle of Camden the next morning proved to be the "southern willows" of which Lee had warned. The battle was a disaster for the Patriots, and Gates's performance ruined his reputation. He attempted to rally the militia, but was caught up in the swarm of running men and carried along back to Rugeley's. Sometime in that retreat, Gates decided that his army was lost and simply continued riding north, first to Charlotte and then as far as Hillsborough, North Carolina, leaving behind the remnants of the army.

At Hillsborough, Gates wrote his battle report and worked to rebuild the southern command. In early October, Congress gave Washington the authority to name a successor to Gates, and Washington appointed Nathanael Greene. Gates went home to await his fate. Congress voted a court of inquiry, but it never convened. Gates was invited to rejoin the army and did so at its Newburg, New York camp. In March of 1783, he retired for good. His wife died that June, and Gates descended into the lowest point in his life.

Slowly Gates recovered, marrying again in 1786, and taking an interest in politics. He was elected to a term in the New York legislature in 1800 and worked hard to restore his reputation. Among his supporters was Nathanael Greene, who ultimately defended Gates's battle plan.[28]

Nathanael Greene (1742–1786)

Nathanael Greene, one of the most underappreciated American generals of the Revolution, was born in Potowomut (Warwick), Rhode Island, to a prosperous Quaker family. His devout father owned a grist and sawmill, warehouse, ironworks, wharf, dam, forge, and small coastal vessel. Greene was an avid reader, and his private collection of books included military writings. As an adult, he settled on a career as a forge-master and merchant. After his father died, Greene's attendance at Friends meetings dropped off, and eventually he withdrew from the Society after being suspended. Greene's first encounter with the British was on February 17, 1772, when the British navy seized a sloop owned by Greene's company for smuggling rum and brown sugar while attempting to avoid the British sugar tax.

The year of 1774 was one of mixed blessings for Greene. He found and married his lifelong partner, Catherine "Caty" Littlefield, and in October he was instrumental in forming a militia company. However, he was mortified that when officers were chosen, his name was rejected, probably because he had limped from childhood. Despite the embarrassment, he joined the ranks as a private. In an amazing turn of events, after Lexington and Concord, Rhode Island sent an "Army of Observation" to Boston, and Greene was made commander and a brigadier general. How Greene went from private to general in a year poses what historian John Buchanan deems "an intriguing historical question." "What matters is that the Rhode Island Assembly, for whatever reason," Buchanan notes, "had chosen most wisely."[29]

Greene quickly became a valuable member of George Washington's councils of war. Congress made Greene a brigadier general in the Continental Army. He commanded the forces on Long Island but was absent during the battle due to sickness. He rallied to the front at Harlem Heights, but unwisely insisted that Fort Washington be held. When it fell, Greene was crushed. He led one of the American columns at Trenton and performed admirably at the battle of Princeton. He may have saved the army at the battle of Brandywine, thwarting a British flank attack. He conducted an orderly retreat at Germantown.[30] With each battle, Washington's confidence in him and their friendship grew.

Then in March 1778, after much resistance, Greene accepted the position of quartermaster general. Under difficult conditions he did an excellent job, establishing a transportation system and field depots, and clothing the soldiers. Despite being an able staff officer, he resigned as quartermaster in August 1780 after sharply criticizing Congress. When Horatio Gates lost the battle of Camden, Washington, in one of his wisest decisions, chose Greene to command the new southern army.

The southern Continental Army was in poor shape when Greene arrived, and one of his first steps was to introduce himself to Francis Marion and Thomas Sumter, asking for their support. Marion and his spies were tasked to act as Greene's eyes in the lowcountry. Then, in a most daring step, Greene divided his army, sending Daniel Morgan into the backcountry to threaten Ninety Six, while Greene marched into South Carolina and camped along the upper Pee Dee River. Part of this decision was tactical, to force the British out of their posts, and the other was logistical, as it made it easier to feed the army.[31]

Morgan's maneuver led British General Cornwallis to detach Colonel Banastre Tarleton to defend Ninety Six. Tarleton caught up with Morgan at Cowpens, South Carolina in January 1781 and fell into Morgan's trap of multiple defensive lines and was defeated. A furious Cornwallis moved north into North Carolina to try to capture the retreating Morgan. Morgan and Greene were able to join up and led Cornwallis on a long chase northeastward across the state, until Greene was able to get across the Dan River to safety.

Greene rested and refitted, and then returned to North Carolina, where he next met Cornwallis at Guilford Court House. Cornwallis won the bloody slug-fest, but was so battered that he limped his way to Wilmington, North Carolina, where he had access to resupply from the sea. Later, Cornwallis would move north into Virginia and surrender his army at Yorktown in October 1781.

Greene then turned south, reentered South Carolina, and with the assistance of Marion, Andrew Pickens, and a reluctant Sumter, forced the British back into Charleston by the end of 1781. Greene engaged the British in three major battles, Hobkirk's Hill, the siege of Ninety Six, and Eutaw Springs. Greene technically lost all three battles, but in each, the British lost irreplaceable manpower, allowing Greene to win the strategic battle of attrition. Meanwhile, his militia captains captured British outposts and harassed supply lines. The war dragged on for another year, but for the most part, the British in the south were loosely confined to Charleston, which they abandoned in December 1782.

After the war, Greene was rewarded with a 2,000-acre plantation in Georgia, 12 miles from Savannah, where he settled. South Carolina also gave him a plantation. He struggled with finances, as he had many debts connected with his providing a guaranteed loan for John Banks and Company, which supplied the southern army and had gone bankrupt. Greene died on June 19, 1786 of sunstroke contracted while returning home from Savannah. No doubt his body had been weakened by the war. Congress paid off most of his debts in his honor.[32]

Peter Horry (1743–1815)

Peter Horry was born on March 12, 1743, in Prince George Winyah Parish and was a boyhood friend of Marion's. Horry inherited 475 acres of land from his father, Huguenot rice planter John Horry, and eventually became a wealthy landowner and planter with plantations on Winyah Bay and the Santee River as well as land in the Ninety Six District and a house in Columbia, South Carolina. At the time of his death, Horry owned as many as 116 slaves.

Horry was commissioned a captain on June 12, 1775, and served with Marion in the Second South Carolina Regiment. Horry fought at the battle of Sullivan's Island in June 1776. He rose to the rank of lieutenant colonel in the Continental Army, and in January 1780, he took command of the Fifth South Carolina, with the rank of colonel in the state militia. When the Fifth and other undermanned regiments were consolidated, Horry found himself without a position and was released from active duty.

When Charleston fell in May 1780, Horry went to North Carolina and joined Major General Johann de Kalb's staff as an observer. He joined Marion and returned to South Carolina with Horatio Gates's army. When Marion was detached southward by Gates, Horry came along and become one of Marion's most valuable and trusted officers. His brother Hugh also served with Marion. Late in the war, when Marion attended the legislature at Jacksonborough, he left Horry in command of his brigade.

When General Nathanael Greene created two new battalions of light cavalry, he placed Horry in command of one and Hezekiah Maham in command of the other, commissioning them both as lieutenant colonels. Since their new commissions bore the same date, Horry and Maham often quarreled over rank, and the friction between them contributed to the defeat of Marion's brigade in late February 1782 at Wambaw Bridge. After the two regiments were consolidated under Maham, Horry was appointed commandant at the important port of Georgetown. The bickering between Maham and Horry caused a falling-out with Marion, but Marion and Horry reconciled after the war and became close friends again.

One problem that plagued Horry was that he was a poor horseman and not naturally suited to command cavalry. He struck an imposing figure, with red hair and weighing 300 pounds (Marion weighed just 110), but his size made it difficult for him to stay in the saddle of his horse or to swim. Once, while chasing the British after they destroyed Marion's camp on Snow's Island, Horry plunged into Lynches Creek and found himself "never so near the other world in my life" when the swift current caught up his horse and swept him downstream.[33]

Horry also had difficulty speaking in public, and he was especially prone to stammering when he was under stress. According to one story, once when leading his troops in battle Horry had difficulty getting out the word "charge." After several futile attempts, he shouted in exasperation, "Damn it, boys, you, you know what I mean, go on!"[34]

After the war, Horry remained in the militia until 1806. He was also active in politics, representing Prince George Winyah Parish in the state House of Representatives in 1782 and from 1792 to 1794. He sat in the state Senate for the same parish from 1785 to 1787. In 1801, when the legislature established new judicial districts, the state honored his wartime service by creating Horry District.

Horry turned his sizable collection of war documents and letters over to Mason Locke "Parson" Weems, who had recently finished a popular and fanciful biography of George Washington. Using similar literary liberalities, Weems wrote the *Life of Marion* in 1809, but Horry was so vexed by Weems's fictions that he disassociated himself from the work. "You have carved and mutilated it with so many erroneous statements that your embellishments, observations and remarks must necessarily be erroneous as proceeding from false grounds," Horry complained to Weems. "Most certainly, 'tis not my history but your romance." Horry died in Columbia in 1815 and is buried at Trinity (Episcopal) Church.[35]

Henry Lee (1756–1818)

Henry Lee, known as "Light Horse Harry," was born into the famous Lee family in Leesylvania, Virginia in 1756. He began his military career in 1776 as a captain in the Fifth Troop of Light Horse of the Virginia State Troops, which soon was incorporated in the First Continental Light Dragoons in George Washington's Continental Army. In January 1778, Lee was surprised by British Colonel Banastre Tarleton at Spread Eagle Tavern, near Valley Forge, Pennsylvania. Lee acted quickly, foiling the attack by barricading his men in the tavern. Congress recognized this "brave and prudent officer," promoting him to major.[36]

In February 1780, Lee formed a Legionary Corps, and by November of that year the corps had grown to three mounted troops and three dismounted or infantry. Lee's Legion, as it became known, acted as the 18th-century equivalent of a combined arms unit today. Lee continued to perform well in Washington's army in partisan actions and was promoted to lieutenant colonel.

Lee and his legion were detached to General Nathanael Greene's southern command when Greene marched south late in 1780. In January 1781, Greene sent Lee into South Carolina to cooperate with Francis Marion. Lee and Marion quickly formed a bond and a plan to attack the British forces in Georgetown; however, the two-pronged assault was mistimed and failed. Greene soon recalled Lee when, after the British defeat at Cowpens, Lieutenant General Lord Charles Cornwallis made a determined effort to catch and destroy Greene's Continental Army in North Carolina.[37] The Legion played an active role in the Race to the Dan campaign and at its climax at the battle of Guilford Court House on March 15, 1781.

When Cornwallis moved north into Virginia, Greene returned to South Carolina, and Lee was again detached to join Marion with the goal of cutting the British supply lines to the backcountry villages they occupied including Camden, Ninety Six, and Augusta. Together, Marion and Lee laid siege to and captured Fort Watson in April and Fort Motte in May. Lee then moved independently to capture Fort Granby and joined Colonel Andrew Pickens to take the forts at Augusta, Georgia. Rejoining Greene at the siege of Ninety Six in June, Lee and his Legion continued to play a vital role in the Southern Campaign throughout 1781 until, feeling he was not being properly recognized by Greene, Lee resigned in 1782. Eventually, the two men reconciled, but Lee did not return to the army.

Lee's post-war career included representing Virginia in the Continental Congress and as a congressman in the United States House of Representatives. He also served as Governor of Virginia. Successful in war and public service, his skills did not transfer to business acumen. Spending wildly and speculating poorly, he eventually became insolvent. Charles Royster would summarize Lee's life noting that: "Few Americans saw as much of the Revolutionary War as Lee did; few Americans suffered reverses so complete in the years that followed; and few Americans grew so isolated from their country."[38]

Hezekiah Maham (1739–1789)

Hezekiah Maham was born on June 26, 1739, and became a successful planter in St. Stephen's Parish, South Carolina. When the American Revolution began, he was representing St. Stephen's in the Second Provincial Congress. He was active in the militia from early 1776 and was promoted to the rank of major in a state regiment of light dragoons in 1779.

After the fall of Charleston in May 1780, Maham joined Marion's brigade and served as a commander of cavalry. During the siege of Fort Watson in the spring of 1781, it was Maham who suggested constructing a log tower with a platform high enough to allow riflemen to fire into the fort. The success of "Maham's Tower" at Fort Watson was repeated by Patriot forces at the sieges of Augusta and Ninety Six later in the year.

On June 21, 1781, Maham was promoted to the rank of lieutenant colonel and appointed to command a battalion of light cavalry which would come to be known as Maham's Legion. Peter Horry was promoted the same day and given command of another battalion. Historian Ray Talbert reports Horry had "a thin skin and a brooding nature."[39] Historian Samuel Fore writes that Maham was "known for his temper" and once forced a deputy sheriff to eat a summons he was trying to serve on Maham.[40] With such personalities, it is no wonder the pair quarreled over rank.

Maham's cavalry followed Henry Lee's lead in the daring assault across Quinby Bridge in the battle there on July 17, 1781. In mid-November, Maham led a raid on a British hospital at Fairlawn Plantation that captured over 100 prisoners. Friction between Maham and Horry hamstrung the Patriots at Wambaw Bridge in late February 1782 while Marion was away on legislative duties with the state Senate. The rivalry ended in March when the two cavalry units were combined under Maham's command. Unfortunately, Maham soon took ill and withdrew to his plantation, where he was captured and paroled by Tories.[41]

Francis Marion (1732–1795)

Francis Marion was born in 1732 to Gabriel and Esther Marion of Goatfield Plantation, St. John's Parish, Berkeley County, South Carolina.[42] There are few primary sources detailing Marion's youth, and to learn anything about this period, one must rely on his early biographers Peter Horry, Mason Locke Weems, William Dobein James, and William Gilmore Simms, none of whom are particularly reliable.[43]

Marion's immediate ancestors were Huguenots who settled along the Santee River in the late 17th century and became middling planters. His family moved to Winyah Bay, near Georgetown, South Carolina, and in his teens Marion reportedly went to sea. Returning from the West Indies, his ship was rammed by a whale, and after six days in a lifeboat, most of the crew survived and made landfall. With that unhappy experience, Marion returned to plantation life and in 1750 assumed management of the family plantation after his father died and his four brothers and one sister had married.[44]

Many scholars attribute Marion's knowledge of irregular tactics to his experience fighting the Cherokees. Marion is listed on the colonial militia rolls in 1756, but his real exposure to military life came when he joined a provincial cavalry unit as a captain in Governor William Lyttelton's expedition against the Cherokees on October 31, 1759.[45] As a lieutenant in Captain William Moultrie's militia infantry company in 1761, Marion was part of an expedition against the Cherokees led by Lieutenant Colonel James Grant. According to Horry and Weems, near Echoe, North Carolina, Marion was given the dubious honor of leading a charge into a mountain pass that was lined with Cherokees. Twenty-one of his detachment of 30 men were killed. Recent biographer John Oller challenges the veracity of the story, pointing out that Grant's whole army sustained only 11 killed that day, and only one was a Carolina provincial. What can be said with some confidence is that Moultrie described Marion as "an active, brave and hardy soldier."[46]

After the expedition, Marion returned to farming and in 1773 purchased a plantation at Pond Bluff along the Santee River, four miles below Eutaw Springs, South Carolina (the plantation house was inundated in the 1940s to create Lake Marion). By the beginning of the American Revolution, Marion was a well-respected member of plantation society exemplified by his being elected a delegate to South Carolina's first Provincial Congress.

As a provincial and militia officer in the Cherokee wars, Marion would have gained leadership experience in both regular and irregular warfare. From 1775, when he was selected a captain in Moultrie's Second South Carolina Regiment of Infantry, until the fall of Charleston in May 1780, Marion worked his way up through the officer corps, gaining additional experience in conventional 18th-century warfare and tactics. He eventually became a lieutenant colonel and commander of the Second South Carolina Regiment.[47] These South Carolina regiments had been taken into the Continental establishment by that time so that his rank was not as a militia officer but as a lieutenant colonel in the Continental Army, a distinction that would become important later in the war.

Furthering his development as a leader of soldiers, Marion held several independent commands. He was in command at Fort Dorchester in 1775 and commanded the heavy guns on the left side of Fort Sullivan during Britain's first attempt to take Fort Sullivan in 1776. Perhaps his most significant test of leadership up to becoming the Swamp Fox of the Revolution was leading his regiment in an all-out assault against the British-held Spring Hill redoubt in the failed 1779 siege of Savannah, Georgia. After the Americans retreated to Charleston, Marion was left with three regiments at Sheldon, South Carolina, with orders to watch the British in Savannah.

In the spring of 1780, the British moved north from Savannah to capture Charleston. Marion was recalled to Charleston in March where a stroke of good fortune made possible his eventual fame as a partisan warrior. The story goes that Marion was attending a dinner party on Tradd Street in Charleston, and the host locked the doors to keep the drinking going long into the night. Since Marion was reportedly a teetotaler, he decided to escape the party and jumped out of a second-story window, breaking his ankle.[48] As the British surrounded Charleston, Marion and all other supernumerary officers and the physically unfit were sent out of town. Marion hid out in the lowcountry and eventually made his way north with a few followers to join the Second Continental Army then forming in North Carolina.[49]

Congress gave the command of this new Continental Army to Horatio Gates, and initially Marion marched with Gates toward Camden. Soon, however, Marion was detached to take command of the Williamsburg militia camped at Witherspoon's Ferry on Lynches Creek. Arriving on August 17, 1780, the day after Gates's army was decimated at the battle of Camden, Marion began his career as a partisan.[50]

Throughout the fall of 1780, Marion was largely alone in the northeastern part of South Carolina, acting without formal attachment to any government. Using Snow's Island and Britton's Neck as a base of operation, Marion made a series of strikes against British and Loyalist detachments, harassing British forces stationed in Charleston, Georgetown, and Camden. Whenever the British would attempt to concentrate against him, Marion would disperse his men and retreat into North Carolina, only to return and raid again.[51]

In December 1780, General Nathanael Greene arrived in South Carolina with the Third Continental Army. Marion and Greene immediately formed a trusting bond, which would remain in place throughout the war. At the end of the month, South Carolina Governor John Rutledge commissioned Marion as a brigadier general, and the South Carolina militia was officially reestablished.[52]

Marion's link to Greene was short-lived. On January 17, 1781, American Brigadier General Daniel Morgan defeated British Lieutenant Colonel Banastre Tarleton at the battle of Cowpens in the upstate.

The commander of the British forces in South Carolina, Lord Charles Cornwallis, was made furious by the defeat and launched his field forces north into North Carolina to keep Morgan from joining Greene. For the next two months, Cornwallis would attempt to bring Greene to battle, chasing Greene's army across the state, always one step behind.

During Greene's brief stay in South Carolina, he had detached Colonel Henry Lee to join Marion. Together the pair attempted to capture Georgetown, which ended in failure, and shortly thereafter Lee was ordered to join Greene. Marion was again alone in the northeastern part of the state. British forces remaining in South Carolina were able to attack and destroy Marion's depot on Snow's Island in March 1781; however, they were also subjected to a hit and run campaign in which Marion continually battered Colonel John W. T. Watson, forcing him to retreat to Georgetown.[53]

Greene and his Continental Army returned to South Carolina in April and from that point on, the Americans were on the offensive. Lee rejoined Marion, and together they captured British Forts Watson and Motte between Charleston and the backcountry strongholds of Ninety Six and Camden. Marion then moved against Georgetown and finally captured the coastal village, an objective that was always in the back of his mind. That July Marion, under the command of Brigadier General Thomas Sumter, engaged in a fierce battle at Shubrick's Plantation in which Marion was ordered to charge headlong into British forces protected in and behind plantation outbuildings. Marion suffered heavy casualties and vowed never to cooperate with Sumter again.[54] Shortly afterward, Governor Rutledge restored civil government and Sumter resigned. Marion was then promoted to command all the South Carolina militia.[55]

By August 1781, the British had abandoned the backcountry including Augusta, Camden, Winnsboro, and Ninety Six, and were now largely confined to Charleston and the region around the town. At the end of August, Marion ambushed a British foraging party at Parker's Ferry and then joined Greene's main Continental Army. On September 8, 1781, Marion commanded his militia in the front line of the last large set-piece battle in South Carolina at Eutaw Springs. The militia, prone to flee in the face of British regulars, fired 17 rounds before retiring in order.[56]

In January 1782, Marion was elected to the State Senate. Although a great honor, it took Marion out of the field, and, without Marion, the brigade deteriorated. Discipline fell, Colonel Peter Horry assumed command but became ill and left, and Colonel Hezekiah Maham also left the field. Now under the command of Colonel Adam McDonald, the brigade was defeated in a skirmish at Wambaw Bridge.[57]

Learning that the British were out in force, Marion was able to get leave from the General Assembly and return to the brigade. On February 25, he was camped at Tidyman's Plantation, on the south bank of the Santee, when a British force appeared at the plantation lane and formed for battle. Marion was able to form and ordered a charge, but unfortunately his cavalry became disordered, and he had to retreat, losing several men when they attempted to cross the river. British newspapers erroneously reported Marion had drowned.[58]

Marion took post at Wadboo Plantation in July 1782, and on August 29 his camp was attacked by Black Dragoons under Major Thomas Fraser. The attack was defeated in what would be Marion's last battle. When the British abandoned Charleston on December 14, 1782, Marion dismissed his militia and returned to his Santee River plantation.[59]

Marion's plantation and fortune were in ruins at the end of the war. As he achieved state and national acclaim for his services, the state made him commandant of Fort Johnson, providing a modest salary. He married Mary Esther Videau, which restored his wealth, but they had no children. He died on February 27, 1795.[60]

Thomas Sumter (1734–1832)

Thomas Sumter was born on August 14, 1734, in Hanover County, Virginia. His controversial military career began as a provincial soldier in the ranks during the French and Indian War. After promotion to sergeant, he was one of four men selected as peace envoys to the Cherokee towns along the Holston River. Three Cherokee chiefs returned with him, and he escorted them to London. Upon returning, Sumter escorted the chiefs back to the Cherokee towns. When he returned to Virginia, he was imprisoned for debt, but with the help of a friend, Sumter escaped to Long Canes, South Carolina.[61]

Sumter soon settled at a crossroads near Eutaw Springs and Nelson's Ferry along the Santee River and opened a store. There he gained in property and slaves, and in 1767, he married Mary Cantey Jameson. She was a wealthy widow, and the couple settled across the river at her Great Savannah plantation. As the rebellion gathered momentum, Sumter was elected to the First and Second Provincial Congresses.[62]

Sumter participated in many early campaigns and battles, including the Snow campaign in 1775. He was promoted to lieutenant colonel in 1776 and commanded the 6th Regiment at Breech Inlet during the battle of Sullivan's Island on June 28, 1776. He then participated in the campaign against the Cherokees in the summer and fall of 1776.[63]

With the fall of Charleston, Sumter's partisan career as "the Gamecock" began. After the British burned his summer home in the High Hills of the Santee, Sumter was elected "general" by various partisan leaders in the backcountry in recognition of his earlier militia service. During the summer and fall of 1780, Sumter operated much like Francis Marion; both partisans only loosely connected to any formal Rebel government and harassing the British as opportunities appeared.

That summer, Sumter had three engagements against the British: Rocky Mount (July 30, 1780), Hanging Rock (August 6, 1780), and Fishing Creek (August 18, 1780). At Rocky Mount, Sumter attacked but failed to seize a British post. At Hanging Rock, he attacked a British camp and after a fierce battle, had to withdraw when Patriot ammunition ran low. At Fishing Creek, his men were surprised by Colonel Banastre Tarleton, and Sumter barely escaped with his life.[64]

Sumter was made a brigadier general on October 6, 1780. Through the fall of 1780 he engaged the British at Fishdam Ford on November 9 and at Blackstock's Plantation on November 20. Both can be considered Patriot victories, but Blackstock's may have been Sumter's finest hour. There, his men stood firm against veteran British regulars under the command of Tarleton and soundly defeated them. Unfortunately, Sumter was wounded and would be out of commission until early in 1781.[65]

When General Nathanael Greene arrived in South Carolina, he requested the cooperation of the South Carolina militias. Marion coordinated with Greene for the rest of the war, but Sumter was more reluctant and eventually became an irritant to Greene. In February 1781, Sumter embarked on a raid southward from the backcountry. He first attacked the British posts at Fort Granby, then moved farther south and attacked Belleville plantation, and finally he attacked Fort Watson. All three efforts failed.

It was around this time that Sumter proposed, and South Carolina Governor John Rutledge agreed to, a scheme to encourage Patriot enlistments which became known as "Sumter's Law." The plan was to build a war chest to provide new recruits with clothing, arms, horses, salt, and slaves. These commodities would be provided by raiding Loyalist plantations. Greene was reluctant and insisted that the Loyalists receive certificates for their seized property. Marion refused to have any part of the plan.[66]

During the campaign against the British posts in the summer of 1781, Sumter captured the British post at Orangeburg. When Greene moved against Ninety Six, Sumter was ordered to delay a British reinforcement but Sumter again failed. Nonetheless, in July 1781, he convinced Greene to have Marion and Lee serve under him in a raid through the lowcountry to capture Dorchester and the British detachment at Moncks Corner. The Patriots chased and cornered the British at Shubrick's Plantation where, against the advice of Marion and Lee, Sumter ordered Marion and Colonel Thomas Taylor to attack the well-situated British posted behind planation buildings. Marion took heavy casualties, and Marion, Lee, and Taylor never cooperated with Sumter again.[67]

When the state legislature met in Jacksonborough in January 1782, Sumter took his seat with the Senate. He stayed until it adjourned on February 26 and then resigned his commission and returned home. After the war, he served in the General Assembly several times until 1790. He served five terms in the United States House of Representatives between 1789 and 1801, and in the United States Senate from 1801 to 1810. He died on June 1, 1832, one of the last surviving generals of the American Revolution.[68]

Campaign Overview

In broad terms, the state of South Carolina is divided by a fall line that is located between the Piedmont and Sandhill regions. North of the fall line is commonly referred to as the "upstate." At the time of the Revolution, this was also called the "backcountry." South of the fall line is the "lowcountry." The lowcountry includes abundant coastline, rivers, creeks, and swamps. The "lowcountry campaign" of the American Revolution refers to the series of battles fought within this geographic area, but these were part of a larger campaign in the Southern Theater that included Virginia, North Carolina, South Carolina, and Georgia. To understand Marion's exploits, which took place predominantly in the lowcountry of South Carolina, it is necessary to understand the larger Southern Campaign.

From the outbreak of hostilities, the British ministry believed there was a large percentage of the colonial population that remained loyal to the king. All that was needed was support from Britain in the form of British regulars, and these "Loyalists" would rally to the king's defense. Reports and letters from Loyalists in the southern colonies reinforced this notion, and while the overall British strategy was first to subdue the rebellion in New England, the British looked for opportunities to harness those loyal southern citizens, regain the deep southern colonies, and then move north.[1]

One of the many Loyalist strongholds, for example, was in the Ninety Six District in the South Carolina backcountry. The American Provincial Congress sent William Drayton to deal with Loyalist militias gathering in that district. Drayton negotiated a truce in September 1775, but the following month, Patriot militia was surrounded by Loyalists at the village

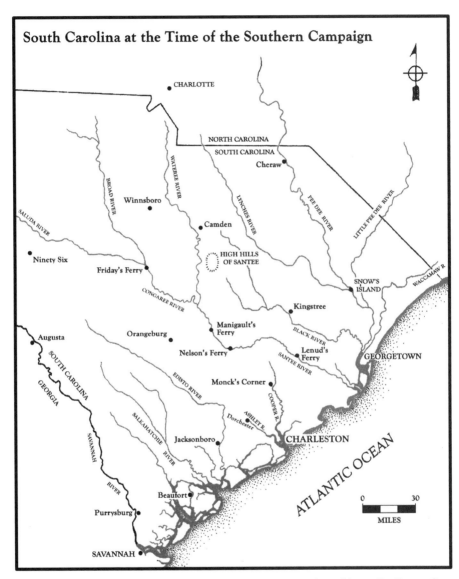

South Carolina at the Time of the Southern Campaign (Adapted by Vally Sharpe from James B. Legg Map, in Oller 2016, xiv).

of Ninety Six. The siege ended with a cease-fire and both sides withdrew only to meet again at the battle of the Great Cane Break.[2] Throughout Georgia and South Carolina, civil war spread.

In North Carolina, Royal Governor Josiah Martin was among those who were convinced that Loyalists support would surge with the arrival of British regulars. As loyal highland Scots gathered at Cross Creek, North Carolina, the British sent Henry Clinton from Boston and Admiral Peter Parker from Ireland to rendezvous off Cape Fear, and support the Loyalists. The Highlanders did not wait, however and marched to Moore's Creek Bridge where they were destroyed in a failed attack against Patriot militia. The defeat set back Loyalist support until the British capture of Charleston in 1780.[3]

Attack on Fort Sullivan

Realizing that their original goal of assisting Loyalists in North Carolina had failed, the British expedition looked for another opportunity and found it at Fort Sullivan in Charleston Harbor. The American Continental Congress also had their eye on the south and had sent Major General Charles Lee to organize resistance. Gaining intelligence that the British fleet had departed Cape Fear, Lee was sure their objective was Charleston. When he arrived in Charleston on June 8, he found that the British were indeed off Charleston Harbor and the city was in a panic. Lee wanted to abandon the fort on Sullivan's Island, across the bay from Charleston. The fort's commander, William Moultrie, and the South Carolina rebel Governor John Rutledge disagreed with Lee and decided to hold their ground.

On June 28, nine British frigates were sent against the fort. Bombs fired from mortars landed in the fort's mud-soaked center and were largely ineffective. Likewise, iron solid shot from British cannon were absorbed by the fort's palmetto log-reinforced walls. Meanwhile, American return fire pounded the British ships, and some, attempting to maneuver to a flanking position, ran aground on a sandbar. The battle continued through the day until at 9:00pm, when the fleet fell back in defeat. During the fight, Clinton's infantry had attempted to support the navy by landing troops north of the fort, but that attack failed also. The Americans lost 12 killed and 26 wounded, the British had 64 killed and 141 wounded, and one frigate sunk. One of the officers in the fort was Francis Marion who commanded the left battery.[4] After the battle, Fort Sullivan was renamed Fort Moultrie in honor of its commander.

British Return to the South

On August 2, 1776, news of the Declaration of Independence arrived in South Carolina, effectively ending hope of reconciliation between England and America. During 1776, some 2,000 South Carolinians enlisted as Continentals or state troops, but as the next year unfolded without a major British threat, enthusiasm for military duty diminished; a problem that continued into 1778. Indeed, no major campaigning occurred in South Carolina in 1777, although it is likely that small parties of Patriots and Loyalists continued to harass each other in the backcountry. For the moment, the backcountry was relatively secure for the Patriots, and a certain amount of complacency set in. Still, South Carolina Continentals, including Marion, remained at their stations in Charleston, training and preparing.

North Carolina remained relatively quiet also, while in Georgia, American Major General Robert Howe led a failed expedition toward British-held St. Augustine early in 1778. The attempt was abandoned in July due to sickness.[5] Perhaps the most significant event of 1778 for the southern colonies happened in Paris, France, where in February, the French signed an alliance with the Americans.

The British ministry, however, was not through with the southern colonies and remained convinced that the population included significant pockets of loyalism. With the northern campaign going nowhere, Lord George Germain looked again to anticipated southern loyalism. He ordered Clinton to mount a campaign southward. Clinton ordered Lieutenant Colonel Archibald Campbell to Georgia. Campbell outflanked Howe and captured Savannah. Howe retreated to Purrysburg, South Carolina, along the Savannah River, joining General Benjamin Lincoln, who had been named commander of the southern Continental army in September 1778. Meanwhile Major General Augustine Prevost took command of the British forces in Georgia and sent Campbell to capture Augusta. Prevost marched for Lincoln at Purrysburg.[6]

Augusta was quickly in British hands at the end of January 1779; however, the British would not be there for long. Disappointed by the lack of Loyalist turn-out, Campbell realized he could not hold the village and abandoned it on February 13. The next day American militia commander Colonel Andrew Pickens proved Campbell correct when Pickens surprised a Loyalist militia force at Kettle Creek, Georgia. Like the defeat at Moore's Creek Bridge, this defeat did much to quell Loyalist ambitions in the Georgia backcountry until the British captured Charleston. Prevost, meanwhile, had also suffered a reverse when he tried to land a force in Beaufort, South Carolina. General William Moultrie met the attackers and forced them back across the river.[7]

The British were far from defeated though and were able to secure a major victory on March 3 at Briar's Creek, Georgia. After heavy fighting, the American militia collapsed before a British bayonet charge. Georgia Continentals held firm until they were surrounded and compelled to surrender. The Americans lost 377 while the British only lost 16.[8]

Now both commanders decided to take a risk. At the end of April, Lincoln left Moultrie in the lowcountry and marched north to Augusta with nearly 4,000 men, ostensibly to reclaim the backcountry for the Patriots and subdue any potential rise in loyalism. Prevost, at the same time, decided to make a thrust at Charleston with around 3,000 soldiers. Crossing the Savannah, Prevost quickly swept away the guard at Purrysburg, and another detachment at Coosawhatchie under John Laurens, and marched north towards Charleston. Moultrie with the remaining American forces in the lowcountry, managed to get ahead of the British and was in Charleston by May 7. British Colonel Mark Prevost, Augustin's brother, arrived before Charleston on May 11 with the van of the British army. Despite Moultrie's protests, government authorities in Charleston wanted to negotiate a peace.

Amazingly, when Prevost was offered Charleston and the colony's neutrality, he refused, saying he was not there for legislative purposes, but in a military capacity. Moultrie then took charge, saying the American army would fight it out. As the Americans were preparing the defenses, Prevost pulled back after learning that Lincoln was in Charleston. He gathered food and forage, building three redoubts on James Island, including a tête-du-pont protecting Stono Ferry. Lincoln responded by attacking the fortification on June 20. A bloody battle, including hand-to-hand fighting, occurred before Lincoln withdrew as the British were reinforced.[9]

Through the hot summer of 1779, both sides accomplished little else. The main British forces were in Savannah, with a detachment at Port Royal, South Carolina. The Carolina backcountry was in the control of the American militias, while Lincoln's army in Charleston withered as enlistments expired. The good news for the Americans was that help was on the way.

The Siege of Savannah

On September 1, 1779, a French fleet arrived off the coast of Georgia under the command of Admiral Charles Henri Hector d'Estaing. A rendezvous was arranged with Lincoln and the Americans for September 11, however, d'Estaing did not wait and by the time Lincoln arrived on September 16, d'Estaing was before Savannah and had given Prevost 24 hours to decide to surrender or fight. Prevost used the time to strengthen his defenses. A siege was now the only option. The allied bombardment began on October 3 and d'Estaing ordered an assault against the British lines on October 9. The focus of the assault was against the Spring Hill redoubt, and Francis Marion was given command of the initial thrust. It was a disaster. Marion's detachment managed to break through the abatis, cross the ditches and plant their flag on the parapet in fierce hand-to-hand fighting, but were then checked and thrown back. Some 1,500 Americans and 3,500 French troops fought in the battle against 4,800 British. The Americans lost 239 killed and wounded, the French 585, and the British 55.[10] That ended the siege. Lincoln was across the Savannah by October 19 and the French on their ships. Lincoln returned to Charleston, as it was obvious that Charleston would be the next target for the British. Marion, with the Second South Carolina Regiment, was left at Sheldon, South Carolina, to watch for the coming invasion.

Fall of Charleston

At the end of January 1780, Clinton arrived in Georgia with a significant reinforcement consisting of some 8,700 men. He sent nearly 2,000 north to recapture Augusta and landed another 2,000 on Simmons (now Seabrook) Island, South Carolina, on February 11 as a first move in the campaign to take Charleston.[11]

Lincoln sent Moultrie and a detachment of light infantry under Marion to harass the invaders, but gradually, the British noose tightened around the city. By the last week of March, Clinton had begun the first siege line on Charleston Neck, 800 yards from the American defenses.[12] On April 8, Clinton closed the harbor when 10 ships of the fleet entered the harbor and anchored off Fort Johnson on James Island. Meanwhile outside of Charleston on April 14, British Colonel Banastre Tarleton surprised a Patriot force at Moncks Corner, South Carolina, capturing many good dragoon horses.[13]

By April 17, the British opened their second line and continued a bombardment against the city. Time was running out, however, and when Tarleton surprised an American detachment at Lenud's Ferry on May 6, and Fort Moultrie fell on May 7, Patriot morale was devastated. Negotiations began on May 8, and Lincoln surrendered on May 12. Patriot losses were catastrophic. Some 89 were killed and 140 wounded, and over 5,600 Continentals and militia surrendered. Three hundred cannon were lost, along with huge amounts of gunpowder, food, and stores, and three frigates. Among the victims were thousands of slaves whom the British gathered and sent to the Caribbean Islands.[14] Among the Americans who escaped was Francis Marion, who had broken his ankle and was sent home before the British closed their noose.

The fall of Charleston dealt a significant blow to the Patriot cause and there would be further defeats. As the main British forces besieged Charleston, Tarleton's legion was released to the backcountry to block American reinforcements still heading for Charleston. On May 29, he caught up with Lieutenant Colonel Abraham Buford and a detachment of reinforcements that had marched from Virginia to Camden, but had fallen back upon learning of the fall of Charleston. Buford's green troops were slaughtered by Tarleton at the Waxhaws in northern South Carolina. The Americans lost 316 men in comparison to Tarleton's 17.[15]

Partisan Warfare

The British wasted no time in subduing and occupying backcountry villages after the capture of Charleston. By May 15, Cornwallis was on his way to Camden. Two other British columns marched for Ninety Six and Augusta, Georgia. Throughout the backcountry, Loyalists and Provincial troops captured small villages in support of the British regulars. Clinton then put Cornwallis in charge of the southern theater with over 6,000 rank and file, and returned to New York. Before leaving, Clinton made a decision that arguably would ultimately lead to the loss of the southern colonies. He issued a proclamation on June 3, 1780, declaring that no person could remain neutral in the present crisis; all had to proclaim loyalty and assist in subduing the rebellion.[16] This forced choice alienated those who simply wished to return to their farms, while at the same time emboldening those who were still in rebellion.

Beyond South Carolina, the British occupied Augusta in June and Georgia Patriots captured at Charleston were allowed to go home where things remained relatively quiet. In North Carolina, Cornwallis pleaded with Loyalists to restrain from uprising until he could move Regulars into the colony. Again, Loyalists would not wait and were defeated at Ramsour's Mill where they had rallied.[17]

In South Carolina, the backcountry erupted in reaction to the fall of Charleston. Between June 1 and August 1, there were 16 small engagements in modern-day Spartanburg, York, Chester, Fairfield, Kershaw, Marlboro, and Lancaster counties.[18] Patriot militias formed under elected leaders such as William Hill, Edward Lacy, William Bratton, Richard Winn, and Andrew Neel. These men cooperated in command, with Lacy, Bratton, and Winn joining together to defeat Loyalists at Gibson's Meeting House and Brierley's Ferry. Meanwhile, British Legion Captain Christian Huck destroyed William Hill's Iron Works on June 18. Huck met his fate, however, in a predawn attack against his camp at Williamson's Plantation on July 12 in which Lacy, Neel, Bratton, and Hill joined forces to surprise Huck's detachment and kill him.[19]

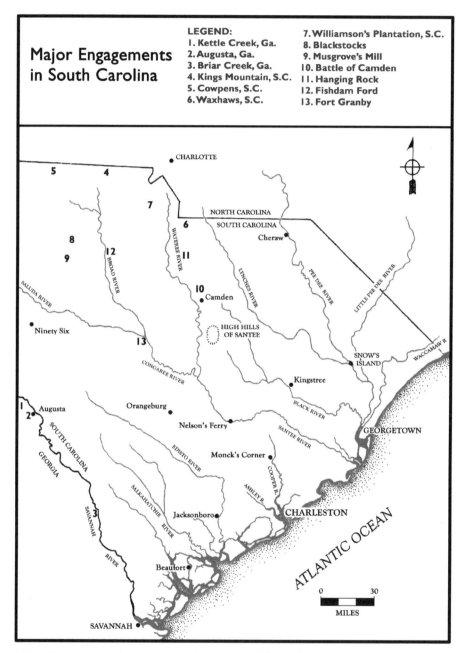

Major Engagements in South Carolina

LEGEND:
1. Kettle Creek, Ga.
2. Augusta, Ga.
3. Briar Creek, Ga.
4. Kings Mountain, S.C.
5. Cowpens, S.C.
6. Waxhaws, S.C.
7. Williamson's Plantation, S.C.
8. Blackstocks
9. Musgrove's Mill
10. Battle of Camden
11. Hanging Rock
12. Fishdam Ford
13. Fort Granby

Major Engagements in South Carolina (Adapted by Vally Sharpe from James B. Legg Map, in Oller 2016, xiv).

The Patriot militia leaders often acted on their own, but were loosely organized under the overall command of Thomas Sumter, whose plantation had been burned by Tarleton. Sumter was elected "general" on June 15, but, with no standing government, Sumter's was largely a ceremonial position. Sumter moved against the British outpost at Rocky Mount on July 30 but failed to capture it. On August 6, he struck a British camp at Hanging Rock, South Carolina, and had the better of the battle, if not a complete victory. Casualty reports in these battles are rarely accurate, but Sumter's biographer lists 20 men killed, 40 wounded, and 10 missing of Sumter's forces, while the British combined regulars, provincials and Loyalists lost 130 killed, an equal number wounded, and 75 made prisoner. The British also lost valuable horses and stores.[20]

Camden

These victories improved Patriot morale, and there seemed cause for optimism. Although the Americans had lost their Continental Army when Charleston fell, prior to the loss, General George Washington had sent reinforcements of Maryland and Delaware Continentals south to assist Lincoln. Following behind was the hero of Saratoga, General Horatio Gates, to whom Congress had given overall command of the Second Continental Army in the Southern Theater. Gates arrived on July 24, and as he surveyed his command, he learned that a large detachment of Virginia militia under Brigadier General Edward Stevens was on its way. With the expected arrival of North Carolina militia under Major General Richard Caswell, Gates was under the impression that some 4,000 men would be under his command. He quickly marched into South Carolina with the aim of taking the British stronghold at Camden.

On the night of August 15, at 10 o'clock, Gates's army marched from his camp at Rugeley's Mill, south along a narrow road toward Camden. Lord Cornwallis, who only recently had arrived in Camden, marched north to surprise Gates, coincidently leaving Camden at the same hour. The two forces met at 2:00am in a deep but open pine forest with high grass all around. After a brief skirmish, both sides fell back and prepared for what was inevitably going to be a major battle when dawn came.

Through the night, Gates worked to deploy his men, with the Continentals on the right of the road and the militia on the left, with his 1st Marylanders in reserve. Cornwallis, pleased that he had caught Gates's army, left his men to rest. As dawn came, Cornwallis deployed with his regulars on the right and Loyalists and Provincials on the left, and the 71st Highlanders and Tarleton's dragoons in reserve. The British immediately charged forward, taking their worst casualties in the battle from Gates's artillery firing canister. Undaunted the British regulars plowed into Gates's militia, who promptly fled, many without firing a shot. The 1st Marylanders opened ranks and let the militia through then checked the British momentarily. On the opposite flank, the battle was hotly engaged until Cornwallis saw his opportunity to send Tarleton and the 71st Highlanders into the gap between the two American lines. Gates's army dissolved, small groups of men fighting their way off the battlefield, while Tarleton's dragoons chased others and Gates's wagon train up the road some 22 miles. Perhaps as many as 800 Americans were killed and wounded, and 700 prisoners taken. The British lost 68 killed, 245 wounded, and 11 missing.[21]

Within four months, the Americans had lost two large Continental armies. As a result, through the fall of 1780 the Patriot cause in the south was held together by partisans, without the support of a functioning Continental force. Francis Marion, who had joined Gates on his march into South Carolina, was dispatched to take charge of the Williamsburg and Britton's Neck militias just prior to the battle of Camden. It was then that Marion began his career in the northeastern part of South Carolina as the "Swamp Fox."

On August 24, Marion surprised a detachment of British at Great Savannah, releasing 150 Continental soldiers captured at Camden. He then defeated Loyalist detachments at Blue Savannah (September 4), Black Mingo (September 29), and Tearcoat Swamp (October 26). He made two unsuccessful raids on the British post at Georgetown and was chased by Tarleton through the lowcountry, but remained out of reach. Marion quickly made himself a thorn in the side of the British efforts to subdue the rebellion in that region.[22]

Thomas Sumter, the "Gamecock," likewise gave the British fits, and often Sumter's excursions would draw off the British from focusing on

Marion. Sumter was surprised by the British at Fishing Creek (August 18) and Fishdam Ford (November 9), but got his revenge by defeating Tarleton at Blackstock's Plantation (November 20). Meanwhile, South Carolina Governor John Rutledge made him a brigadier general in command of the South Carolina militia on October 6.[23]

Sumter and Marion were not alone in helping revive backcountry morale after the disaster at Camden. The battles of Musgrove's Mill and King's Mountain were especially important. At Musgrove's Mill, militia colonels Elijah Clark, Isaac Shelby, and James Williams rode some 40 miles to intercept a British detachment camped along the Enoree River. When they arrived, they found they were outnumbered by more than two to one. They formed a defensive line and drew the British into a trap, inflicting 63 killed and 90 wounded casualties, with 70 prisoners taken on the same day Tarleton surprised Sumter at Fishing Creek.[24]

Even more significant was the defeat of Patrick Ferguson at King's Mountain on October 7, 1780. In September, Ferguson had marched into North Carolina and camped at Gilbert Town. There he issued a proclamation to the backcountry "Overmountain Men" of eastern Tennessee and western North Carolina to surrender, or he would march over the mountains and burn them out. In response, Patriot militia leaders Isaac Shelby, John Sevier, and William Campbell rendezvoused at Sycamore Shoals on September 25. When Ferguson learned of this threat, he began a surprisingly slow retreat toward Cornwallis who was near Charlotte, North Carolina. Eventually some 900 militia men caught up with and surrounded Ferguson who had camped atop Kings Mountain, South Carolina. The militia repeatedly charged up the hill to fire their rifles, then retreated down the hill when the British charged with the bayonet. As casualties mounted, the British circle constricted and the British attempted to break out. Ferguson and some 157 Loyalists were killed, another 163 were too wounded to be moved and 698 prisoners were taken. The loss caused Cornwallis to withdraw from North Carolina back to Winnsboro, South Carolina, and further significant attempts to rally Loyalist support in the far backcountry were over.[25]

Greene Takes Command

After the defeat at Camden, Gates retreated to Hillsborough, North Carolina, and remained in command of the remnants of the Continental forces in the south. Washington appointed General Nathanael Greene to replace Gates in October; however, Greene did not take formal command until December 3, the day after he arrived at the American camp near Charlotte, North Carolina.

Greene was a solid tactician, master planner, and the right man for the job. On his way south, he studied the Virginia and North Carolina topography and ordered surveys of the rivers and streams; information that would prove vital for his strategic plans. Upon arrival he introduced himself to Marion by letter, asking Marion to keep up his partisan war. Greene also rode to Sumter, who was still recovering from his wound, to coordinate strategy in the backcountry. Then Greene acted boldly. He divided his army, sending recently arrived Brigadier General Daniel Morgan and a large detachment west of the Catawba River to take command of all militia forces in the upcountry. On December 20, Greene marched with the rest of the army into South Carolina and camped along the upper Pee Dee River.

With Morgan moving west and Greene toward the Southeast, Cornwallis, at Winnsboro, South Carolina, was in a quandary. If he advanced on Greene, he would leave the British posts at Ninety Six and Augusta exposed to Morgan. If he went after Morgan, the low-country between him and Charleston was open to Greene. On the other hand, located between the two American forces with superior numbers, it might be possible to defeat both in turn. He decided to attack Morgan first. Tarleton was ordered west to destroy Morgan while Cornwallis moved north to block Greene from supporting Morgan. Tarleton characteristically acted aggressively, making a forced march to catch Morgan. Meanwhile, Morgan called in the militia to meet him at Cowpens, South Carolina.

At the Cowpens, Morgan prepared for battle. Morgan's tactical deployment continues to be studied today, and throughout the rest of the war, Greene would make successful use of it with modifications.

Morgan arrayed his forces in three lines, each line being stronger than the former. His front skirmish line consisted of South Carolina and Georgia riflemen. His second line consisted of South Carolina militia under Pickens, and his third line consisted of Maryland, Delaware, and Virginia Continentals, Virginia militia and State Troops. William Washington's Continental Light Dragoons and mounted militia made up the reserve. Using the local topography, the second and third lines were higher than the first line and were out of sight of Tarleton. When Tarleton arrived on January 17, 1781, he spent little time evaluating the scene.

In typical British fashion, Tarleton charged forward in a frontal attack against the first line of Patriot skirmishers. The skirmishers, as ordered, fired and fell back in good order. Tarleton's regulars continued forward to meet the second line who waited until the British were close, then let loose a volley of well-aimed fire. The British line was momentarily stunned, but reformed and attacked several times until the American line gave way. It was, however, a planned withdraw and not a rout. Seeing the retreat, the British believed they were winning, but their advance was checked by a third line of Patriot regulars. An intense battle followed, with both sides firing at close range. Tarleton committed his reserve cavalry and 71st Regiment, attempting a double envelopment. Strong leadership by Morgan and his subordinates, however, kept the men in order, giving the shocked British a well-aimed volley. This was followed by a charge and the arrival of Washington's cavalry. It was too much for the British who broke and ran.[26]

Casualty figures, as usual, are inconsistent across sources, however, Lawrence Babits places the American losses between 127 and 148 killed and wounded. The British lost 100 killed, 200 wounded, 29 officers and 500 privates taken prisoner, and two artillery pieces, 35 baggage wagons, 800 muskets, and 100 dragoon horses captured.[27] Tarleton's defeat had the twin effect of lowering British morale and boosting Patriot morale; not only in South Carolina but also in the north where Congress voted Morgan a gold medal. Tarleton's losses reduced Cornwallis's army by one-quarter, mostly made up of the light troops who had served as scouts, foragers, and screeners for the main army.

Race to the Dan

Despite the loss, a furious Cornwallis carried on with his plans to enter North Carolina, and his hopes were lifted by a reinforcement of Hessians, regulars, and Loyalist militia. Leaving Lieutenant Colonel Lord Francis Rawdon in charge of South Carolina, Cornwallis marched north to Ramsour's Mill, attempting to cut-off any chance of a rendezvous between Morgan and Greene. There, Cornwallis burned his baggage and most of his wagons, hoping that traveling light would ensure his catching Morgan. For his part, Morgan had not lingered after the battle but had quickly marched to Gilbert Town, North Carolina, knowing Cornwallis would not be far behind. Thus, began a Race to the Dan River across North Carolina as Cornwallis tried to catch the Americans under Greene and Morgan.

From that point on, the Americans stayed just ahead of Cornwallis, crossing the Catawba and Yadkin Rivers and leaving detachments at the fords to delay the British. On February 7, Morgan and Greene arrived at Guilford Court House with their armies intact. At that point, Morgan was granted a medical leave and Greene turned to Otho Williams with orders to take 700 light infantry and cavalry and screen the main army from Cornwallis as the main army made its way to the safety of the Dan River in Virginia. For the next four days, Williams skirmished with Cornwallis's van. On the evening of February 14, Greene was across the Dan.[28]

Cornwallis was now some 240 miles from his supply base at Camden, and Greene was beyond reach on the north side of the Dan. Cornwallis decided to march to Hillsborough, North Carolina, arriving on February 22 and issuing a proclamation inviting Loyalists to join him.[29]

There were few supplies in Hillsborough, and the Loyalists failed to rally around Cornwallis. Meanwhile, Greene rested his army and sent his cavalry across the river to harass Cornwallis. For the next couple of weeks, British cavalry and Patriot cavalry met in several skirmishes. In one clash, Patriot Colonel Henry Lee's dragoons disguised as Tarleton's Legion, walked into a Loyalist detachment and hacked to death nearly 90 of them at what became known as Pyle's massacre.[30] Both sides maneuvered westward, with Cornwallis seeking food and forage, and Greene growing stronger and looking for an opportunity to fight, but only on his own terms.

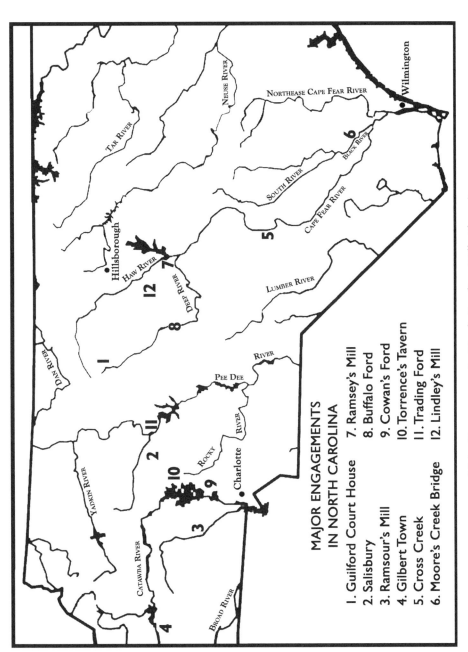

MAJOR ENGAGEMENTS
IN NORTH CAROLINA

1. Guilford Court House
2. Salisbury
3. Ramsour's Mill
4. Gilbert Town
5. Cross Creek
6. Moore's Creek Bridge
7. Ramsey's Mill
8. Buffalo Ford
9. Cowan's Ford
10. Torrence's Tavern
11. Trading Ford
12. Lindley's Mill

Major Engagements in North Carolina (Vally Sharpe).

Guilford Court House

Eventually, Cornwallis camped at New Garden, and Greene at Guilford Court House about 12 miles away. Cornwallis, with 1,900 men, was desperate to fight, and Greene, having been reinforced and now numbering some 4,300, was ready. Greene made use of Morgan's basic deployment at Cowpens, placing his army in three lines.[31]

Cornwallis and his army appeared before the Americans at 1:30pm, on March 15 and the battle began with artillery fire from both sides. As the British moved forward, the center of the American front line gave way, but the flanks held, forcing Cornwallis to commit his reserves to fill the center as his front line split to face the American flanks. When the British met the American second line, a vicious battle began, and although the British eventually pushed through to Greene's third line, Cornwallis was in such a desperate way, he ordered his artillery to fire into the melee to stop an American cavalry charge.

Greene wisely decided it was best to withdraw at this point, having given Cornwallis a hard punch and not wanting to risk any more. The British were too exhausted to follow. As usual, divergent numbers of casualties were reported. Greene's count was 22 militia killed, 73 wounded, and 885 missing, while the Continentals lost 57 killed, 111 wounded, and 161 missing. Greene also lost four cannon. Cornwallis' losses were catastrophic—532 officers and men who would never be replaced. Before Cowpens, Cornwallis had some 3,300 men. Now, after Cowpens, the Race to the Dan, and Guilford Court House, he was down to some 1,400.[32]

Greene retreated north to Speedwell's Iron Works to await the enemy's next move. Cornwallis fell back to New Garden Meeting House, then left most of the wounded there and began a slow retreat toward Ramsey's Mill. Greene followed, but once Cornwallis left Ramsey's eastward for Cross Creek, North Carolina, Greene halted the pursuit. His army was tired, and, as it consisted mostly of militia, it daily diminished in size.[33]

Greene Returns to South Carolina

At the end of January 1781, the British under Major James Craig had captured Wilmington, North Carolina, as a place to resupply Cornwallis and to rally the Loyalists. Cornwallis marched for Wilmington and established a camp near there by April 7. By that time, Greene had decided to return to South Carolina, turning his back on Cornwallis and going on the offense against the British forces further south. He crossed the state line around April 16.

In leaving Cornwallis in his rear, Greene was taking a calculated risk. Furthermore, traitor Benedict Arnold was in Virginia with another British army.[34] Greene would continue to worry about Cornwallis for several weeks, wondering whether Cornwallis would follow him or move toward Virginia.

As part of the movement into South Carolina, Greene detached Colonel Henry Lee with his Legion first to watch Cornwallis and then to turn south and join Marion in the lowcountry. Greene's strategy was to advance on Lord Francis Rawdon's command at Camden. While militia forces under Andrew Pickens kept the British busy in the upcountry, Sumter was to join Greene, and Lee and Marion would slip below Camden and attack the British posts between Camden and Charleston.[35]

Lee and Marion were already acquainted. Greene had detached Lee to join Marion in January, and the pair had made an unsuccessful attack on the British at Georgetown. Lee's Legion, consisting of dragoons and light infantry, had worked well with Marion's mounted militia until Lee was recalled to assist Greene in the Race to the Dan campaign.

Much had happened in South Carolina since Cornwallis had left the colony to go after Greene. With no Continental Army in the colony, partisans under Pickens, Sumter, and Marion were left to fight the British. Some 25 partisan battles and skirmishes, including those outlined below, occurred between the battle of Cowpens and Greene's return to South Carolina.[36]

After Lee left, Marion was unsupported in the eastern part of the state. Rawdon went after Marion and chased him to the Pee Dee River until being recalled to Camden because Sumter was harassing British outposts west of the Congaree and Santee. Then at the beginning of March, a British detachment at Fort Watson along the Santee and under the command of Colonel John Watson was ordered to find and destroy Marion. Watson marched from the fort along the north bank of the Santee River towards

Marion's camp on Snow's Island. Marion harassed Watson's detachment in a series of hit and run attacks, which eventually forced Watson to break off his campaign and march to the safety of Georgetown. Meanwhile another British detachment from Camden, under Colonel Welbore Ellis Doyle, found Marion's camp and destroyed it. Marion left his harassment of Watson and attempted to catch Doyle but failed. Marion was camped some 20 miles north of Snow's Island and was contemplating retreating into North Carolina when he learned of Greene's return and the pending arrival of Lee.[37]

Meanwhile, since Cowpens, Sumter had engaged in a series of largely unsuccessful attacks against the British outposts at Fort Granby and Belleville Plantation along the Congaree, and Fort Watson along the Santee. Sumter had captured a British supply train, however he promptly lost the supplies in a failed attack on Fort Watson. Nonetheless, Sumter's efforts did have the positive effect of drawing the British away from Marion.[38] In the far backcountry, Elijah Clarke and Andrew Pickens threatened the British around Ninety Six, and Clarke defeated a Loyalist party at Beattie's Mill on March 23.[39] In Georgia, Loyalists and Patriots skirmished in raids and ambushes, while the British in Savannah and Augusta strengthened their defenses.

As Greene approached Camden, Marion and Lee rendezvoused and marched for Fort Watson. This fort was a stockaded post sitting atop a Native American mound along the Santee River. Watson had shaved the top and sides of the mound and added three rows of abatis to make it a strong defensive position. Marion and Lee besieged the fort from April 15 to April 23. The British were compelled to surrender when the Americans built a tower allowing some soldiers to fire down into the fort while others attacked the main gate.[40]

Greene arrived near Camden on April 19. After a reconnaissance and skirmish, he decided the heavily fortified village was too strong to siege. He settled on Hobkirk's Hill, a moderate wooded ridge, a mile and a half north of the post. He hoped to draw Rawdon out for a fight, and Rawdon obliged.

On the morning of April 25, Rawdon, who had just been ordered to abandon Camden, armed all men fit for duty and marched for Greene. Although they were seeking battle, the Americans were quite possibly surprised. Greene's men were cooking breakfast or washing up when Rawdon struck the American left flank. Greene countered by attempting to flank Rawdon on both sides, but Rawdon threw in his reserves and lengthened his lines.

Greene had his artillery fire canister into the British lines, then ordered a bayonet charge and his cavalry to charge the rear of the British. Unfortunately, a confused American officer ordered a central unit to fall back at a critical point in the battle, causing disorder along the line. Greene, ever cautious, withdrew. Losses were approximately even: Greene's army of around 1,550 men lost 266, of which 18 were killed. Rawdon's 900 lost 258, of which 38 were killed.[41] On the day of battle, unbeknownst to Greene and Rawdon, Lord Cornwallis abandoned Wilmington and marched to Virginia.

After the capture of Fort Watson, Lee and Marion moved closer to Camden under orders to block Watson in Georgetown from joining Rawdon in Camden. After Hobkirk's Hill, Greene ordered Lee and Marion to cross the Santee and see if they could capture the British western posts of Fort Motte, Fort Granby, and Orangeburg. Crossing the Santee, they just missed Watson's detachment.

On May 6, Lee and Marion arrived before Fort Motte and began a siege. Greene had by this time retreated to Rugeley's plantation—where Gates had camped before the disastrous battle of Camden—then Greene crossed the Wateree River. Rawdon, meanwhile, was contemplating his own situation, and felt he had to at least make one more attempt to throw off Greene before abandoning Camden. On the evening of May 7, Rawdon crossed the Wateree and marched for Greene. He found Greene on a high and well-protected ridge along Sawney's Creek. There was no possibility of success against Greene in that position, so Rawdon reversed his course and returned to Camden on the afternoon of May 8. The next day, he posted orders for the evacuation of Camden.

With Marion and Lee at Fort Motte, Sumter moved farther south and captured the British post at Orangeburg on May 12.[42] Fort Motte fell that same day. Greene then rode to Fort Motte, where he met Marion for the first time. Afterward, Marion moved to a camp on the Santee. Then, with Greene's reluctant approval, Marion marched on Georgetown and took it without firing a shot on May 28. Meanwhile, Lee had marched north and taken Fort Granby, and with the captured stores from both Motte and Granby, Greene detached Lee to capture Augusta while Greene marched for the British at Ninety Six.

Siege of Ninety Six

Like Camden, Ninety Six was a fortified village, well defended with outlying redoubts and a palisade around the village, and communication trenches between the village and the outposts. Ninety Six also included a star-shaped fort northeast of the village. Unlike Camden, Greene decided to lay siege to this British stronghold. Greene's army initially consisted of 908 Maryland, Delaware, Virginia, and North Carolina Continental soldiers, plus 66 North Carolina militia, and three, six-pounder cannon. An unknown number of militia patrolled the outlying region, attempting to block Loyalist reinforcements to the British. Inside the fortifications, were between 550 and 850 British provincials consisting of New Jersey Volunteers, New York Loyalists, and South Carolina Loyalist militia.[43]

Siege operations began on May 22, 1781, but were unsuccessful, largely because of poor decisions by the Americans and strong leadership by the British commander, Lieutenant Colonel John Cruger. After a tour of the British defenses, Greene turned over the siege operations to Colonel Thaddeus Kosciuszko. Kosciuszko decided that the focus of the siege would be against the star fort, the strongest British position. The next several weeks consisted of the Patriots bombarding the British, while attempting a variety of siege tactics including digging zig-zag formal siege trenches to get close to the fort, a Maham tower like the one used to capture Fort Watson, raised artillery positions, and a mine. They even fired burning arrows into the village in an attempt to burn out the British, who responded by removing the roofs from the village structures. The British also launched nearly nightly sorties to disrupt the Americans progress. Colonel Henry Lee arrived on June 8 and placed his troops on the opposite side of the village and began to harass the British redoubt there.

As the British tactical situation became more desperate, help was on the way. A reinforcement of 3,000 British soldiers arrived in Charleston, and part of that force under the command of Lord Rawdon was assembled to relieve Ninety Six. Upon learning that the relief party was en route, Greene ordered Pickens, Sumter, and Marion to assemble whatever forces they could to stop or delay Rawdon. Even though the British march northwest in the June heat was devastating to the unacclimated British, the Americans were unable to stop them. The militia failed to assemble, and Sumter was out-maneuvered. Each day Rawdon grew closer to Ninety Six, and Greene's siege was increasingly threatened. Greene decided he had to act before Rawdon reached Ninety Six. According to Lee, Greene's men were also pressing him to take action. On June 18, Greene ordered an attack on two sides of Ninety Six, the main one being against the star fort. The initial rush, called the "forlorn hope," became entangled at the bottom of the ditch while the British fired down on them and used long spears to repel any of those who made progress up the fort's glacis. Then, two detachments of British sallied out of the back of the fort, one going right, the other left, and flanked the forlorn hope in the ditch, where British bayonets were well-employed. The main American attack never materialized, as the men were pinned down by British fire. Greene, seeing the carnage, decided to withdraw without ordering more men forward. Across the way to the west, Lee was able to take the redoubt, but found it empty. Soon the order came to prepare to leave Ninety Six before the arrival of Rawdon. Total American casualties for the siege were 58 killed, 76 wounded, and 20 missing. The British lost 27 killed and 58 wounded.[44]

Greene withdrew on June 20, and Rawdon arrived the next day. Rawdon attempted to catch Greene, but Greene was able to make his escape and Rawdon returned to Ninety Six. Rawdon immediately set in motion what Greene had failed to do; destroy Ninety Six. Leaving 1,400 men with Cruger for this task, Rawdon began his march back to the Charleston area.

The British Confined

By the end of June 1781, the British strongholds of Camden, Augusta, Ninety Six, and Georgetown, and their posts at Fort Watson, Fort Motte, and Fort Granby had been lost, captured, or abandoned. The British still held the coastal cities of Charleston and Savannah where they were too strong for the Americans to dislodge.

Despite the summer heat, the skirmishing continued. From the first of July to the end of August, another 17 engagements occurred in South Carolina, mostly between partisan and Loyalist militias. Marion was involved in two of the bloodiest.

The first began when Greene, whose army was in camp in the High Hills of the Santee, gave Sumter the mission to attack the British posts at Moncks Corner and Dorchester. Marion and Lee were included in the plan and encouraged to cooperate under Sumter's command. They did so reluctantly, and the results proved them right.

A British detachment was operating in the Moncks Corner region and Sumter ordered Marion and Lee to attack. Realizing the Americans were after him, British Lieutenant Colonel James Coates made a run for Charleston. As he retreated, Coates destroyed bridges until he stopped his march at Shubrick's Plantation and placed a howitzer at Quinby Bridge immediately east of the plantation. Lee came up first and charged the British at the bridge. Lee was unable to get his entire force across because the British had loosened the bridge timbers, which fell off as horses dislodged them.

After a skirmish, the British retired to the plantation and settled into the plantation house, barns, and slave quarters. Marion and Lee consolidated their forces but decided the British were too strongly posted to be attacked. When Sumter arrived late in the afternoon, he disagreed and ordered an attack. Marion's detachment was ordered to cross an open field under fire, but returned to help Colonel Thomas Taylor's men who were heavily engaged. Although Marion's reinforcements forced back a British counterattack, the Patriots took heavy casualties until Sumter finally called off the attack. Taylor was furious with Sumter, and although Marion never officially complained, he and Lee left Sumter that evening and marched 15 miles away without saying goodbye. That was the last time either officer would serve with Sumter.

For his part, Sumter resigned shortly afterward, not because of the failure at Shubrick's, but because South Carolina Governor John Rutledge issued a proclamation against looting of Loyalists in August, which effectively nullified Sumter's Law. This "law" was an edict that allowed new recruits, both officers and men, to be paid in horses, clothing, and slaves for enlisting in the Patriot militia. These commodities and slaves would come from Loyalists plantations. Marion disagreed with the edict and refused to support it.[45]

The second action involving Marion that hot summer was on August 30. Marion had been asked to come to the aid of Colonel William Harden in the lowcountry southwest of Charleston where a British foraging party was operating. Marion made a remarkable forced march across the Edisto River to find Harden's troops dispersed and Harden ill. Marion spent the next few days gathering Harden's militia and seeking an opportunity to attack the British. On August 30, he set up an ambush in a thick wood along a well-used road leading northeast toward Parker's Ferry with about 445 men that included about 80 saber men. He assumed the British force of about 500 Hessians, British regulars, and mounted Loyalists, and two artillery pieces would pass there on their way back to Charleston. Once there, he learned that 100 additional Loyalists were at the ferry.

Just before sunset, a few of the Loyalists from the ferry came down the path and saw Marion's men in the woods. Shots were exchanged, and the Loyalists turned back to the ferry, chased by some of Marion's swordsmen. The noise of that exchange attracted the British column that was indeed heading into the ambush. The Loyalist dragoons rushed ahead and ran into Marion's ambush, and were destroyed. The remnants were unable to turn around under fire and drove ahead toward the ferry. Then the British infantry came up and a full-scale battle seemed to be brewing. Some of Marion's men panicked, however, when they thought they were being flanked and Marion was unable to rally them. The British too seemed stunned and fell back, especially after all their artillerymen became casualties. The British lost some 20 killed and 80 wounded. The Americans only lost one killed and three wounded. It was Marion's most brilliant tactical success.[46]

Eutaw Springs

While Marion was heading across the Edisto River to assist Harden, Greene decamped on August 23 to engage the British. By this time,

Lord Rawdon's health had deteriorated and he had returned to England to recuperate. Colonel Alexander Stewart replaced him in the field. Greene made a circuitous route toward Charleston, writing Pickens and Marion to join him. Stewart, not knowing where Greene was, encamped at Eutaw Springs around a strong brick house, along the Santee River near the old crossing and post at Nelson's Ferry.

Marion made another forced march and joined Greene and Pickens at Burdell's Plantation, about seven miles north of Stewart's camp on September 7. Greene had managed to gather some 2,276 regulars and militia against Stewart's 1,793.[47] Although Greene would repeat the tactical deployment used at Guilford Court House and Cowpens, this time the Americans would be on the offense. The Patriot front line consisted of four battalions of North and South Carolina militia with Marion in overall command. Behind these were three brigades of regulars. Both lines had artillery. Lee's Legion protected the right flank, and South Carolina state troops were on the left. William Washington's cavalry and Captain Robert Kirkwood's Delaware Continentals formed a reserve.

Learning of the American approach, Stewart sent out a detachment to gain intelligence. The detachment found Greene's van and a short fight ensued. A British foraging party was also in the area and was rounded up by Greene who now had as many as 400 prisoners before engaging the British main line, which was still three miles away. At around 9:00am the two main lines met. The British had formed in front of their camp with the Santee on their right and veteran light infantry under a Major John Majoribanks in a thicket next to the river.

The American militia, led by Marion, did not falter, standing and firing multiple volleys before retiring. The British then met the second line and began to fall back. Majoribanks's light infantry in the thicket supported their retreat and checked the American left flank. The American cavalry attempted to push them out but, unsupported by infantry, they failed. Nevertheless, the main British line was nearly routed. As they fell back through their tents, the Americans followed and became entangled in the camp. A British detachment made it into the brick house and began a galling fire. Greene ordered his artillery forward to pound the house, but all of the artillerymen were killed or wounded. At that point, Majoribanks's men charged forward and captured the guns. Greene recalled his troops. They were exhausted, low on ammunition, and had been without water for the day.

The casualties at Eutaw Springs were high for both sides. The British lost 84 killed, 351 wounded, and 257 missing. The Americans suffered 139 killed, 375 wounded, and eight missing.[48] Among the casualties on the American side were many officers, including Andrew Pickens wounded and William Washington wounded and captured. The British would lose the brave Majoribanks to a mortal wound. Both sides declared victory.

The War Winds Down

Eutaw Springs would be the last large engagement between the Patriots and the British in South Carolina. Marion and Lee kept eyes on the British immediately after the battle and while Stewart was reinforced by General Paston Gould, the British did little other than march up and down the south bank of the Santee River. Greene eventually returned to the High Hills of the Santee to rest and refit, and again dealt with a dwindling army as the militias returned home.

Back in April when Lord Cornwallis marched to Virginia, he took up a campaign against the Marquis de Lafayette but failed to draw him into a major battle. By August 22, Cornwallis had settled into Yorktown, Virginia. In what turned out to be the decisive battle of the American Revolution, he was trapped by the Americans and French on land, and by the French by sea, and surrendered his army on October 19. Despite the defeat, there was still over a year to go before the British would completely abandon the southern colonies and two years before the Treaty of Paris was ratified on September 3, 1783, officially ending the war. Until then, there were still more soldiers and civilians who would die.

In spite of the Patriot victories, a resurgence of Loyalism emerged in South Carolina. William "Bloody Bill" Cunningham's band and others went on a raid laying out a circular a path of destruction from Charleston, westward to Ninety Six to the Congarees and back. Historian John Buchanan states that Cunningham himself engaged in 22 separate actions.[49]

Greene eventually moved south and on December 1 arrived at Dorchester, South Carolina, and after a skirmish the British abandoned the post. Then on December 9, his army arrived at Round O, across the Edisto River southwest of Charleston. General Arthur St. Clair arrived from Virginia with reinforcements on January 4, 1782.[50] With him was Major General Anthony Wayne who was sent south to take control of Georgia. Wayne harassed the British and forced them to abandon their posts and retreat into Savannah, where he kept them bottled up until the British finally abandoned the city on July 11.[51]

In addition to Savannah, the only other British stronghold in the South at the beginning of 1782 was Charleston. There Greene again found himself in a situation in which victory was just out of reach. He had the British loosely confined to Charleston, however, he lacked the necessary numbers to tightly bottle-up the enemy or conduct an actual siege. Meanwhile, he was losing many of his officers. Colonels John Eager Howard, Otho Williams, Henry Lee, and Thomas Sumter all retired through the winter and spring of 1782. Marion and Sumter were appointed as Senators in the state legislature and Andrew Pickens to the House of Representatives. Greene was also losing many men. Throughout the year, Greene would have to combat rumors that the war was ending, desertions, and mutinies.

The British continued to break out, raiding and foraging around Charleston. In one major raid in late February, Lieutenant Colonel Benjamin Thompson surprised Marion's men at Durant's planation on Wambaw Creek while Marion was serving in the legislature. Marion left the legislature and gathered his dragoons in search of Thompson. At Tidyman's Plantation, Marion was resting his troops when Thompson suddenly appeared. Marion deployed his men and attacked, but his cavalry became confused maneuvering around a pond and they fell back when Thompson countercharged. Marion was able to rally the men, but the damage had been done, and the battle lost. Thompson killed several men and captured many horses. A false rumor circulated that Marion was drowned in the battle.[52]

Skirmishing continued through the spring and summer, but no major battles took place until late in August when two significant actions occurred. The first was at Tar Bluff on August 27, 1782. The British were conducting raids in the lowcountry south of Charleston. Greene sent

General Mordecai Gist to intercept them. He ordered fortifications to be built 12 miles south of Combahee Ferry at Tar Bluff to harass the British as they came downstream. John Laurens asked to command the work. When a number of British boats came downriver, Laurens fired upon them and the British deployed. Although Gist was on his way to reinforce, Laurens chose to attack and was killed along with several other men. Gist came up, exchanged fire with the British and forced them to retreat, but not before they captured the howitzer at the fort.[53]

The second action was Marion's last engagement on August 30. Marion was camped at Wadboo Plantation east of Moncks Corner, across the Cooper River. Here he could watch the activities of the British to the north and east of Charleston. A detachment of British provincial cavalry and African American dragoons were foraging in the area under the command of Colonel Thomas Fraser. Both sides learned of the other's presence at about the same time.

Marion prepared for battle by placing his men along an avenue of cedars in front of the plantation house and in various outbuildings. Then he sent some cavalry out to lure Fraser to the plantation. Fraser took the bait and followed the cavalry up to the plantation where Marion's men were hiding in the cedars. Fraser lost some 20 men, including four killed. He was able to capture an ammunition wagon, which caused Marion to withdraw, however, Marion returned to the plantation when Fraser left.[54]

Still the war was winding down, and the British House of Commons voted to abandon the war in February 1782. The new commander of British forces in Charleston, General Alexander Leslie, sent a proposal for a cease fire to Greene in May. Greene was skeptical but passed it on to Congress.

Although Greene did not know it, Leslie had received orders to quit Charleston on August 1. Nonetheless, it would take another four months to gather enough ships to evacuate soldiers, Loyalists, and slaves.[55] Also unknown to the South Carolina armies, in November, America and Britain had signed a preliminary treaty in Paris. On December 14, 1782, the British army finally left Charleston. As Greene's army entered the town at last, Francis Marion said goodbye to his men at Wadboo Plantation and rode home to his destroyed plantation along the Santee River.

The Campaigns of Francis Marion (Adapted by Vally Sharpe from James B. Legg Map, in Oller 2016, xv).

PART TWO

Leadership Lessons and Vignettes

Francis Marion and a Leader's Frame of Reference

"None of us see the world as it is but as we are, as our frame of reference, or maps, define the territory."

STEPHEN COVEY

Frame of Reference

Effective leaders build a personal frame of reference from schooling, experience, self-study, and assessment. They reflect on past experiences in order to learn from them and to help place their current organization and situation in strategic context.[1] Some of this learning is gained as a result of naturally occurring experiences, but the leader can also build a frame of reference based on simulations and imagination that stretches them to practice and prepare for situations in the future.[2]

This frame of reference, however, is designed to expand, not limit, the leader's horizons. The leader cannot unimaginatively apply a course of action that may have worked once to a new situation for which it is inappropriate. They must be mentally agile enough to understand the circumstances around them and adjust. The goal of a properly applied frame of reference is not to inappropriately create an over-simplified certainty based on a past experience, but instead to facilitate improved clarity and contextual understanding of a new experience.[3]

Francis Marion and Fighting the Cherokees

Throughout the French and Indian War, the Cherokee Indians had been loyal allies of the British, but they also had come to feel that the British had failed to compensate them for horses lost during the campaign and that they had been generally cheated by White traders and land grabbers. Returning from the Ohio Valley where they had helped the British secure Fort Duquesne, the Cherokees absconded with some horses belonging to colonists along the Virginia frontier. In retaliation, the Virginians killed and scalped a number of Cherokees, and the Cherokees responded with violent raids against settlers in the Carolina backcountry.[4]

As the British royal governor William Lyttelton was preparing a force to meet this threat in October 1759, the Cherokee warrior Oconostota led a peace delegation to Charleston, proposing a treaty based on mutual forgiveness. Lyttelton not only rejected Oconostota's overtures, he took the Indians hostage and carried them with him on a march west to settle the matter by military means.[5]

Lyttelton had assembled a composite army of British regulars, South Carolina provincial troops and militia, slaves, vagrants impressed into service, and assorted Indian enemies of the Cherokees. Among the soldiers was 27-year-old Francis Marion who had joined Lyttelton's force on October 31, 1759, and became a captain in a troop of provincial cavalry headed by his brother Gabriel.[6]

Lyttelton's campaign was short-lived. The governor concluded a hasty treaty with the Cherokee statesman Attakullakalla before any shots were fired and returned to Charleston. Although Lyttelton claimed a victory, his actions, especially his mistreatment of Oconostota, actually did little more than foment the Cherokees' discontent and resentment.[7]

Although Marion saw no combat on this brief military venture, he was exposed to British army training and methods. He also saw how colonial militia resented what they interpreted as high-handedness in British officers and how they resisted British attempts to impose strict discipline. These were lessons that Marion would file away for future use.[8]

The fragility of Lyttelton's peace soon manifested itself when Cherokees began attacking South Carolina's western frontier settlements. After an expedition led by Colonel Archibald Montgomery failed to end the

Cherokee raids, the British assembled a stronger force led by Lieutenant Colonel James Grant. Grant commanded a mix of British regulars, South Carolina provincials, specially trained rangers, various Indian allies, and slaves. Marion was commissioned as a lieutenant in the provincial infantry and served directly under Captain William Moultrie.[9]

Grant's expedition was both more active and more successful than Montgomery's, and the Cherokee were forced to sue for peace. While Marion's precise role in the campaign is uncertain, he obviously gained additional experience in frontier warfare characterized by ambush, wanton violence and cruelty, and irregular tactics.[10] Moultrie proclaimed Marion to be "an active, brave and hardy soldier and an excellent partisan officer." Marion had also been part of a cause that, in addition to Moultrie, included such future military and political leaders of the American Revolution as Thomas Middleton, Henry Laurens, Andrew Williamson, Isaac Huger, and Andrew Pickens. Such associations no doubt were another important by-product of Marion's experience as part of Grant's campaign.[11]

Once Marion's regiment was disbanded, he returned to a life of farming the fertile lands above the swamps on the western side of the Santee River.[12] His experience fighting the Cherokees had given him a valuable frame of reference from which to draw on in the American Revolution. He had served with his future enemy and learned something of the British Army's tactics, organization, and leadership. He had witnessed the unique character, strengths, and limitations of the colonial militia. He had fought in the irregular and ruthless style of Indian warfare. He had forged relations and the bonds of shared hardship with several future colleagues in the struggle for American independence. He had learned how to use rugged terrain to military advantage. It is for good reason that Robert Bass aptly titles this chapter of his biography of Marion, "Apprentice to Mars."[13]

★★★

One very basic frame of reference involves how the leader views the nature of the organization. This perspective no doubt informs a leader's decision making and response to various situations. Lee Bolman and Terrence Deal identify four frames or lenses through which leaders perceive organizations: structural, human resource, political, and symbolic.[14]

In any situation there is simply too much going on at once for the leader to attend to everything. Bolman and Deal argue that frames are useful in helping the leader understand what is important and what can safely be ignored. Frames also allow scattered bits of information to be organized into manageable patterns. This ability is increasingly important as leaders are exposed to more and more data sources.[15]

But as a leader goes through this filtering process, part of their self-awareness must be an understanding of what their default frame is because such a "habit of mind" naturally influences what they see and what they may miss or misread. In order to avoid the narrowness inherent in a habitual reliance on the leader's default frame, Bolman and Deal argue that multi-framing and reframing are necessary skills for a leader to respond with imagination and courage in complex situations.[16] Indeed, Marion demonstrated a use of all four of Bolman and Deal's frames.

The Structural Frame

The structural frame "depicts a rational world and emphasizes organizational architecture, including planning, goals, structure, technology, specialized roles, coordination, formal relationships, and metrics." Structures are designed to fit the organization's environment and technology, and allow organizations to allocate responsibilities or create "divisions of labor." The organization's myriad diverse activities are coordinated into a unified effort by roles, policies, procedures, systems, and hierarchies. Progress is measured by objective indicators. In short, a leader with a predominantly structural frame of reference "treats an organization like a factory." If the leader becomes too comfortable with this frame of reference, problems can arise when the existing structure does not align well with changing circumstances or when performance declines.[17] Leaders relying on the structural frame must be careful not to let rules and manuals take the place of communication and the use of judgment.[18]

Francis Marion and the Second Continental Regiment

On June 21, 1775, the First and Second South Carolina Regiments were organized, and Marion was elected as captain of a company in the Second Regiment. On February 22, 1776, he was promoted to major, and when Isaac Motte, the regimental commander, was promoted to colonel on November 23, Marion was promoted to lieutenant colonel and named his successor. By then the repulse of the British at the battle of Sullivan's Island on June 28 had created a time of quiet around Charleston, and Marion's men soon began to succumb to boredom. Many filled their idle hours with misbehavior such as drunkenness, stealing from each other, pillaging from nearby plantations, exceeding leaves of absence, general slovenliness, and even "runnin with one another intirely naked" about town.[19]

As a partisan leader, Marion would respond differently, but in dealing with Continental soldiers, he drew on his experience with the British Army and viewed the Second Regiment through the structural frame. Such an organization required disciplined soldiers who performed their roles and responsibilities with the precision necessary to create unified action. Only by repetitive musket loading and firing drills could soldiers gain the proficiency necessary to deliver the expected three shots per minute. Hours on the parade field were necessary to perfect the ability to maneuver without loss of the formations that battlefield tactics required. Only by well-honed obedience and discipline would soldiers respond to the order to launch a bayonet charge.[20]

In meeting these requirements through the structural frame, Marion was quick to impose harsh punishment on his misbehaving soldiers. The Continental Congress authorized military flogging of up to 100 lashes, raised from 39 in 1776. In the British Army, Marion recalled punishments still more brutal.[21]

Marion made liberal use of the lash. Between 1775 and 1777, more than one out of four men in the Second Regiment received court-martial-ordered whippings. One especially egregious repeat offender received a total of 749 lashes as a result of six courts martial.[22]

While such measures would be considered abhorrent today, it was not so in Marion's era and very compatible with a structural view of a

Continental infantry regiment. The structural frame emphasizes "organizational architecture," and Peter Horry, who served as a major under Marion, declared, "I am not afraid to say that Marion was the architect of the Second Regiment and laid the foundation of that excellent discipline and confidence in themselves, which gained them such reputation whenever they were brought to face their enemies."[23] Buoyed by the structural frame, Marion built an organization of disciplined members who could perform their assigned roles in precise and expected ways to deliver unified action.

The Human Resource Frame

The human resource frame "sees an organization as an extended family, made up of individuals with needs, feelings, prejudices, skills, and limitations." The key leadership challenge from this largely psychological perspective is to tailor the organization to its individual members in a way that allows them to accomplish their tasks while simultaneously feeling good about themselves and their work. From this frame of reference, it is the organization's responsibility to create an environment where the members feel secure, adequately compensated, sufficiently trained, and trusted.[24] A leader who relies primarily on this frame of reference may encounter difficulty when the organization simply lacks the financial and other resources necessary to continue to meet the increasing socio-economic expectations of its members.

Francis Marion and Motivating Militia and Partisans

If Marion tended toward the structural frame in leading Continental soldiers, he relied more on the human resource frame when leading partisans. His experience fighting the Cherokees again provided useful and had left Marion with a keen awareness of the psyche of the partisan soldier he would lead in the American Revolution. Even allowing for the hagiographic nature of his biography, Mason Locke Weems provides valuable insight in reporting that "the world, perhaps, never contained a partisan officer who better understood the management of militia than did General Marion."[25]

The British used an indirect approach in their 1780 siege of Charleston that avoided Charleston's impressive harbor defenses enveloping the city from the rear. General Sir Henry Clinton set this plan in motion on February 11 by landing troops on Simmon's Island. At the time, Marion had been dispatched to train soldiers at a receiving station at Bacon's Bridge near Dorchester, but with this new threat, he was returned to his regiment on February 19 to help strengthen the fortifications around Charleston. The British steadily advanced, capturing Fort Johnson on March 6 and beginning siege operations around Charleston on April 1.

After Charleston surrendered on May 12, Hillsborough, North Carolina was designated as the general rendezvous point for the scattered Continental soldiers still in the South. Marion made his way there and reported to Major General Johann de Kalb. In spite of Marion's intimate familiarity with the local terrain, Major General Horatio Gates, who on June 14 had been named commanding general of the Southern Department, had little interest in a man he dismissed as a "hopping South Carolina colonel without a command [who] can tell me nothing."[26] With such limited opportunities under Gates, Marion asked to be released from the army in order to assume command of the militia in the Williamsburg District. Gates acquiesced and on August 15, Marion and a small party left the army with orders "to go Down the Country to Destroy all boats & Craft of any kind, we found on Santee River in Order to prevent Cornwallis & his Troops Escaping him."[27]

As a leader of farmer-partisans and militia of the lowcountry, Marion relied on the human resources frame rather than the structural frame that had been more appropriate with the Second Continental Regiment. If Marion failed to make this transition, he ran the risk that his independent-minded soldiers would simply leave camp and never return.[28] Thus, Weems reports that Marion sought to cultivate a willingness in his soldiers that grew from a conviction that it was in their interest to serve the Patriot cause. By appealing to their sense of liberty and their love of their families, Marion fostered internally, rather than externally, sustained commitment.[29] Because of this self-motivation, Marion was able to forsake the cruel discipline with which officers in Regular units kept their soldiers in line. Rather than the "rule of the lash," Marion led his partisans with tact, caring, and persuasion, being especially mindful to the concerns they had for their families and farms.

Marion's ability to transition between frames and apply them appropriately based on the audience and situation shows his great flexibility as a leader. His understanding of the psychological motivations of partisans and militiamen allowed him to tailor his relationship with them to create the environment they needed. He deftly used frame of reference to expand rather than limit his options.

The Political Frame

The political frame "sees organizations as arenas, contests, or jungles." Deeply rooted in political science theory, this perspective recognizes the competition that occurs when parochial interests battle for finite resources. This competition breeds conflict that must be resolved by routine bargaining, negotiation, coercion, and compromises. The leader must exercise political skill and acumen to keep things moving. Both ad-hoc and long-term coalitions form around issues. Problems arise when the leader cannot adjust to power being concentrated in the wrong places or being so widely dispersed that paralysis results.[30]

Francis Marion and Nathanael Greene

Nathanael Greene was quite decided in his feelings about the relationship between the Continental Army and the partisan forces. "The salvation of this Country don't depend upon little strokes," he told Thomas Sumter. Partisan victories were "like the garnish of a table, they give splendor to the army and reputation to the officers, but they afford no substantial national security." In Greene's mind, only a large regular army could bring decisive victory and that is where he assigned his priority for the allocation of limited resources.[31]

While pressing Sumter for horses, Greene added, "General Marion I am told has a considerable number of [dragoon horses] on which he has mounted Militia. It is a pity that good horses should be given into hands of people who are engaged for no limited time." To Marion directly, Greene wrote, "Get hold of all the good dragoon horses you can to mount our cavalry." When Marion took no action and Greene received intimation from Henry Lee that Marion had extra chargers, Greene sharply wrote Marion, "You would promote the Service greatly if you could furnish us with sixty or eighty good dragoon horses."[32]

With each request, Marion's frustration grew. Finally he wrote Greene, "I acknowledge that you have repeatedly mentioned the want of Dragoon horses & wish it had been in my power to furn[is]h them but it is not nor never had been. The few horses which have been taken from [Tories?] has been kept for the service & never for private property, but if you think it best for the service to Dismount the Malitia now with me I will direct Col. Lee … to do so, but am sertain we shall never git their service in future."

Marion wanted Greene to understand that such compliance would come with a price: "This would not give me any uneasiness as I have sometime Determin to relinquish my command in the militia as soon as you arrived in it & I wish to do it as soon as this post [Fort Motte] is Either taken or abandoned," he wrote Greene. "I shall assist in reducing the post here and when Col. Lee returns to you I [will] Take that opportunity in waiting on you when I hope to get permission to go to Philadelphia."[33]

Philadelphia, of course, was the home of the Continental Congress and a popular destination for disgruntled officers to lodge complaints. Greene knew he could ill afford to lose Marion and quickly went into what Andrew Waters calls "damage control mode." Greene wrote to Marion on May 9, commending him for "the important service [he had rendered] to the public with the Militia under your command" and wished him success in his current efforts against Fort Motte. There was no more talk of horses.[34]

Greene and Marion demonstrate the political frame in their competition for horses and the implications it had for the Continental Army and the militia. By threatening to resign, Marion brought the competition to the point of crisis and placed the onus on Greene to resolve the matter. Greene showed great restraint in dealing with the reliable but sometimes prickly Marion, and for his part, Marion also let the incident quickly dissipate.[35] While the issue did not go away, it seems as if there was a tacit mutual agreement to talk of it no more. Consistent with the political frame, both men did their part to "keep things moving."

The Symbolic Frame

The symbolic frame emphasizes "culture, symbols, and spirit as keys to organizational success." It draws on social and cultural anthropology to treat organizations as temples, tribes, theaters, or carnivals. Rather than the rationality common in the three other frames, the symbolic frame replaces rules, policies, and managerial authority with rituals, ceremonies, stories, heroes, and myths as the stuff that propels organizations. Leaders comfortable with this frame of reference may encounter problems when the actors in the theater misplay their roles, when symbols lose their meaning, or when rituals lose their potency.[36]

Francis Marion as the "Swamp Fox"

On August 16, 1780, the day after Gates sent Marion to Williamsburg, Gates suffered a catastrophic defeat by Lord Charles Cornwallis at the battle of Camden. Nearly 1,500 of Gates's 3,052 men were killed, wounded, or taken prisoner. The British, who began the battle outnumbered nearly two to one, suffered only 324 total casualties.[37] Just two days later, on August 18, Thomas Sumter's company of 800 partisans was surprised and overwhelmed by Lieutenant Colonel Banastre Tarleton at Fishing Creek, four miles north of Camden. Sumter lost 150 men killed or wounded and another 300 captured. Tarleton suffered just 16 men killed or wounded.[38] Like Gates, Sumter fled into North Carolina, his men scattering in all directions. The twin disasters created what John Oller concludes may well have been the Patriots' "darkest hour."[39] The defeats at Camden and Fishing Creek left Marion to stand alone as the only organized fighting force to oppose the British onslaught in South Carolina. He thus became the symbol of the Patriot resistance in South Carolina.

After the battle of Camden, Cornwallis sent a large number of prisoners taken there toward Charleston under an escort of 36 guards. Marion learned from a deserter that the guard and their prisoners were encamped at Sumter's abandoned plantation on Great Savannah, six miles east of Marion's location at Nelson's Ferry. Marion struck the unsuspecting British before dawn on August 20 and liberated some 150 prisoners, mostly Maryland Continentals. This small victory was a glimmer of hope in an otherwise dismal season for the Patriot cause. Gates passed the good news on to the Continental Congress, and newspapers including *The Boston Gazette*, *The Country Journal*, *The Connecticut Courant*, and *The Pennsylvania Journal* reported the story. With such publicity, biographer Hugh Rankin declares that Marion "was on his way to becoming something of a folk hero."[40]

Marion's rise drew the attention of Lieutenant Colonel Banastre Tarleton, who was perhaps Marion's chief adversary on the British side. In his 1787 memoir, Tarleton recalled that "Mr. Marion, by his zeal and abilities, showed himself capable of the trust committed to his charge. He collected his adherents on the shortest notice, in the neighborhood of Black River, and, after making excursions, he disbanded his followers. The alarms occasioned by these insurrections frequently retarded supplies on their way to the army; and a late report of Marion's strength delayed the junction of the recruits, who had arrived from New York for the corps in the country."[41]

Tarleton was willing to expend considerable resources to bring such a nemesis to bay; perhaps most famously on November 8, 1780, when he chased Marion for seven hours and 26 miles through the thick swamps near the Santee River. Eventually, an exhausted and frustrated Tarleton reportedly told his men, "Come, my Boys! Let us go back, and we will find the Gamecock [Thomas Sumter], but as for this damned old fox, the Devil himself could not catch him." From Tarleton's lament, Marion acquired the nickname "Swamp Fox" and took on an even greater symbolic role in the Patriot cause.[42]

Faced with a much better organized and equipped, and numerically superior foe, the Patriots in South Carolina found in Marion a symbol of pride and hope. He was the defense against what would otherwise have been an unchecked British juggernaut. The idea of Marion as a symbol of Patriot strength is captured in the opening lines of William Cullen Bryant's "Song of Marion's Men":

Our band is few, but true and tried,
Our leader frank and bold;
The British soldier trembles
When Marion's name is told.[43]

As a symbolic leader, Marion and his exploits quickly assumed legendary proportions, and any biographer faces the daunting task of separating the complex web of fact and fiction that has enmeshed Marion's life. (For a thoughtful analysis of this challenge, see Chapter Nine of *Francis Marion and the Snow Island Community*.) It is not the purpose of this vignette to untangle this web. Instead, it is to acknowledge the web's existence as evidence of how Marion and his partisans illustrate the symbolic frame of reference by using heroes, myths, spirit, and stories as leadership tools to influence people and action.

Francis Marion and the Responsibility of Leadership

"Duty then is the sublimest word in the English language. You should do your duty in all things. You can never do more, you should never want to do less."

ROBERT E. LEE

Willingly Accepting Responsibility

Regarding responsibility, John Gardner requires leaders to possess "the impulse to exercise initiative in social situations, to bear the burden of making the decision, to step forward when no one else will," and to do so with willingness and eagerness.[1] Gardner is making the distinction between a grudging or half-hearted approach to responsibilities and an attitude of affirmative and enthusiastic choice. Joseph Badaracco contrasts the somewhat passive "accepting" of responsibilities with leaders who "take" responsibility by wresting it "from a hard, recalcitrant world."[2] In so doing, they demonstrate that they have "not only the skills but also the determination and personal strength to be a leader."[3] As Badaracco describes it, "taking" responsibility implies a greater emotion, assertiveness, energy, and psychological commitment than does merely "accepting" responsibility.[4] Marion showed this elevated sense of responsibility in his decision to join the Patriot cause.

Francis Marion and the Patriot Cause

Although Marion escaped from Charleston before it fell, the city's ultimate surrender posed a new threat to his safety. Additional British troops could now be released to scour the countryside for suspected rebels and eradicate the uprising. In fact, General Sir Henry Clinton soon sent three columns of men into the interior of South Carolina to strengthen British control. The situation worsened still for the Patriots when Lord Charles Cornwallis succeeded Clinton and dispatched Banastre Tarleton to pursue what remained of the organized resistance. Tarleton caught up with Colonel Abraham Buford's 350 Virginia Continental dragoons at Waxhaws near the North Carolina border and decimated his enemy. Three hundred and sixteen Virginians were killed and 200 were wounded, compared to just 17 British killed and wounded. In the wake of Tarleton's rampage, even Governor John Rutledge was forced to flee to North Carolina.[5]

Charleston's *Royal Gazette* boasted that there was "NOT A REBEL IN ARMS IN THE COUNTRY," and rumors circulated that the Continental Congress was preparing to cede the three southernmost colonies to Britain. On May 22, Clinton issued a proclamation offering pardon to anyone who professed allegiance to the Crown, and many people flocked to take the oath.[6]

Given such circumstances, Scott Aiken concludes, "History would not have condemned [Marion] had he, a supernumerary officer without a command, limping on an ankle not yet healed, faded into the woods of the South Carolina lowcountry. He had already served in his state's militia against the Cherokees and earlier in the American Revolution."[7] Instead, Marion willingly accepted responsibility to make even greater contributions, in spite of the risks and sacrifices associated with his decision. He made his way to Hillsborough, North Carolina, the designated rendezvous point for Continental troops in the South after the fall of Charleston, arriving there sometime after July 27.[8]

Major General Horatio Gates, the commander of the Southern Department, gave Marion a cool reception, and Marion's prospects for being given significant responsibilities under Gates were slim. What seemed much more promising to Marion was news of the recent exploits of Thomas Sumter. After his home near Statesburgh was burned by men from Tarleton's Legion within two weeks of the fall of Charleston, Sumter had initiated what Hugh Rankin calls "the second revolution in South Carolina." On May 28, Sumter took to the field, collecting a partisan force, harassing British foraging parties, and disarming Loyalists. At Williamson's Plantation on July 11, forces under Sumter's general command soundly defeated a detachment of Tarleton's dragoons and Loyalist militia commanded by Captain Christian Huck. The victory attracted even more men to Sumter's group, swelling his ranks to about 600. More importantly, Sumter's resistance gave pause to British assumptions that South Carolina was on the verge of being restored to the authority of the Crown.[9]

Rather than while away his time under Gates's obvious lack of interest, Marion asked to be released from the army and build off Sumter's partisan success as commander of the militia in the Williamsburg District. It was a bold and uncertain move, and one for which John Oller notes there was "no script telling [Marion] what to do or where to go."[10] Such a circumstance clearly demonstrates how far Marion was willing and eager to go to take responsibilities on behalf of the Patriot cause.

Accountability

Badaracco argues that leaders take responsibility not when they merely know a job and its requirements, but "when they feel it is theirs."[11] This sense of ownership and personal attachment builds the perseverance a leader needs to see a task through to completion; not just grudgingly, but with eagerness. Henry Browning uses this elevated commitment and connection to make a distinction between responsibility and accountability. "Responsibility" for a task is generally extrinsically delegated to an individual by a senior, the organization, or by virtue of a position, but "accountability," Browning says, comes when that individual intrinsically takes ownership for the task and with it the consequences that come from success or failure.[12]

Francis Marion and Blue Savannah

Major General Horatio Gates gave few instructions to Marion, but when Marion left Gates in August 1780, Gates had told him "to go Down the Country to Destroy all boats & Craft of any kind, we found on Santee River in Order to prevent Cornwallis & his Troops Escaping him."[13] Such was fairly broad guidance, but it did represent an extrinsically assigned specified task. Gates told Marion what he was responsible for doing, where to do it, and even why to do it. Marion pursued this responsibility at Nelson's Ferry on August 20 where he struck a body of British troops and wagons. After the raid, Marion escaped Tarleton's pursuit and encamped at Port's Ferry on Britton's Neck.

Major Micajah Ganey had raised a regiment of Loyalist militia in the area, and when he learned of Marion's whereabouts, Ganey called up his men. He assembled a force of at least 250 men, including a troop of dragoons commanded by Captain Jesse Barefield. On September 4, Ganey led his men from their camp on the Little Pee Dee River in an attempt to surprise Marion.[14]

Marion, however, had learned of the Loyalist mobilization and had begun his own march along the Little Pee Dee in search of Ganey. Since both forces wore homespun, Marion instructed his 50 or so men to place white cockades in their caps to distinguish friend from foe. To preserve secrecy, Marion did not tell his men their destination, but placed the capable Major John James and a group of select horsemen as an advance guard.[15]

After about two hours of movement, one of James's scouts reported a Loyalist company of 45 mounted men blocking the road. James ordered his men to attack, and the startled British scattered and fled. James lost one man wounded, and only 15 men from Ganey's advance guard escaped; the rest were killed, wounded, or captured.

Marion learned from the prisoners that the main body of Loyalists was about three miles away and began moving in that direction. In about 10 minutes he ran into Barefield's men, who had been alerted of the action and were waiting in battle line. Barefield had a force of 200, and Marion wisely decided to retreat. As he did, he feigned fear and using his tactic of retreat, enticed Barefield to pursue.[16]

Marion halted his men at Blue Savannah, an open sandy swale surrounded by a screen of pine saplings and undergrowth, and set up an ambush. Thinking Marion was on the run, Barefield pressed onward without proper security into the ambush. As Marion's mounted men attacked, the unprotected Loyalist infantry broke and ran into the surrounding woods and the Little Pee Dee Swamp.[17]

Marion pursued the British to the edge of the swamp and then returned to camp. At this point, Marion was beginning to expand beyond mere responsibility and into accountability. He knew that following the enemy into the swamp would be dangerous and time consuming, but his decision to end the engagement was based on more than just immediate caution and convenience. It also reflected Marion's consideration of the longer-term consequences of unnecessary Loyalist bloodshed.[18] As Marion's biographer Robert Bass explains, "the wounds of civil strife would heal more quickly if there were no dead kinsmen to remember."[19] As an accountable leader, Marion considered these consequences and decided not to pursue the enemy further.

At Blue Savannah, Marion successfully accomplished his mission to harass and attrite the British. Beyond this assigned responsibility, however, were important considerations about how he should proceed. British support had never been strong in the country along the Pee Dee River, and Marion understood that long-term interests required him to use the minimum force necessary.[20] His restraint and accountability were well rewarded. The Loyalist hold east of the Pee Dee was largely broken, and 60 new volunteers soon rode in to Marion's camp, doubling his strength.[21]

Share of the Task

Borrowing from part of the United States Army Ranger Creed, General Stanley McChrystal titled his memoir *My Share of the Task*. The implication is that a leader accepts responsibility in the context of being but one player on a much bigger team. Their responsibilities do not impact only themselves; they are part of a whole that is greater than the sum of its parts. The leader must determine not just what their "share" is, but how it fits in to the broader "task." They must build the situational awareness needed to understand their role and to fulfill their responsibilities not as ends unto themselves but as parts of the whole.

Francis Marion's Support to the Overall Strategy

General George Washington had originally favored Nathanael Greene to command the Southern Department, but the Continental Congress instead appointed Horatio Gates to the post on July 25, 1780. Gates largely ignored Marion, answering few of his letters and leaving him mostly unaware of the plans of the Southern Army and how he could support it. That all changed in October when, after the defeat at Camden, Congress voted to allow Washington to name a new commander. Washington selected Greene who proceeded to the Southern Department, reaching Charlotte on December 2 to relieve Gates.[22]

By temperament, Greene would have preferred to have a body of American regulars who had the discipline, unit cohesion, and officer leadership necessary to defeat the British on equal terms. He knew, however, that he lacked such a force at the moment and would for the immediate future. Instead, Greene found in North Carolina a force of just 1,482 men, only a fraction of which were Continentals. They were poorly trained and equipped, and save for some limited successes in backcountry actions, had largely been defeated in the last six months of fighting. Lord Charles Cornwallis, on the other hand, commanded an army of disciplined British regulars some three times greater than Greene's and was fresh from the victory at Camden. Greene knew that he needed time to recruit and train men, to gather supplies, and to build confidence.[23]

To gain that time, Greene would rely on irregulars like Marion to keep Cornwallis occupied. Greene wrote Marion on December 4, "Until a more permanent Army can be collected than is in the Field at present, we must endeavor to keep up a Partizan War and preserve the Tide of Sentiment among the People as much as possible."[24] Greene also knew, however, that he could not give Cornwallis a free hand against the much smaller partisan bands. To relieve that pressure, Greene advanced his small Continental force into the Cheraw area of South Carolina to serve as a target for Cornwallis. He tempted Cornwallis further by dividing his force, sending Daniel Morgan toward Ninety Six with 600 men. Greene also ordered Lieutenant Colonel Henry Lee and his Legion to join forces with Marion.[25] The result was a mutually supporting relationship of which Bruce Lancaster quipped, "without Greene, Marion could not have existed. Without Marion, Greene could hardly have survived."[26]

By the spring of 1781, Greene's South Carolina strategy had evolved in to the so-called "War of the Posts." The British had established a supply line that pushed inland from Charleston and Georgetown. A series of relatively isolated posts both guarded the supply line and gave British forces bases from which to operate. Greene hoped that by nearly simultaneously attacking several key posts he could prevent the posts from reinforcing each other. Without their posts to guard their supply line, the British would be forced back to Charleston.[27]

Marion reveled in the role he played within Greene's larger strategy, and his attacks on the British supply lines had multiple-order effects. Obviously, they disrupted the British ability to logistically support on-going operations. Moreover, the constant threats caused Banastre Tarleton and other British commanders to divert soldiers from offensive operations in order to guard baggage trains and depots. Finally, the supplies that Marion captured helped equip his men and the Continental Army.[28]

In his classic description of guerrilla warfare, Mao Tse-tung describes three phases that culminate in conventional battle. That great battle in the American Revolution would ultimately occur at Yorktown, Virginia in September and October 1781, but until then, partisans like Marion contributed to the overall American strategy by accomplishing the preservation and expansion Mao requires of the first two phases.[29] Understanding how his responsibilities fit into the overall scheme of things, Marion found his "share of the task" and excelled at it.

Responsibility to Principles

While all roles come with a certain set of responsibilities, the leader cannot let their role define them. Instead, leaders should be defined by their values and their character.[30] The very expression "play a role" connotes a certain inauthenticity and an emphasis on image rather than reality. "Playing a role" requires constant maintenance and often involves making your followers think you are something you are not. Being yourself comes naturally and allows for transparent and trusting relationships. An authentic leader behaves in a way that subordinates the expectations of their professional role to who they are as a person. Leaders are true to themselves and responsible to their principles.[31]

Stephen Covey makes an interesting distinction between principles and values. Values are the social norms of the organization, and like all values, they are personal, emotional, subjective, and arguable. The particular values are unique to the given organization, and all organizations, even criminal, hateful, and selfish ones, have some set of values that they embrace. But principles, Covey argues, are impersonal, factual, objective, and self-evident. They transcend other factors in that even though different cultures or individuals may translate principles into different practices and the wrongful use of freedom may obscure principles over time, the principles remain. Covey equates them to natural laws that operate constantly. Values may govern behavior, but principles, he argues, govern consequences, and principled leadership aligns the organization's values with nature's changeless principles.[32]

Francis Marion and Sumter's Law

In March 1781, Brigadier General Thomas Sumter announced a plan to raise a regular, standing militia of 10-month enlistments. Known as "Sumter's Law," the plan proposed paying officers and men in slaves that were anticipated to be captured from Loyalists. A colonel was "to receive three grown negroes and one small negro." A private was authorized "one grown negro." Each rank in between had its own allotment.[33] While Colonel Andrew Pickens adopted this recruiting incentive and Nathanael Greene tacitly approved of it, Marion rejected it, stating that it was "inhuman, immoral, and violative of due process."[34]

Sumter's Law had its intended effect in drawing recruits. In fact, Sumter's ranks were so swelled that he could not pay their promised bonuses. To pacify his complaining soldiers, Sumter resorted to plunder, such as in July 1781 when he ordered Captain William Ransome Davis to seize the slaves, horses, salt, indigo, and medical supplies in and around

Georgetown. Georgetown was Marion's territory and the incursion cost him. While it "may Interfer with my Command," Marion reported, "[I] suppose I must submit." When Greene belatedly learned of the situation, he noted, "General Sumter's taking the goods at Georgetown was certainly wrong, but it is now too late to prevent it."[35]

Marion issued strict orders to protect slaves from falling victim to Sumter's seizures. Colonel Peter Horry was among those officers in South Carolina who attempted to lease black laborers to support military operations. While Marion provided Horry the Continental currency for hiring slaves, Marion charged that he would "not suffer Negroes to be seized on or taken out of his Brigade."[36] This was in fact his attitude toward all seizures. "Any soldier taking any article from any plantation from white or black," he warned his men, "will be deemed a marauder & plunderer & shall suffer immediate death."[37]

In 1784, the General Assembly passed a law exempting all officers who had seized private property for public use from liabilities of civil suit. Sumter readily accepted this exemption—in fact he had lobbied heavily for it—but Marion steadfastly rejected it. "If, in a single instance, in the course of my command," he wrote, "I have done that which I can't justify, justice requires that I should suffer for it."[38]

On similar principle, Marion objected to the Confiscation Acts passed in 1782 which authorized the state to seize the real and personal property of known Loyalists, in part to pay off Sumter's troops. In 1783, Governor John Matthews hosted a dinner for a number of senators, most of whom were opposed to pardoning any Loyalists. Matthews called upon Marion to make a toast. Marion's biographer William Boddie surmises that, because Marion was known to favor showing mercy to the Loyalists, Matthews may have intended the dinner as a means of weakening Marion's resolve. If so, Matthews was to be disappointed. Raising his glass and pausing to gain the audience's full attention, Marion forcefully said "Here's damnation to the Confiscation act."[39]

Marion's respect for personal and property rights was based on his principles. He had many opportunities to "play a role" and act according to expediency, convenience, or external pressure. Instead, he remained true to his authentic self and followed his principles.

Francis Marion and the Interpersonal Component of Leadership

"The greatest leader is not necessarily the one who does the greatest things.
He is the one that gets the people to do the greatest things."

RONALD REAGAN

Dealing with People

Leadership is about mobilizing others to achieve a common goal. It requires a relationship between the leader and the follower, and it is the nature of that relationship that determines the quality and quantity of what gets done and the ease or difficulty it takes along the way. Because leadership is a team event rather than a solo performance, leaders should remember advertising executive Charlie Brower's observation that "few people are successful unless a lot of other people want them to be."[1]

Francis Marion and the Conniving Lieutenant

On September 14, 1775, Marion sailed from Gadsen's Wharf in downtown Charleston to an anchorage a mile from James Island as part of an expedition led by Colonel William Moultrie to capture British-held Fort Johnson. In addition to 50 men under Marion's command, there were 50 more under Charles Cotesworth Pinckney and 50 more under Barnard Elliot. The next morning, the force prepared to storm the fort only to find a British guard of five men waiting to surrender it.[2]

In November, Moultrie ordered Marion to move with 90 men to defend an arsenal at Dorchester, a village 20 miles outside Charleston, in anticipation of a British attack there. When the attack failed to materialize, Marion was called back to Charleston and was helping repair Fort Johnson in January 1776 when an incident occurred that illustrates his skill in dealing with people.

By this time Marion was a captain. Under his command was an unnamed lieutenant who had previously served under other captains, all of whom the dramatic Parson Weems reports had "spoken of him as a slippery, worthless fellow, whom they knew not what to do with."[3] The lieutenant was, according to Weems, "destitute of soul as a monkey."[4]

The lieutenant became aware of a cockfight in Dorchester that he wanted to attend and in order to obtain leave from the fort, concocted a story that he wished to visit his dying father. Marion quickly assented, telling the deceiver, "To be sure, lieutenant, go, by all means, go and wait upon your father; but return as soon as possible, for you see how much we have to do."[5]

As was his plan, the lieutenant abused Marion's trust, and it was some two weeks later before he returned to duty. Marion was at the time sitting with his officers and pretended not to notice the lieutenant. Embarrassed and trying to recover himself, the lieutenant said, "I am sorry, sir, to have overstayed my time so long; but—but I could not help it—but now I am returned to do my duty." By this time, Marion was wise to the charade and, with what Weems describes as "a most notifying neglect," replied, "Aye, lieutenant, is that you? Well, never mind it—there is no harm done—I never missed you."[6]

The lieutenant slunk away and soon found himself the source of his comrades' great amusement. He had to admit that in Marion he had met his match. "I was never at a loss before," he lamented, "to manage all other officers that were ever set over me. As for our colonel [Moultrie], he is a fine, honest, good-natured old buck. But I can wind him round my finger like a pack thread. But as for the stern, keen-eyed Marion, I dread him."[7]

Marion knew exactly how to deal with a pompous and self-serving character like the lieutenant. Even after the initial rebuke, Marion kept him at arms' length and "when visited on business, he would receive and treat him with a formality sufficient to let him see that all was not right." But Marion's distance was not without purpose. Weems notes that Marion "wished his officers to be gentlemen. And whenever he saw one of them acting below that character, he would generously attempt his reformation."[8]

And so it was with this case. Weems reports the lieutenant soon "became remarkably polite, and also attentive to duty. In short, no sub-altern behaved better." As the lieutenant improved, so did his relations with those around him, to include with Marion, and the two grew to become both brothers-in-arms and friends.[9]

Even allowing for Weems's characteristic embellishments, Marion's treatment of the lieutenant illustrates the need of leaders to meet people where they are. To some, a stern rebuke is needed where for others a word of encouragement is in order. Marion was able to deal with people in a range of ways in order to bring out the best in them.

Understanding Followers' Needs

The traditional yardstick for interacting with others is the Golden Rule's admonition to treat others as we would like to be treated our-selves. Marshall Goldsmith notes that a better standard might be to treat others as *they* would like to be treated. His logic is that we all have different levels of tolerance for life's inconsistencies, annoyances, and difficulties. If it is within our ability to absorb some circumstance, we sometimes have a hard time understanding why other people can't also just suck it up and deal with it. Real understanding of others requires us to see things not from our point of view but from the other person's. Leaders must remember that they are leading other people; not themselves.[10]

Servant leadership is a leadership approach that embodies this awareness and empathy. The servant leader meets the subordinate's legitimate needs—which might include such concerns as training, encouragement, resources, or help with personal issues—in order to allow the subordinate to better focus on and accomplish the organizational mission.[11] While the traditional authoritarian leader asks, "What can the organization do for me?" the servant leader asks, "What can I do for the organization?"

Servant leadership requires attention to the subordinate's situation, humility, and hard work. The servant leader must figure out what their subordinates need, put their own needs aside, and devote time and energy to creating the environment where the subordinates are both cared for and empowered. The idea is that if the leader meets their subordinates' needs, they can then concentrate on and are empowered to pursue the organization's needs. They also build a genuine trust in their leader based on responsiveness to their needs.

Some leaders shy away from servant leadership because of its demands, but Major General William Cohen argues, "Many times the dilemma between accomplishing the mission and taking care of the troops is a false one. Many times both objectives can be achieved if the leader is willing to work a little harder himself."[12] Servant leaders must do that hard work.

Francis Marion and Leading Partisans

Many of Marion's men were small farmers who lived along the Black and Pee Dee rivers.[13] As such, they were beholden to the agricultural cycle for their livelihood and survival. They were also responsible for the safety of their families and the security of their property. Whenever they were in the field with Marion, his men had understandable concerns for their crops and loved ones. As William Simms explains, the planting of crops "though not allowed by the regular disciplinarian, was, in the mind of the militiaman, a duty quite as imperative as any that he owed to his family. Indeed, it was inseparable from his necessities that, when the Government did not give him bread, he must make it for himself. His family could not starve, and if he could fight without pay, it was not possible to do so without food."[14]

Marion understood these needs and accepted that his men would come and go as they felt necessary to tend to their responsibilities at home. As a result, Hugh Rankin estimates that Marion seldom had the same people under his command for longer than two weeks.[15] This significant turnover created numerous difficulties for Marion in terms of training, readiness, and predictability, but he did not interfere with it because of his sensitivity to the situations of his men.

Marion's commitment to his men's domestic responsibilities was tested late in 1780. After the Patriot successes at Great Savannah and Blue Savannah, the British sent units commanded by Major James Wemyss and Major Micajah Ganey to punish Marion. Marion dispersed his men and retreated to the Great White Marsh in North Carolina to avoid the converging British forces, but while he was away, Wemyss took out his frustration by ransacking the Williamsburg District, cutting a swath of destruction 70 miles long and in places 15 miles wide. Recovering from this loss, Williamsburg militiamen returned to Marion's Great White Marsh encampment, and on September 29, 1780, Marion conducted a swift attack at Black Mingo Creek. Marion inflicted about two dozen British casualties, and, still possessing the element of surprise, wished to press the attack against Colonel Joseph Wigfall's 50 Loyalists stationed at Black River Church. Instead, however, Marion acknowledged the concerns of the men who had withdrawn with him from Blue Savannah to the Great White Marsh. These men had not seen their families since Wemyss's rampage through Williamsburg and were anxious to learn if he had harmed their homes. As Simms explains, in such cases, "the necessity of providing for, and protecting destitute families, starving wives and naked children, was more imperative than that of a remote and fancied liberty."[16] Instead of pressing the attack, Marion conducted a retrograde to safety at Ami's Mill on Drowning Creek, asking the men who departed for home to return as soon as possible.[17]

With these reductions, Marion found himself bivouacked at Port's Ferry with just 60 men. He was impatient to resume activity and had perhaps underestimated the difficult conditions that his men had to rectify back with their families.[18] Nonetheless, having tended to their interests at home, the militiamen slowly returned to camp, and Marion's strength had risen to 150 men by the time he attacked a lax Tory camp at Tearcoat Swamp on October 26. After still more time for his men to recuperate, Marion sent out a call for additional manpower in preparation for the December 12–13, 1780 battle at Halfway Swamp. Soon his force swelled to 700 men. In explaining the timing of the resurgence, Scott

Aiken notes that "since the crop cycle was complete, times on the farm were slower, and the militia and partisans responded well."[19]

By accepting that his men needed the freedom to come and go, Marion was modelling servant leadership. He was meeting his subordinates' legitimate needs in order to allow them to better focus on and accomplish the organizational mission.[20] Of course, such accommodation of his men placed a burden on Marion by limiting his freedom of action. All told, however, it was a wise decision. Marion's men responded to his obvious concern for their needs by giving him their steadfast loyalty.

Presence

Belle Linda Halpern and Kathy Lubar call for a "leadership presence" that represents "the ability to connect authentically with the thoughts and feelings of others, in order to motivate and inspire them toward a desired outcome."[21] A leader's presence helps show subordinates their genuineness, approachability, and humanity and that the activity is truly a priority of theirs. But because leaders cannot be everywhere at once, the presence they impart is the result of choices they make and actions they take or fail to take.[22] By being present in one place, they are necessarily absent in another. They must make a conscious decision to be where their presence can have the most impact.

In Marion's day, a leader's presence was especially important because of the demand for "heroic leadership." In that era, society worked "to accentuate and exaggerate the characteristics of those to whom it conceded leadership for war and conquest." Heroic leaders were "champions of display, of skill-at-arms, of bold speech but, above all, of exemplary risk-taking." John Keegan notes that such a leader had to make a mask: "a mask made in such form as will mark him to men of his time and place as the leader they want and need."[23]

Francis Marion and the Leader's Location

Leaders need to be where they can understand and influence events. That does not necessarily mean they always need to be in the tactical thick of things. In fact, sometimes such closeness can limit rather than enhance a leader's ability to understand and influence. In many cases, Marion led from a distance that allowed him to see the big picture and make decisions. Other times, Marion felt he needed to be in the midst of the action. The battle at Quinby Bridge on July 17, 1781, was such a case, and Marion's decision to take a forward position offers a contrast from Thomas Sumter's decision to stay further back.

The battle of Quinby Bridge was part of Sumter's "Dog Days Campaign," so called because it took place in the hottest part of the South Carolina summer. Sumter had long desired to subdue the British post at Moncks Corner, and Nathanael Greene finally acquiesced to letting him try with Marion and Henry Lee under his command.

The British force commanded by Lieutenant Colonel John Coates had taken up a nearly impregnable position behind the three-foot thick brick walls of Biggin Church across the Cooper River. At about 3:00am on July 17, Coates set fire to the church and moved down the Cooper. Eighteen miles later Coates's infantry reached Quinby Creek, crossed it, and began throwing planks off the bridge to thwart the Patriot cavalry that had been following them. The British had already created a significant gap in the bridge when Lee rode up with his cavalry, but Lee boldly pressed across. He was followed by a contingent of Marion's cavalry led by Lieutenant Colonel Hezekiah Maham.[24]

The British repulsed a disorganized series of Patriot charges and then withdrew a short distance to the covered positions of the main house and outbuildings of the Shubrick Plantation. Marion and Lee assessed the situation and decided they would need their own infantry to attack the well-protected British. The pair also wanted to wait for their sole artillery piece to be brought forward to assist with the attack. While these preparations were being made, Sumter rode up and ordered an immediate attack. Marion and Lee pointed out the disadvantage of the present odds, but Sumter insisted.[25]

Sumter ordered a South Carolina militia unit of 45 men under Colonel Thomas Taylor to occupy a fence a short distance from the Shubrick house. He ordered Marion to move across an open field to a fence some 50 yards on the other side of the house. As for his own brigade, Sumter took up a position behind some slave quarters outside of shooting range.[26]

Nathanael Greene (Artist, Charles Wilson Peale, 1783, Wikimedia Commons).

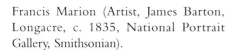

Francis Marion (Artist, James Barton, Longacre, c. 1835, National Portrait Gallery, Smithsonian).

Francis Marion (Artist, P. P. Carter, South Carolina House Chamber Portraits, Columbia, SC).

Horatio Gates (Artist, James Peale, c. 1782, National Portrait Gallery, Smithsonian).

Henry Lee (Artist, James Herring, c. 1834, National Portrait Gallery, Smithsonian).

Thomas Sumter (Artist, William Armstrong, c. 1835, National Portrait Gallery, Smithsonian).

Francis Rawdon-Hastings (Artist, Martin Archer Stone, National Gallery of Ireland, Wikimedia commons).

Lord Cornwallis (Artist, Thomas Gainsborough, 1783, National Portrait Gallery, London).

Banastre Tarleton (Artist, Joshua Reynolds, 1782, National Gallery).

Miniature of young man in uniform, possibly Peter Horry (Courtesy of the South Caroliniana Library, University of South Carolina, Columbia, S.C.).

Revolutionary Militia crossing a river (Artist, William Ranney, c 1854).

Marion crossing Pee Dee (Artist, William Ranney, 1850, Amon Carter Museum of American Art).

Mrs. Motte directing Generals Marion and Lee to burn her mansion (Artist, John Blake White, c. before 1859, U.S. Senate).

Battle of Fort Moultrie, 1776 (Artist, John Blake White, 1826, Wikimedia Commons).

General Marion inviting a British Officer to share his meal (Artist, John Blake White, U.S. Senate).

Battle of Eutaw Springs (Artist, Alonzo Chappel, c. 1858, Wikimedia Commons).

Marion's tomb near Pineville, South Carolina (Photo by Steven D. Smith).

Statue of Francis Marion at Venter's Landing, South Carolina, formerly Witherspoon's Ferry (Photo by Steven D. Smith).

Taylor's men quickly came under fire and were running low on ammunition. The British were poised to charge them with their bayonets when Marion launched an oblique attack under heavy fire to come to Taylor's aid. Marion's attack forced the British to call off their bayonet charge, and the battle continued for another 45 minutes. Then Marion withdrew in good order to a bivouac 15 miles away.[27]

Marion's position at the decisive point of the attack allowed him to lead by example, understand the situation, and influence the action by assisting Taylor. This location at the front stands in sharp contrast to Sumter's position of safety. Taylor was furious at the battle's mismanagement and went looking for Sumter. Instead of anywhere near the action, Taylor "found Gen. Sumter sitting coolly under the shade of a tree."[28] John Oller describes Taylor as having a "longtime, dutiful" relationship with Sumter, but that Taylor could not now suppress his disgust.[29] "Sir," he told Sumter, "I don't know why you sent me forward on a forlorn hope, promising to sustain me, & failed to do so, unless you designed to sacrifice me. I will never more serve under you."[30] Marion also noted Sumter's distance from the action, telling Greene in his report of the battle, "I cannot give any perticulars of Gen. Sumters Brigade as they was too great a distance from me with fences & Corn fields which Interupted the sight."[31]

Marion was not reckless or foolhardy in selecting his position as a leader. Henry Lumpkin notes that Marion led by "riding into battle at the head of his men, but seldom participating in the actual fighting. Instead, he directed and controlled the action with calm brilliance, attacking savagely or pulling back from an engagement as the situation required."[32] Marion always selected positions that allowed him to "direct and control." At Quinby Bridge, that position was in the front.

Unity of Effort

Dating back to at least 1921, US Army doctrine has cited nine "principles of war" as being fundamental to successful military operations. Over time, the exact names of the principles have fluctuated to reflect a particular emphasis. One good example of this phenomenon is the distinction between "unity of command" and "unity of effort."

Unity of command is the traditional principle of war. In pure cases of unity of command, there is a single commander who has authority over all the forces involved in the operation. As the military began conducting more and more operations involving host nation forces, irregular units, civilian agencies, and non-governmental organizations, cases of pure unity of command became increasingly rare. What such situations required was not unity of command, but "unity of effort." Unity of effort is "coordination and cooperation toward common objectives, even if the participants are not necessarily part of the same command or organization, which is the product of successful unified action."[33]

The globalized era and the changing nature of society have also affected the ability of non-military leaders to leverage unity of command in its traditional hierarchal form. Instead, they must recognize the large degree of free will that various stakeholders wield in any situation and seek the function provided by unity of effort. To do so, they must draw heavily on their conceptual and interpersonal skills.

In many areas, the unity that could safely be assumed in years past is declining as extreme positions and polarization become increasingly commonplace. Many adherents to single-issue agendas are particularly strident in their rhetoric and in their confidence that theirs is the only legitimate position. When trying to build unity of effort with such stakeholders, the first task of the leader is often to reestablish a dialogue where one has ceased to effectively function. In such situations, the leader must practice graceful listening and acknowledge hearing the other person's point of view as a prerequisite to building the trust necessary to establishing unity of effort.[34]

This is not to say that groups need to reach accord on everything. The strength of diversity is the different perspectives that different people bring to the organization. Nonetheless, leaders must build on the agreement found in common values in order to achieve unity of effort.[35] They must look past themselves and their strict agendas, and seek the bigger picture.

Friedrich Nietzsche cautioned that "many are stubborn in pursuit of the path they have chosen, few in the pursuit of the goal." Unity of effort occurs when people focus on the goal and find common purpose in achieving it.[36] It requires communicating to all involved "how the dream is a shared dream and how it fulfills the common good."[37]

Francis Marion, Thomas Sumter, and Andrew Pickens

While there was no formal unity of command among them, South Carolina's three partisan leaders—Francis Marion, Thomas Sumter, and Andrew Pickens—certainly achieved unity of effort. With the British closing in, on April 12, 1780, Major General Benjamin Lincoln persuaded Governor John Rutledge to leave Charleston "to preserve the Executive Authority of the State." There was only one escape route: to follow the Cooper River to the Wando River and then to the hinterland. While Brigadier General Isaac Huger held the upper approaches open at Moncks Corner, some 30 miles above Charleston, Rutledge and a few key members of his council made their escape. Rutledge eventually found safety in North Carolina, where he used the special emergency powers that had been granted him to keep the Patriot resistance alive. Key among Rutledge's initiatives was his sanction of the activities of Sumter, Marion, and Pickens.[38]

Sumter was the first of the three to launch partisan activities on a broad scope. Winning the nickname of the "Gamecock," for his fierceness in a fight, Sumter operated in what is now known as the "midlands" section of South Carolina, but ranged into North Carolina as well. Marion picked up the sobriquet of the "Swamp Fox," because his territory was below Sumter's in the "lowcountry" swamps of the Pee Dee River. The third partisan leader, Andrew Pickens, carried with him the moniker "Skyagunsta" or "Wizard Owl" from his days fighting the Cherokee. He operated in the foothills of South Carolina's "upstate" region. No one coordinated or assigned these geographic boundaries. Instead, Sumter, Marion, and Pickens simply began fighting where they lived.[39]

The three had much in common. They were all born in the 1730s, were products of the South Carolina backcountry, and had extensive service in militia, provincial, or Continental forces. There were also some differences. Only Marion was a native of South Carolina. Sumter was born in Virginia and Pickens in Pennsylvania. Marion was a Huguenot and Pickens a Presbyterian, and their religions were very influential in their lives. At least at the time of the American Revolution, Sumter appears to have been less shaped by his religion. Growing up, he attended St. Mark's Episcopal Church, but after the war he became a regular worshipper at High Hills Baptist Church.[40] Sumter and Marion immediately continued the fight after the defeat at Charleston. Pickens was so discouraged by the loss that he initially took the oath of loyalty to the Crown required by Henry Clinton to obtain "protection." Subsequent British atrocities convinced Pickens to violate his parole and rejoin the Patriot cause in December 1780.[41]

South Carolina became the focus of the British efforts to regain the southern colonies, and it was the independent guerrilla efforts of Sumter, Marion, and Pickens that initially thwarted their plans. With the arrival of Nathanael Greene's army, regular and partisan forces combined in an overall campaign that led to Cowpens and Guilford Court House. These successes were the result of unity of effort rather than unity of command.

Commons

In the globalized world, leaders spend less time commanding and more time engaging. Thus, Bob Johansen challenges leaders to be "ravenous networkers with active links all around the world."[42] This connectivity creates "commons" which are the platforms of shared resources that individuals and groups use for the greater good. Commons can grow out of ad hoc arrangements, but generally they take a long-term view toward sharing assets and continuing value for the participants over an extended period of time. Sometimes the leader will personally create the commons, but in other situations their task may be to step back to create a space for others to fill and then to hold that space open for the common good. An effective leader knows that creating commons builds unity of effort by using cooperation to take competition to a higher level. Commons make win/win situations possible by expanding the playing field and improving conditions so that everyone can benefit.[43]

Francis Marion and Snow's Island

One example of a commons was Marion's secret camp at Snow's Island, a triangular-shaped, three-mile-long by two-mile-wide plateau in the swamps in the southeast corner of what is now Florence County. Bordered by the Pee Dee to the northeast, Lynches Creek to the north, and Clark's Creek to the west and south, Snow's Island offered Marion the seclusion and protection he needed to rest and refit his brigade. Its proximity to Witherspoon's, Port's, and Britton's Ferries facilitated control of well-travelled transportation arteries and gave Marion the opportunity to "sally forth, as occasion offered, to harass the superior foe, to cut off his convoys, or to break up, before they could well embody, the gathering and undisciplined Tories."[44] On the northern tip of the island there was dry, higher ground surrounded by marsh, canebrakes, and thick undergrowth which afforded a protected and snug campsite.[45] Before the American Revolution, this northern section was owned and farmed by William Goddard, and the only buildings that existed there were Goddard's cabin and barn.[46]

Marion established a camp at Snow's Island sometime around mid-November 1780 and quickly set out to improve these natural advantages with his own protective measures. His men created obstacles by dismantling bridges and felling trees. They collected up all the boats of the neighborhood and kept them on the island side of the rivers and creeks so attackers could not use them. Frequent patrols saturated the area and provided early warning of approaching traffic. Marion reinforced Goddard's barn, transforming it into the "Bull Pen" used to house captured prisoners. On the east side of the Pee Dee, across from Snow's Island at Dunham's Bluff, Marion built a small earthwork to protect his flank. He also established a small camp at Dunham's Bluff. In fact, he may very well have had several camps on and around Snow's Island that allowed him to vary his location and keep the enemy guessing.[47]

The Snow's Island community was dominated by Whigs, and even if many of the men were off fighting, women and slaves kept the local farms and plantations running and able to provide reliable sources of supply.[48] Marion and the Snow's Island community had a symbiotic relationship in which the community provided Marion with men, food and forage, and intelligence and Marion offered security and protection from Loyalist antagonists.[49] His rank as a lieutenant colonel in the Continental Army tied his followers to the overall greater Patriot government, both at the state level and national level, as militia soldiers rather than being illegitimate civilian bandits or outlaws. Peter Horry described the citizenry's role as being both "generous stewards and faithful spies, so that, while there, we lived at once in safety and plenty." Marion exercised his characteristic respect for private property, refusing to request more than was necessary and issuing receipts to allow reimbursement from the government for the supplies he took. He also launched raids against nearby Tories to dissuade them from antagonizing the Patriots. One such operation into the Waccamaw Neck region north of Georgetown netted 150 precious bushels of salt. After supplying his brigade's needs, Marion distributed the remainder, "in quantities, not exceeding a bushel for each Whig family; and thus endeared himself the more to his followers."[50]

Snow's Island was a commons that mutually benefited Marion and the community. John Oller notes that this symbiotic relationship was "one reason Marion gained the hearts and minds of his countrymen, whereas the British, with their threats and reprisals against the inhabitants, failed to do so."[51] Commons create win-win situations, and that is exactly what Snow's Island was for Marion and the Whigs around it.

Cooperating with Peers

John Maxwell refers to peer-to-peer leadership as "leading across" in a way that helps peers win. To do so, leaders must establish relationships based on a "follow me, I'll walk with you" philosophy.[52] Leading peers requires a particularly nuanced approach to cooperation, explanation, and persuasion to create win-win situations.

Maxwell emphasizes that especially when dealing with peers, leadership must be viewed as a long-term, on-going process. Because leading peers is based on personal rather than positional power, it requires the investment in time necessary to build human relationships. Expedient short-cuts and desire for quick results generally are counterproductive to such efforts.[53]

An example of the leadership challenge of cooperating with peers is present in institutions such as the many universities that govern themselves according to the collegial system. Even though the university president may have extraordinary powers based on their position, they are largely viewed by their colleagues as "first among equals" rather than the "boss." Therefore, university presidents are "expected to influence without coercion, to direct without sanction, and to control without inducing alienation."[54]

Robert Birnbaum suggests that to be effective in such situations, leaders must be especially purposeful in serving as role models and facilitating communication. "Exemplify[ing] the values of the group to an exceptional degree" is critical, Birnbaum explains, because it "engenders trust ... and the leverage it confers."[55] Because there is no official authority that the leader can draw on, trust is what they use to gain the followership of their peers. Such leaders also gain influence by placing themselves "at the center of the communications web." From this position they serve to create interaction, while at the same time listening to other people state their views and overcoming the leader's tendency to talk and pass judgment. Birnbaum explains that "in permitting others to talk or argue, the leader is not abrogating responsibility, because in any social exchange the leader's values will ultimately carry more weight than those of others."[56]

Francis Marion and Henry Lee

The fluid nature of partisan warfare placed a premium on unity of effort. Marion had to manage interactions with the local population, squabbles over rank among subordinates such as Hezekiah Maham and Peter Horry, and his own dealings with Continental officers such as Henry Lee. Of this last matter, Gregory Massey and Jim Piecuch write that Nathanael Greene "showed an uncanny knack for pairing Continental and militia/ partisan officers for operations," including the "volatile" Lee with the "steady" Marion.[57]

Marion was 20 years Lee's senior, but their differences went well beyond age. Ryan Cole paints a stark contrast between "Lee, who drank wine from silver chalices, and Marion, who subsisted strictly on a mixture of vinegar and water." Their troops were also markedly different, with Lee's arrayed in "immaculate uniforms," while many of Marion's "scruffy men" did not even have uniforms.[58]

In spite of their differences, Marion and Lee worked together successfully on several occasions. The partnership began on January 20, 1781, when Greene ordered Lee's 300 Continental cavalry and infantry to reinforce Marion's scant brigade of approximately 90 men. Together the men planned what would be Marion's third attack on Georgetown.

The two forces were closely integrated during the movement from Snow's Island to Georgetown. Lee's infantry and Marion's dismounted men moved by river, with Marion's men serving as guides. This contingent departed on January 22. A day later, Lee's cavalry and Marion's mounted men began an overland movement. Unfortunately, poor road conditions delayed the overland force, and, fearful that waiting would lead to their detection, the infantry attacked early on January 24. The initial attack caught the British off guard, but they soon rallied and took up strong defensive positions in their fortifications and buildings. Lee and Marion decided their incomplete force was insufficient for the task, and ordered a withdrawal.[59] Although this attempt on Georgetown was unsuccessful, Marion and Lee worked well together in developing a plan, integrating and organizing their forces, and ultimately agreeing to withdraw.

Lee and Marion cooperated again at Fort Watson in April. When the two reunited, Marion had first proposed another attack on Georgetown, but Lee objected that it would put their force too far to the east if Greene decided to move against Camden. Marion saw Lee's point, and the two began planning to attack Fort Watson. While Marion acquiesced to Lee's strategic thought, Lee agreed to place his legion under Marion's direction, something Lee hesitated to do with others.[60]

Fort Watson was a formidable position that Thomas Sumter had failed to capture on February 28. To overcome the stout defenses and lack of cover, Hezekiah Maham proposed building a tower that would allow the Patriots to deliver protected fire down into the fort. The structure would have to be built under the cover of darkness to avoid the British interrupting the work, and on the evening of April 22, construction began. Working with only two percent illumination from the moon, Lee and Marion's men had less than 10 hours to complete the task.[61]

With the help of Maham's Tower, the Patriots attacked and captured Fort Watson the next morning. In testimony to the cooperative nature of the enterprise, Marion and Lee each provided a captain to negotiate the terms of surrender.[62] As an indication of the relationship growing between the two men, Marion wrote Greene that he was "particularly indebted to Colonel Lee for his advice and indefatigable diligence in every part of these tedious performances."[63] For his part, Lee, who was generally loath to give credit to others, had come to recognize Marion's leadership ability, and he asked Greene to be formally assigned to Marion's command "in some degree."[64]

Lee and Marion also found common cause at Quinby Bridge in July 1781 when both cautioned Sumter not to launch a hasty attack without artillery support. When the attack failed, both men failed to disguise their disgust, withdrawing 15 miles from the site of the battle and pitching camp without informing Sumter of their actions.[65]

This is not to say that Marion and Lee agreed on everything. They had different opinions about such things as providing horses to Greene and treatment of prisoners.[66] Rather than the joint effort at the surrender of Fort Watson, at Fort Motte some friction had developed, causing Lee to receive the surrender of the British regulars and Marion that of the Loyalists.[67] Such ebb and flow is not uncommon when working with peers, but overall common cause—in Marion and Lee's case, the cause of American independence—can help ensure unity of effort in the long run.

The Law of the Niche

One of John Maxwell's "seventeen indisputable laws of teamwork" is "the law of the niche." According to this law, "all players have a place where they add the most value," and it is the responsibility of the leader to put people in such situations where they can maximize their effectiveness. If that does not happen—"when people aren't where they do things well,"—Maxwell cautions, "things don't turn out well."[68]

In order to put people in the places that best utilize their talents and maximize the team's potential, Maxwell says leaders must know the team, know the situation, and know the player. Knowing the team involves understanding its vision, purpose, culture, and history. Only by knowing where the team is now and where it is trying to go and why, can a leader know what types of talents the team members must have. Knowing the situation is important because teams pass through certain life cycles. A team that is just forming has different talent requirements than a team that is mature or one that is undergoing significant change, crisis, or growth. Knowing the player includes understanding their experience, skills, temperament, passion, people skills, discipline, emotional strength, and potential. Leaders must resist the temptation to assume all team members are similar to the leader in these areas.[69]

Maxwell also notes that "the idea that one person is always doing all the leading is false."[70] The challenge of the moment may suggest that the person whose strengths are best aligned with that niche lead in that particular situation. The effective leader is aware of the talents that are present on the team and is willing to empower individuals with the leadership authority needed to optimize those talents. To do so, they can't be obsessed with protecting their own position and hoarding their own power.[71]

The law of the niche usually is applied when the leader fills an open position with the right person. This individual can be an existing member of the team or one who is specifically recruited for that position. Sometimes, however, the leader becomes aware of an exceptionally talented person for which there is no existing position open. The person's potential contribution may be so great that the leader creates a position in order to bring them into the organization. Usually, the niche exists and the leader matches the person to fill it. In this case, the leader creates the niche for the person.[72]

The whole idea of the law of the niche is to understand the places and the people available to fill them, and to then align the two in a way that maximizes effectiveness. As part of organizational and individual growth, Maxwell acknowledges that leaders will sometimes place people in positions that stretch their "comfort zones," but he advises to never move them outside their "gift zones." Such misplacement is more likely to result in frustration than growth.[73] On the other hand, having the right people in the right places multiples the overall effectiveness of the team.[74]

Francis Marion and Eutaw Springs

At Eutaw Springs, Nathanael Greene commanded between 1,900 and 2,100 men. He faced between 2,200 and 2,400 British commanded by Lieutenant Colonel Alexander Stewart. John Oller notes that "probably no two armies in any large-scale engagement during the southern phase of the war were as evenly matched."[75] "The biggest question mark," for Oller, "was how the American militia, a third of Greene's total force, would perform."[76]

Eutaw Springs would be the first large pitched battle that Marion's militia would fight under him. Up to this point, the Patriot militia had a spotty record in such circumstances. At Camden they had turned and run when they saw the British bayonets bearing down on them. At the battle of Cowpens on January 17, 1781, things were different. There General Daniel Morgan had found an effective niche for his militia, and the result was a decisive Patriot victory.

At Cowpens, Morgan deployed his force in three lines. First was a line of sharpshooters, tasked to disrupt the British attack and focus their efforts against officers. Behind them was a second line of militia commanded by Andrew Pickens. Morgan knew the militia could not stand long against the British regulars so he asked them to fire just two volleys. Then they were to retreat behind the safety of the third line made up of Colonel John Howard's Continentals.

The militia did as they were asked during the battle, and as they fell back, Banastre Tarleton's dragoons pressed the pursuit, sensing victory. Instead, Tarleton was being drawn into Morgan's trap, as Colonel William Washington's cavalry rushed to the scene. Tarleton committed his reserve, but Morgan was able to reform his lines and rout the British with a double envelopment. In less than an hour, the Patriots inflicted British losses of 84 killed, 351 wounded, and 257 missing, while the Patriots suffered 139 killed, 375 wounded, and eight missing. The decisive Patriot victory proved to be the turning point of the war in the Southern Theater.

In March, Greene tried a modified version of Morgan's tactic at Guilford Court House, North Carolina. The militia performance there was "a mixed bag."[77] Undeterred, Greene resolved to try the formula again in September at Eutaw Springs. Employing what Rod Andrew describes as the now "standard American practice whenever patriot militia and Continentals fought together,"[78] Greene put his militia from North Carolina and South Carolina in front. Marion's men formed the right flank of this line. Behind them was a line of over 900 Continentals from Maryland, Virginia, North Carolina, and Delaware. In the rear, Greene formed his horse, consisting of Henry Lee's Legion, Washington's dragoons, and Lieutenant Colonel Wade Hampton's cavalry.[79] Hugh Rankin describes the mission of the militia as to "absorb the initial shock of the enemy, with the better trained and better disciplined Continental troops making up the second line."[80] Marion understood the limited role his men were expected to play and asked them to fire at least 12 shots.[81]

As the British approached, Marion's men moved forward about half a mile, firing slowly and accurately. When the British charged, the militia retreated to steer clear of the enemy's bayonets. They never broke though, and would reform and push forward again. Rather than the expected 12, Marion estimated each man fired an average of 17 shots. When the militia had done its duty, Marion's men stayed in the rear and the British ran headlong into the steady second line of Continentals. The British front line collapsed, and Greene ordered Washington's cavalry forward.

The Patriots seemed on the verge of a great victory, but two things changed the course of the battle. The first was that much forward motion was lost as the advancing Patriots stopped to enjoy the considerable provisions they found abandoned in the British camp. The second was the wise decision of British Major John Majoribanks to withdraw to a strong defensive position from which he could deliver effective fire against the Patriot left flank. Majoribanks's timely intervention slowed Greene's attack and helped set up a British counterattack on the Patriot right. Greene had no choice but to fall back and leave the British in possession of Eutaw Springs.[82]

Although the battle of Eutaw Springs ended in a draw, Marion felt that "my Brigade behaved well." Greene agreed that "the Militia fought with a degree of spirit and firmness that reflects the highest honor upon this class of Soldiers." Morgan, Greene, and Marion understood that militiamen were not Continental soldiers, and that they could not expect from them the same type of performance. What these leaders did do, however, was apply the law of the niche, and give the militia a role for which they were well suited and by which they could contribute to the overall effort.

Francis Marion and Communicating as a Leader

"You can have brilliant ideas, but if you can't get them across, your ideas won't get you anywhere."

LEE IACOCCA

Communicating Expectations

An essential subset of interpersonal skill is effective communication. Leaders should strive to be consistent, clear, and courteous in their communication.[1] Consistent communication builds the predictability and dependability that are critical to trust. Clarity provides the understanding necessary for hearers to act on the communication. Courtesy fosters mutual respect, even when the subject of the communication may be difficult.

One reason that leaders communicate is to set expectations. Expectations can be both implicit and explicit. Because implicit expectations have usually not been openly discussed, they are often a source of ambiguity and friction. It is incorrect for a leader to assume their expectations are self-evident and understood and shared by others. Leaders can reduce this inefficiency by actively looking for clues about their subordinate's unstated expectations and by, to the fullest extent possible, explicitly stating their expectations. Explicitly stating expectations can be labor-intensive and at times awkward, but it is a sound investment that pays great dividends in the long run.[2]

Members come to organizations with all sorts of expectations, some of which may be implicit. Not all of these personal expectations align with the organizational expectations. Leaders must draw out these cases of conflict and be able to clearly and compellingly communicate to subordinates the value of the organizational expectations.

By communicating expectations, leaders and subordinates become synchronized about what is going to happen, why it is worth the effort, and how, in general terms, it will occur. The expectations then become the "consistent norms governing how the game is played."[3] Clearly communicated expectations let subordinates know what is required of them so they have every chance of doing the task correctly. It is also helpful for subordinates to understand why they are doing what they are doing. Understanding the rationale behind or the importance of the task helps subordinates see their effort as purposeful and of benefit to themselves and the organization. Such expectations become "compelling" rather than merely perfunctory. Additionally, if subordinates are given a general idea of what to expect in terms of how the event will unfold, it helps reduce the "fear of the unknown" and the stress associated with it.[4]

Expectations are fundamental to any relationship. In a system that is built on mutual respect and trust, clearly understood expectations allow the senior and the subordinate to work together with cooperation rather than conflict. Shared expectations help build unity of effort.

Thoroughly communicated expectations should address five areas. First, desired results should be articulated by focusing on *what*, not *how*. This emphasis on results rather than methods gives maximum freedom of maneuver and flexibility to subordinates. Second, guidelines that identify the parameters within which the individual should operate must be understood. Again, these should be as few as possible in order to optimize subordinate initiative, but if there are restrictions, the subordinate needs to know them. Third, the subordinate should be told the human, financial, technical, or organizational resources they can draw on to accomplish the desired results. Fourth, accountability is established through identifying the standards of performance and procedures that will be used in evaluation. Finally, the consequences, good or bad, that will occur as the result of the evaluation should be made known.[5]

Following these five elements gives agreements "a life of their own" because they create a standard against which people can measure their own success and achieve their own feelings of self-actualization. Indeed, most subordinates prefer a leader who, having established the standard, leaves them alone, lets them do their jobs, and appreciates work that is done well. There is also a synergy that develops when people know that others around them are also being held accountable. People are more confident in doing their part if they know others are doing theirs. As a result, in a high trust culture with clearly established expectations, the leader can "get out of the way" and assume a role as helper and monitor of progress, intervening only as the situation warrants.[6]

Properly communicating expectations is fundamental to the success of any activity involving leaders and subordinates. Leaders must resist the temptation to jump immediately into a relationship with their subordinates without first clearly setting expectations. Anyone who has used a compass to navigate from one point to another can appreciate the importance of properly setting their azimuth before they begin. If they are off even just a few degrees, that small error compounded over distance can lead them far away from their objective. It is the same with expectations. Clearly established expectations guide teams to the desired results while incorrect or unclear expectations take teams off course.

Francis Marion and his Orders to John Postell

Leaders interact with all sorts of people, and they must master techniques that are appropriate for each individual. The same is true for their communications. In Marion's situation, many of his officers and most of his men had little in the way of formal military training and education. By necessity, then, Marion developed a very simple and direct style of communication.[7]

An excellent example of Marion's written communication style is his orders to Captain John Postell regarding a mission to the Wadboo Bridge area to the northeast of Moncks Corner. Raised on a plantation above Georgetown, Postell was intimately knowledgeable of both the local terrain and its inhabitants. In addition to this personal competence, Postell had a close relationship with Marion. They served together fighting the Cherokees and were both Huguenots.[8] In communicating with Postell, Marion had the benefit of dealing with a capable and trustworthy subordinate.

On January 29, 1781, Marion wrote to Postell:

Dear Sir,

You will cross the Santee River with twenty-five men, and make a forced march to Wadboo bridge, then burn all the British stores of every kind ... You will return the same way, and recross the river at the same place, which must be done before daylight next morning. After effecting my purpose at Wadboo, it will not be out of your way to come by Monck's Corner, and destroy any stores or wagons you may find there. You can learn from the people at Wadboo what guard force is at the corner; if it should be too strong you will not attempt the place ... The destruction of all British stores in the above-mentioned place is of the greatest consequence to us, and only requires boldness and expedition. Take care that your men do not get at liquor, or clog themselves with plunder so as to endanger your retreat.

I am with regard, dear Sir,
Your obedient servant,
Francis Marion

When giving missions to subordinates, today's military commanders are admonished to include both "task" and "purpose." Tasks are specific activities that contribute to accomplishing missions or other requirements.[9] Marion articulated his tasks to Postell by telling him to "cross the Santee River with twenty-five men, and make a forced march to Wadboo bridge, there burn all the British stores of every kind."

The purpose of each task should connect to some other task, objective, or end state.[10] Marion is less specific in providing Postell the purpose, but certainly implies it in saying that "the destruction of all British stores in the above-mentioned place is of the greatest consequence to us." At the time of Postell's mission, Nathanael Greene was leading his army through North Carolina toward Virginia, with Lord Charles Cornwallis in a hot pursuit. The supplies that Postell destroyed would have otherwise made their way to Cornwallis who was presently living off land that had already been picked clean by Greene's army ahead of him.[11] Postell no doubt understood this purpose from orders Marion had given him a month earlier to prevent movement of any supplies to "where the enemy can get them."[12]

Marion's instructions to Postell also provided a particular perspective that Marion thought bore emphasis. His caution to "take care that your men do not get into liquor" was based on a previous experience in which Colonel Peter Horry's men had consumed alcohol while on patrol and become temporarily combat ineffective. Through this combination of clearly stated task and purpose, and specific restraints, Marion gave his subordinates orders that allowed him to decentralize operations and expand control over larger parts of the South Carolina lowcountry.[13]

Information Flow

Leaders manage the flow of information up, down, and laterally throughout their organization. From higher to lower, leaders transmit instructions, orders, and guidance. From lower to higher, they report statuses, relay concerns or questions, and provide feedback. Laterally, they share implementing instructions, lessons learned, and awareness. Effectively communicating information to others allows them to make decisions and take action. If it is true that "information is power," leaders must get the correct information to the correct people in order for them to have the power they need to act.

Effective information flow involves redundancy which means that the information is delivered in more than one way. This redundancy serves not only as a failsafe, but also reflects the fact that different people process information in different ways. One person might better comprehend written communication such as an email while another might prefer verbal communication such as an announcement at a meeting.

Effective information flow also involves confirmation. The leader does not just disseminate the information. They ensure the intended audience both receives and understands the message. Sometimes this can be a simple email response of "got it," and other times it will require a more detailed report to demonstrate thorough understanding.

Effective information flow is designed to be easy to understand and to process. Disseminating information in a consistent, standardized format such as the "5Ws" of who, what, when, where, and why promotes understanding by its familiarity. Requesting information in a prescribed format such as a fill-in-the-blank form reduces ambiguity and increases validity. Organizational tools like spreadsheets allow the same information to be manipulated and processed to serve several purposes.

Information flows from the leader to followers in the form of instructions, orders, and guidance. As it passes through each level, leaders do the necessary analysis to make it relevant to their team members. As a result, the leader may omit some irrelevant information, amplify existing information, or add new information to make the message clear and specific to their level.

As leaders tailor information to their specific audience, however, they must not become a gatekeeper who filters out information their subordinates need. Nor can they change the intent of the original author. Finally, they must refrain from negatively editorializing about the information or being disloyal to its originator.

In addition to disseminating information to subordinates, leaders also receive it and either act on it themselves or relay it up the organization's hierarchy. Sometimes leaders will request information of their subordinates such as whether or not they have accomplished assignments. Other times, subordinates will request information such as about how to solve a problem.

Francis Marion and Leadership after Camden

The August 16, 1780, battle of Camden was disastrous for the Patriots. Nearly 700 Patriots were killed, wounded, or captured, and the British suffered just half that many losses. After the defeat, General Horatio Gates fled to Charlotte and over the following weeks collected the remnants of his command at Hillsborough, North Carolina, almost 200 miles away from the battle.

When Thomas Sumter learned of the rout at Camden, he retreated his command to what he thought was a safe distance from the battle and camped on Fishing Creek just north of Great Falls. He posted sentries, but otherwise exercised poor security. As Sumter's men relaxed, Banastre Tarleton pressed his men in pursuit. By the time Tarleton reached

Fishing Creek, he had just 160 men against Sumter's nearly 800, but his rapid attack on August 18 overwhelmed the lax Patriot security. Sumter suffered 150 killed or wounded and 350 captured. Tarleton lost just 16 killed or wounded. The humiliation at Fishing Creek combined with the defeat at Camden to mark the low point of the Patriot cause in South Carolina.[14]

About this time, Marion was moving from the Williamsburg militia camp at Witherspoon's Ferry up the Santee when he met some civilians who secretly told him of Gates's defeat at Camden.[15] Marion now had a decision to make. If he told his men of the Patriot disaster, discouragement and panic might infest the ranks. Instead, Marion decided to tell the men only that he had learned that a British force with a number of American prisoners was en route from Camden to Charleston and nearing Nelson's Ferry.[16] Marion led his men on an attack there at first light on August 20, liberating some 150 Maryland Continentals that had been captured at Camden. This success, as well as a victory at Musgrove's Mill on August 18, provided a small glimmer of hope in an otherwise bleak situation for the Patriot cause.

It was the prisoners liberated at Nelson's Ferry who told Marion's men about the defeat at Camden.[17] Marion even waited until August 27 to confide the terrible news to his trusted subordinate Peter Horry. "I am sorry to acquaint you that Gen. Gates is defeated with great loss," Marion wrote Horry. "He was obliged to retreat to Charlotte, which obliges me also to retreat."[18]

Scott Aiken credits Marion for withholding information about Camden for the sake of keeping his fledgling command cohesive, but also notes that Marion was quick to spread good news such as the British surrender at Yorktown. Aiken quotes the Chinese military theorist Sun Tzu's admonition that "when the outlook is bright, bring it before [your soldiers'] eyes, but tell them nothing when the situation is gloomy."[19] After Camden and Fishing Creek, Aiken describes Marion's tactical situation as "lonely indeed."[20] Rather than share the burden of the dismal nature of the Patriot circumstances with his men, Marion chose to bear it himself and time the release of the information accordingly. This is a difficult decision for a leader. On the one hand, leaders owe their subordinates the information they need to make decisions. On the other hand, in some cases the leader is right in protecting subordinates from the fickle ebb and flow of events as the organization presses on with the vision. A few of Marion's men did leave him when they learned of the defeat at Camden, but this was also typical behavior of partisan soldiers who left and returned to camp frequently.[21] When weighed in the balance, the glimmer of hope wrought by Nelson's Ferry and its positive effect on Patriot morale throughout the region seems to support Marion's decision in this particular case.

Charismatic Rhetoric

In "A 1976 Theory of Charismatic Leadership," Robert House declines to offer an operational definition of the charismatic leader, but he does in detail discuss the *behaviors* of a charismatic leader. These he identifies as goal articulation, role modeling, personal image building, demonstration of confidence and high expectations of followers, and motive arousal behaviors.[22] Peter Northouse and Jay Conger offer a clear summary and explanation of House's five behaviors.

First, Northouse states that charismatic leaders "are strong role models for the beliefs and values they want their followers to adopt."[23] Conger adds that such leaders "build exceptional trust by demonstrating a total dedication to the cause they share with followers."[24] Second, charismatic leaders "appear competent to followers."[25] They instill confidence in their subordinates by their own abilities.[26] Third, charismatic leaders "articulate ideological goals that have moral overtones."[27] Fourth, "charismatic leaders communicate high expectations for followers, and they exhibit confidence in their followers' abilities to meet these expectations."[28] Conger adds that charismatic leaders make "extensive use of personal example and role modeling ... [and] empowerment practices to demonstrate how their vision can be achieved."[29] Such empowerment influences followers to now perceive as feasible tasks once judged as being too difficult and becomes a significant force multiplier.[30] Fifth, charismatic leaders "arouse task-relevant motives in followers that may include affiliation, power, and esteem."[31] They "create among subordinates a compelling desire to be led in the direction of the vision despite its often significant hurdles."[32] In short, charismatic leaders not only have special personality characteristics that facilitate their leadership; their charisma is also validated by their followers.

Francis Marion and his Loyal Band

Loizos Heracleous and Laura Alexa Klaering note that "powerful rhetoric, the ability to capture an audience through outstanding oratorical skills, is … tightly intertwined with charismatic leadership."[33] Recognizing "an important aspect of charisma is the relationship among leader, audience, and context," they identify the criticality of a "leader's ability to customize their rhetoric."[34] Marion demonstrated such charismatic rhetoric in a speech to his men as they prepared to engage the British near Halfway Swamp in December 1781.

The action began with Major Robert McLeroth and the 64th Regiment on a mission to escort newly arrived British Army recruits of the Royal Fusiliers from Charleston to the High Hills of Santee. Learning of McLeroth's movement, Marion called up a force of 700 militiamen and took off after McLeroth, surprising him after passing through Halfway Swamp, 20 miles above Nelson's Ferry.

Marion had McLeroth at a disadvantage because the British lacked the cavalry to protect their infantry from the Patriots' mounted charges. Against this pressure, the British fell back to a field enclosed by a rail fence and took what little shelter the rails had to offer. McLeroth also sent out riders to request help from Captain John Coffin who, with 140 mounted infantrymen, was moving forward to pick up the recruits and escort them to Camden. Instead of coming to McLeroth's aid, Coffin took up a defensive position behind Swift Creek, thinking he also faced an attack.

As Marion and McLeroth squared off, a British officer approached the Patriot lines under a flag of truce. He vehemently protested that in shooting at pickets, Marion's men had violated the rules of civilized warfare. He challenged Marion to bring his men out into the open and fight like traditional soldiers.

Marion brushed aside the comments about the rules of warfare, countering with examples of British officers burning civilian property. As for the challenge to fight in the open, Marion considered it to be the last resort "of a man in desperate circumstances," but if McLeroth "wished to witness a combat between picked men on each side, he was ready to gratify him." McLeroth agreed to the terms, and the two sides began selecting their best marksmen.

Marion choose Major John Vanderhorst to command the Americans, with Captain Samuel Price as his deputy. Marion then wrote on a piece of paper the names of men he thought would perform well and handed the list to Gavin Witherspoon, one of Marion's best sharpshooters. When the roll was called, all 20 men stepped forward to take on the task. Marion then addressed them with a short speech that connects the elements of leader, audience, and context so essential to charismatic rhetoric. "My brave soldiers," Marion began. "You are twenty men picked this day out of my whole brigade. I know you all, and have often witnessed your bravery. In the name of your country, I call upon you once more to show it. My confidence in you is great, and I am sure it will not be disappointed. Fight like men, fight as you have always done, and you are sure of the victory."[35]

Marion used charismatic rhetoric to appeal to his men as their leader when he told them, "I know you all." He assured them, "My confidence in you is great, and I am sure it will not be disappointed." Through such rhetoric, Marion reminded his men of the relationship they shared and communicated to them his personal belief, trust, and support of them.

Marion also used charismatic rhetoric to personally motivate his audience. They were not just "brave soldiers," but "my" brave soldiers, and he had not merely heard of their bravery, he had witnessed it. They were hand-picked, again out of "my" brigade. With such language, Marion was not only complimenting his men, but was further solidifying the bond they shared.

Finally, Marion used charismatic rhetoric to establish the context necessary to connect past, present, and future. After lauding them for their past bravery, he said, "I call upon you once more to show it." He reminded them that they had always fought like men and assured them that if they do so again in this present challenge, they will be "sure of the victory."

In the end, McLeroth's theatrics were just a ruse to gain time, and the planned showdown between the two 20-man teams never occurred. Instead, McLeroth withdrew under cover of darkness, leaving Marion in command of the Santee River and road. Lord Francis Rawdon, who had assumed responsibility for the defense of South Carolina when Lord Charles Cornwallis advanced north after Cowpens, was frustrated with McLeroth's lackluster performance, but confessed that he too lacked a solution to the Swamp Fox. "I must drive Marion out of that Country," he declared, "but I cannot yet say what steps I shall take to effect it."[36]

It should be noted that in reporting his encounter with McLeroth, Marion mentions he only had "skirmaged" with the enemy. The details of the proposed unorthodox duel come from William Dobein James as reported to him by Witherspoon, and John Oller notes, "maybe the whole story was made up."[37] Apocryphal or otherwise, the speech still illustrates an excellent example of charismatic rhetoric.

Mission Orders

As subordinates grow, leaders transition from the authoritative end of the leadership style continuum to more participative and delegative approaches. They increase their use of "mission orders" that emphasize to subordinates the results to be attained, but not how they are to achieve them. This technique provides the subordinate maximum freedom of action in determining how best to accomplish the mission.[38]

Being able to operate based on mission orders requires a thorough understanding of the leader's intent. The leader's intent transcends the particular components of the plan and describes what constitutes overall success. It also places the particular activity in the broader context of other activities going on around it. Subordinates who understand their leader's intent are able to make decisions in a fluid and changing environment as their leader would. They focus not just on actions as ends unto themselves, but on the impacts and effects of those actions on the desired end state.[39]

Francis Marion and Orders to Peter Horry

In early August 1780, Marion was released from Major General Horatio Gates's army in order to assume command of the militia in the Williamsburg District. Marion left with orders "to go Down the Country to Destroy all boats & Craft of any kind, we found on Santee River in Order to prevent Cornwallis & his Troops Escaping him."[40] Gates's intent was clear—to prevent Lord Charles Cornwallis from escaping.

On August 17, 1780, Marion passed these orders on to Lieutenant Colonel Peter Horry, telling him to "take the command of such men as will be collected from Capts. Bonneau's, Mitchell's, and Benson's companies, and immediately proceed to Santee, from the lower Ferry to Lenud's, and destroy all the boats and canoes on the river, and post guards at each crossing place, to prevent persons from crossing to or from Charleston, on either side of the river."[41] Marion preserved Gates's intent about blocking escape routes, but he added a key task for Horry—to post guards. Marion knew that just destroying boats and leaving the area would merely slow the British down. They could get other boats. If success meant no one crossing the river, posting guards would also be necessary.

Horry clearly understood Marion's intent and the bigger picture. "Not content with destroying the common scows and flats at the ferries," Horry wrote, "we went on to sweep the river of every skiff and canoe we could find." Because he understood what was at stake, Horry continued with his work, even though "it was a serious thing to the planters, and their wrath waxed exceedingly hot against us." So faithful was Horry to the task that he even destroyed a boat and scow "that belonged to my excellent old uncle," 73-year-old Elias Horry. Surveying the damage, Elias demanded of his nephew, "Breaking up our boats! Why, how are we to harvest our rice?" The younger Horry was able to place the matter in context and replied "Uncle, you had better think less of harvesting your rice, and more of catching the muskrats," by which Horry meant the British.[42]

Understanding the leader's intent and desired end state helps promote unity of effort and unified action among partners.[43] While it might be a stretch to say that, at the moment of his boats' destruction, Elias Horry was fully unified with Marion, Marion's intent did equip Peter Horry to make the difficult decision he did. By understanding the need to not just destroy boats but to guard crossings, and by being armed with Marion's order to destroy "all" boats—even his uncle's—Horry was able to conduct himself in a manner consistent with Marion's intent.

Francis Marion and a Leader's Need to Solve Problems

"The significant problems we face cannot be solved at the same level of thinking we were at when we created them."

ALBERT EINSTEIN

Intelligence and Judgment in Action

John Gardner distinguishes between merely being smart and the ability to use that attribute to do the work of a leader. He also distinguishes between "judgment" and "judgment in action." Gardner defines judgment in its simple form as "the ability to combine hard data, questionable data and intuitive guesses to arrive at a conclusion that events prove to be correct." Judgment in action transcends this ability so as to also include "effective problem solving, the design of strategies, the setting of priorities and intuitive as well as rational judgments. Most important, perhaps, it includes the capacity to appraise the personalities of coworkers and opponents."[1]

In a fashion similar to Gardner's linkage of intelligence and judgment, the United States Army links initiative and judgment. Initiative is "the ability to be a self-starter—to act when there are no clear instructions, to act when the situation changes or when plans fall apart." As critical to leadership and organizational growth as initiative is, however, it must be combined with good judgment to be productive. The army's goal then is not mere impulsive or ill-advised action, but initiative, balanced with sound judgment, to produce "disciplined initiative."[2]

Disciplined initiative requires opportunity, ability, action, and risk management. It strikes the balance between "judging too soon and deciding too late," while reflecting a leaning toward action. Judging too soon is often the result of "knowing the answer before considering the question." Deciding too late is often the result of an unrealistic demand for complete certainty. Leaders must be able to reflect while withholding judgment until sufficient facts are in, but then be able to make a decision and act while it is still meaningful to do so.[3] It is this enlightened action that separates leaders from the mere intelligent.

Francis Marion and Great Savannah

From his bivouac at Nelson's Ferry, Marion learned that some 150 American prisoners captured at the battle of Camden were being held at Thomas Sumter's abandoned plantation on Great Savannah. Marion had only days before formed his unit around the Williamsburg militia, and they had no experience fighting together.

Marion had assumed command from Lieutenant Colonel Hugh Horry, and Horry became Marion's second-in-command at Nelson's Ferry. On August 17, 1780, Marion had dispatched Horry's brother Peter with three or four companies on a mission along the Santee River to Lenud's Ferry. This left Marion and Hugh Horry with just 52 mounted partisans and greatly outnumbered by the British forces in the area.[4]

As events unfolded, Marion and Horry exercised two specific instances of intelligence and judgment in action in order to seize a fleeting opportunity and to maintain initiative. The first came on August 19 when Marion learned from his scouts about the prisoners being held at Sumter's Plantation. The scouts also reported that British security there was lax. Believing that Patriot activity had been largely suppressed by the defeat at Camden, the British guards were complacent, and many were sleeping in the house with their weapons stacked at the door. Only a few guards manned posts around the prisoners and a group of supply wagons. Armed with this intelligence, Marion resolved to seize the element of surprise that the situation offered. He developed a plan to attack before dawn the next day. Horry would lead a force of 16 men to block the road that led from the plantation house at a ford across Horse Creek.

Marion, with the majority of the men, would then attack from the rear, providing the hammer against Horry's anvil.

The second instance of judgment in action came when an alert British sentry observed the approach of Horry's men. The soldier opened fire, alerting his fellow guards and spoiling Marion's expectation of surprise. At this point, decisive action was necessary if the Patriots were to maintain their advantage. Horry responded with speed and certainty. Instead of occupying the static blocking position as planned, he ordered his 16 men to charge toward the house at full tilt, making as much commotion as possible in hopes of convincing the British they were facing a much larger force. Horry's bold move paid off, and his men reached the stacked weapons and overwhelmed the token guard force before the rest of the British troops could spring into action. Leaving a few men to secure the weapons, Horry burst into the house with the rest of his team and demanded the British surrender. While all this was going on, Marion executed his charge from the rear and engaged the other British.[5]

In just a matter of minutes, the fighting was over. Marion and Horry herded the British into a harmless group near the house and took 22 British regulars and two Tories prisoner. They also freed some 150 Continental soldiers from Maryland and Delaware. All this was gained with just two Patriots wounded.[6]

Marion and Horry's conduct at Nelson's Ferry was indicative of Gardner's demand that judgment in action include "the capacity to appraise the personalities of coworkers and opponents." Scott Aiken notes that Marion's tactics "were ideal for minimizing the partisans' weaknesses in personnel strength and firepower, while at the same time they capitalized on the partisans' strengths of surprise, mobility, and knowledge of the land." Moreover, it was Marion's excellent intelligence of the British situation that allowed him to "split his attacking force and maintain a preponderance of combat power."[7]

Both men, especially Horry, also demonstrated "disciplined initiative" in their reaction to being observed by the British sentry. Horry had mere seconds to assess the situation and make a decision. His aggressive response clearly shows his propensity to act and his ability to rapidly process information under crisis conditions.

Innovation

"Innovation and leadership," James Kouzes and Barry Posner argue, "are nearly synonymous."[8] They describe leaders as experimenters and tinkerers.[9] To this end, leaders must possess what Bob Johansen calls the inner drive of a "maker instinct" to build and grow things.[10] He confesses that when it comes to how best to shape the future, leaders "don't always know the answer, but they're working on it."[11]

Because innovation often shatters the status quo, John Gardner notes that it is "sometimes dramatized as a powerfully disruptive force." He counters this perception by explaining how innovation is often the response to a crisis that allows survival. Gardner cautions, however, that "the fact that innovation may come in the role of savior does not necessarily ensure acceptance by those who cherish the status quo."[12] While historical analysis is yet to reveal its efficacy, a recent example is the national response to the COVID-19 pandemic that has generated innovations in medical care, social norms, and governance, as well as resistance and skepticism. Still, the innovator must see the wisdom of Paul Romer's charge that "a crisis is a terrible thing to waste."[13]

Francis Marion and Maham's Tower

For Marion, a crisis at Fort Watson in April 1781 led to an excellent example of innovation. This strategic location stood on the road to Nelson's Ferry as part of the British communications network that led from Charleston to the interior of South Carolina. It was manned by a force of 114 British regulars and Loyalists normally under the command of Lieutenant Colonel John Watson. Watson had left the fort on March 5, however, on a joint operation with Lieutenant Colonel Welbore Doyle in an attempt to destroy Marion's camp on Snow's Island. In Watson's absence, command of Fort Watson fell to Lieutenant James McKay.[14] General Nathanael Greene sent Marion and Lieutenant Colonel Henry Lee to reduce this strongpoint.

Although Lee's Legion numbered 300 and Marion had 80 men of his own, Fort Watson was "a tough nut to crack." Marion had resisted Greene's encouragement to attack it in January, deeming the defenses too formidable, and Brigadier General Thomas Sumter had failed miserably when he tried in February. A conventional assault would be suicidal, so to reduce Fort Watson would require a siege, a tactic with which Marion had little familiarity.[15]

Fort Watson was relatively small—measuring less than 20 yards on each side—but what it lacked in size was more than compensated for by the terrain. The fort was built on top of a 23-foot high, pyramid-shaped Indian temple mound and surrounded by three rows of abatis. The British had cleared away all the trees and brush around the fort to rob the attackers of cover and to provide the defenders with excellent fields of fire.[16]

Marion and Lee arrived at Fort Watson on April 15, surrounded it, and promptly demanded that McKay surrender. With plenty of food and ammunition, and confidence in the strength of his position, McKay refused, telling the Patriots that "if they wanted [Fort Watson], they must come take it."[17]

At first Marion tried to reduce the fort by cutting it off from its water supply at Scott's Lake. Marion positioned riflemen between the fort and the lake to interdict any watering parties, but rather than challenge Marion, McKay began digging a well inside the stockade. On April 18, the British struck water, thwarting Marion's plan.[18]

Fort Watson normally had two three-pound cannons, but Watson had taken these with him when he left in March. Lee realized that if the Patriots could get a cannon, they would have a great advantage. He asked for Greene to supply one, boasting that he would use it to "finish the business" in "five minutes" and promptly return it. Greene agreed and dispatched a six-pounder, but the infantry transporting it got lost and returned to Camden.[19]

Having anticipated a quick victory, the men in the Patriot ranks soon became restless with the siege. The digging was slow and difficult. Morale declined and men began to desert, in spite of Marion's threats of capital punishment. Moreover, cases of smallpox began to appear. Lee's men had been inoculated, but Marion's had not. The disease cut a three-fold swath through Marion's ranks. Some healthy men fled to avoid it. Others such as Samuel Jenkins, who had been with Marion since August 1780, caught it. Still others, such as Jenkins's brother Britton, carried infected comrades home.[20]

In the midst of this deteriorating situation, Major Hezekiah Maham approached Marion and Lee with an idea. Maham proposed building a log tower some 30 feet high to enable marksmen to shoot down into the fort. It would be an immense undertaking, but Marion determined it was worth a try.[21]

The Patriots gathered axes from the nearby plantations and began cutting pine saplings that could be fashioned into slender poles. These were carried to a position just outside of British rifle range, and the Patriots began assembling the logs into an oblong tower on the afternoon of August 21. A floor was built at a point higher than the British fort and the front protected with a wall of logs. The tower was completed under cover of darkness and moved to its final position with a party of Captain William McCottry's riflemen at its apex. A contingent of Maryland Continentals posted themselves behind a nearby breastwork to protect the tower from attack.[22]

As dawn began to break, Marion's sharpshooters opened fire. Under this protection, other Patriots sallied forth and began dismantling the abatis and breaching the stockade walls. Behind them was Lee's infantry with bayonets fixed and ready to charge. By the time Marion issued his surrender demand, McKay had been wounded and two of his soldiers were killed. Furthermore, McKay found that "a majority of the men [had] grounded their arms and refused to defend the post any longer." McKay had little recourse but to surrender.[23]

Marion was quick to give Maham credit, writing Greene that it was his innovation that "principally occasioned the reduction of the fort." "Maham's Tower," as the structure became known, was copied to capture Fort Cornwallis in Augusta, Georgia and during the siege of the star fort at Ninety Six. Even in the American Civil War, Federal forces used such a structure to fire on the besieged Confederates at Vicksburg.[24]

Pragmatic Problem Solving

Pragmatic leadership champions a very practical approach to problem solving. Its goal is to maximize benefit, minimize costs, and meet an objective need.[25] As a result, the emotional involvement of followers in this model is of much less importance than one would find in transformational or charismatic leadership.[26]

Leaders face a continual tension between their principles and pragmatism. When exercising pragmaticism, leaders do not so much abandon their ideals as they simply consciously deemphasize them.[27] It is often a necessary trade-off. Joseph Badaracco notes that "Principles alone qualify men and women to be preachers or saints. They can inspire and guide us, but usually don't make the trains run on time. Pure pragmatists can open their toolkits and go to work, but their amorality makes them dangerous." Badaracco says "of course, we want leaders to be both principled and pragmatic," but confesses that "combining principles and pragmatism is among the most difficult challenges leaders face."[28] It requires the wisdom that the Enlightenment philosopher Frances Hutcheson describes as "the pursuing of the best ends by the best means."[29]

Francis Marion and Fort Motte

Fort Motte was a somewhat grandiose name for what was essentially the Motte family's house at Mount Joseph Plantation. The British had seized this strategic location near the confluence of the Congaree and Wateree Rivers. They had improved the site by adding palisaded walls, earthworks, and an outlying ditch. The road from Charleston passed nearby the location, and the British were using it as a supply depot. A 140-man force of British, Hessians, and Loyalists were garrisoned at Fort Motte.

Marion and Lieutenant Colonel Henry Lee had begun formal siege operations at Fort Motte on May 6, 1781, but word of Lord Rawdon's abandonment of Camden instilled a sense of urgency to capture the position before he could arrive and lift the siege. Indeed, the Americans could see Rawdon's campfires on the High Hills of Santee. At Fort Watson, Lee and Marion used "Maham's Tower" to allow the Patriots to fire down on the British position, but there was no time for such a tactic now. Fort Motte's defenders could also see Rawdon's campfires, and their resolve was strengthened with the knowledge that help was on the way. Buoyed by this optimism, the British commander, Lieutenant Daniel McPherson, rejected two demands that the fort surrender.

Lee and Marion developed a very pragmatic solution to their problem. They would compel the British to surrender by firing flaming arrows to set the house's roof on fire. It was determined that the more polished Lee was the better candidate to discuss the matter with Rebecca Brewton Motte, the plantation owner. Motte was a stalwart Patriot whose husband Jacob had died in January of 1781. She could ill afford to lose her home, but, according to legend, she not only acquiesced, but proclaimed that "if it were a palace, it should go" and reportedly provided Lee with a bow and arrows that he could use for the purpose. One of Marion's privates, Nathan Savage, claimed instead that he made a ball of rosin and brimstone which he set on fire and slung on top of the roof. The more likely scenario, and one described by a British officer, is that the arrows were fired from muskets.[30] Regardless of the actual means of delivery, the tinder-dry shingles were soon set ablaze. British efforts to put the fire out were stymied by canister fire from the Patriots' six-pounder cannon, and at 1:00pm on May 12, the British surrendered.[31]

At Fort Motte, Marion and Lee were faced with a problem that demanded immediate action. Setting a Patriot widow's home on fire certainly was not a decision they reached lightly, especially since Mrs. Motte was one of the wealthiest Patriots in the colony at the time, having inherited land and slaves from her late husband and her late brother Miles Brewton. However, when weighed in terms of costs and benefits, Marion and Lee—and seemingly Mrs. Motte as well—reached a very pragmatic solution to the problem.

What perhaps is most interesting is that with the crisis solved, both Motte and Marion immediately demonstrated very principled behavior. Mrs. Motte invited both the British and American officers to a sumptuous dinner, and Marion interceded when he learned that some of Lee's Continentals were in the act of hanging some of the Loyalist prisoners.[32]

Nuanced Assertiveness

Joseph Badaracco writes that "leaders have a deep conviction that they must make something happen and they devote themselves to making it happen—despite obstacles, frustrations, failures, and very steep costs."[33] "Because leadership is often a long, hard struggle against opposing forces," he continues, "it requires determination, commitment, strength, and sheer will." Under such circumstances, the leader must be able to muster "an almost superhuman intensity of focus and effort."[34]

John Gardner notes that successful leaders "are apt to have a fairly strong impulse to take charge," and he adds that such leaders also desire "to leave their thumbprints on events."[35] He cautions, however, that this requirement does "not necessarily conform to the stereotype of the visibly forceful leader." Gardner seems to be emphasizing the leader's ability to dominate the situation more so than to be suggesting an authoritarian leadership style. This is the assertiveness needed to take action, overcome inertia, generate change, and make improvements. Such nuanced assertiveness comes in many forms.

Francis Marion and the Tactic of Retreat

While Marion used persuasion and tact when dealing with his partisans, he used the sort of nuanced assertiveness that Gardner advocates when dealing with his enemies. To do so, Marion made use of the military concept of the "culminating point," which is the point at which a force no longer has the capability to continue its form of operations. In the offense, the culminating point is reached when continuing the attack is no longer possible and the force must consider reverting to a defensive posture or attempting an operational pause. In the defense, it is the point at which counteroffensive action is no longer possible.[36]

Marion frequently used the tactic of retreat to force the British to their offensive culminating point. By breaking contact and withdrawing from an engagement, Marion used his superior mobility to gain an advantage over his foe. His pursuers became disorganized, had to reduce speed in order to maintain security, were vulnerable to ambush, and became emotionally exasperated. This was especially true of an aggressive adversary such as Banastre Tarleton. It seems counterintuitive to consider retreat as a method of gaining ascendancy, but that is exactly what Marion did.[37]

An example of Marion's skillful use of the retreat to bring his opponent to culmination was November 8, 1780, when Tarleton chased Marion for seven hours and 26 miles through the thick swamps near the Santee River. Tarleton's exasperating chase came as a result of the havoc Marion had been sowing along the roads between Charleston and Camden. On November 1, Colonel George Turnbull, the British commander at Camden, sent Tarleton an urgent request to bring his legion to bear against this threat to the British supply line. Tarleton forwarded Turnbull's letter to Lord Charles Cornwallis who was somewhat befuddled. "I can make nothing of Turnbull's letter to you," he told Tarleton, "as he only seems to describe Parties of 10 or 12 Rebels, which of course is not intended to employ the Legion to hunt." Nonetheless, Cornwallis gave Tarleton permission to embark on the mission.[38]

Tarleton was joined by Major John Harrison's North Carolina Loyalists, and the combined force left their camp at Brierly's Ferry on Broad River, crossing the Wateree River at Camden on November 3. Turnbull briefed Tarleton on his understanding of the situation, including the mistaken belief that Marion had established a headquarters at Singleton's Mills in the High Hills with a force of some 4,000 men. The British set out after Marion on November 5, a fact that Marion's vast intelligence network soon reported to him.[39]

Marion's plan to ambush the British at Nelson's Ferry came to naught, and Tarleton established a camp on the plantation of Patriot Mary Richardson, hoping to draw Marion into an ambush. Richardson's husband, Brigadier General Richard Richardson, had died about six weeks earlier, and her son, Captain Richard Richardson, was a paroled Continental officer now hiding on the plantation. Fearful that Marion would be lured into Tarleton's trap, Mrs. Richardson dispatched her son to warn Marion. Captain Richardson found Marion about two miles away and reported to him that Tarleton was waiting for him with two pieces of artillery, 100 cavalry, and 300 infantry. Armed with this warning, Marion reversed direction and rode to safety six miles away on the far side of Richbourg's Mill Dam.[40]

A prisoner escaped from Marion's camp that night and reported to Tarleton that Richardson's intelligence had spared Marion from falling into Tarleton's trap and that Marion was now at Richbourg's Mill. Tarleton immediately roused his riders and took off in that direction, but Marion, assuming the prisoner would report his location, was also on the move. Marion assigned the rear guard mission to the capable Major John James. Using local guides who knew every inch of the trackless swamps, Marion preceded Tarleton on a 35-mile course from Richbourg's Mill to the head of Jack's Creek, around to the Pocotaligo River, back to Black River, and ending at an excellent defensive position at Benbow's

Ferry. After seven hours and 26 miles, Tarleton reached Ox Swamp on Pocotaligo River and decided he had had enough. Exasperated, he reportedly told his men, "Come, my Boys! Let us go back, and we will find the Gamecock [Thomas Sumter], but as for this damned old fox, the Devil himself could not catch him."[41]

Scott Aiken asks a fair question: was Tarleton's culminating point a physical or a mental one?[42] It makes for an interesting discussion, but either way, the result is the same. By using the unlikely tactic of retreat, Marion asserted himself over the seemingly more powerful Tarleton.

Adaptation and Flexibility

While there is a necessary overlap of the skills required of leadership and management, the basic purposes of the two activities are different. Peter Northouse notes that "The overriding function of management is to provide order and consistency to organizations, whereas the primary function of leadership is to produce change and movement. Management is about seeking order and stability, leadership is about seeking adaptive and constructive change."[43] Both leaders and managers need to understand *how things work*, but it is the leader that is driven *to make things work better*.[44]

Northouse challenges leaders to "act to expand the available options to long-standing problems" and to "change the way people think about what is possible."[45] James Kouzes and Barry Posner agree, adding that "change is the work of leaders. It's what they do …. They experiment. They tinker."[46]

Still, leaders must guard against losing this innate spirit of dynamism. German military strategist Helmuth von Moltke is often paraphrased as declaring, "No plan survives contact with the enemy." Nonetheless, the immense mental and physical effort involved in making a plan has tempted many leaders to "fight the plan instead of the battle," even when changing circumstances have rendered the plan irrelevant. In such instances, John Gardner cautions that leaders cannot cling stubbornly to an approach that is not producing results.[47] Instead, they must continually seek adaptive and constructive change.[48]

Francis Marion and Interior Lines

Swiss military theorist Antoine Henri, Baron de Jomini studied Napoleonic warfare in an effort to make sense of those elements that he found chaotic and indiscriminate. In their place he endeavored to use order and logic to define the principles of war in a way that formed a neatly organized system. The result was an almost geometric approach to warfare.

For Jomini, the problem was to bring the maximum possible force to bear against an inferior enemy force at the decisive point in the theater of operations. This condition could best be achieved by properly ordering one's lines of communication relative to the enemy's so that the friendly force possessed "interior lines." Interior lines allowed the friendly commander to move parts of his army more rapidly than could an enemy operating on exterior lines. In this way, the force operating on interior lines could defeat in detail an enemy operating on exterior lines.[49] By the time of the Civil War, Jomini had become the principal interpreter of Napoleonic strategy for the American military, but even before then, Marion seemed to intuitively grasp the concept of interior lines as a means of adapting to developing situations and gaining flexibility.

One way to achieve interior lines is by central position, placing one's army between segments of the enemy force and dealing with each force sequentially to prevent the enemy from massing. Marion used central position in his general area of operations by operating from a base protected by the swamps of the Pee Dee River. This interior position allowed him to move against his enemies in a zone stretching from Charleston to Georgetown, and inland to Camden and the area of present-day Columbia.[50] More specifically, Marion used this technique between the engagement at Wiboo Swamp on March 16, 1781, and the siege of Fort Watson on April 15. At the beginning of that period, Marion located his men near the Lower Bridge on the Black River. From this advantageous position, Marion could either move south toward Georgetown or north toward the British inland forts.[51]

After the action at Wiboo Swamp, Marion and British Lieutenant Colonel John Watson became tangled in a series of running engagements. Marion's successful defense at Lower Bridge on March 8 or 9 sent Watson to an encampment at Blakely Plantation, and Marion continued to harass the British until Watson became seriously fearful of being isolated from any hope of reinforcements. Watson decided his best course was to withdraw to the safety of Georgetown, but Marion was one step ahead of him and cut trees across the road and destroyed the bridges at Ox Swamp, seven miles from Blakely Plantation. To bypass the obstacle, Watson turned southward in hopes of reaching the Santee Road, 15 miles away. Marion trailed him, harassing the British rear guard. As the British slowly made their way toward the Sampit River, just nine miles from Georgetown, Marion dispatched Lieutenant Colonel Peter Horry to destroy the bridge over the Sampit. He also positioned riflemen to overlook the site. When the British arrived at the destroyed bridge, they began wading across. Marion tried to thwart the crossing, but the British were able to beat him back and moved to a camp at Trapier Plantation while Marion bivouacked on the banks of the Sampit. While Marion was in camp, he learned that Colonel Welbore Doyle had destroyed his supply base at Snow's Island. This development caused Marion to turn his attention toward Doyle, allowing Watson to limp the nine miles into Georgetown unmolested.[52]

Marion caught up with Doyle and bested him at Witherspoon's Ferry on April 3. With Marion hot on his trail, Doyle hastened his retreat toward Camden. Marion then realized that Doyle's departure from the area had left Watson almost isolated at Georgetown. It being planting season, Marion could not call up his militia in time to strike this tempting target, but he was in excellent position when on April 14, Lieutenant Colonel Henry Lee and his legion of 300 Continental cavalry and infantry united with Marion near the bridge over the Black River. The two joined forces in an effort to capture Fort Watson, a position along the Santee River that formed part of the British supply chain between Charleston and the outposts further inland.[53]

Marion used central position to adapt to various British threats and to build flexibility into his offensive actions. Leaders who create such conditions have the resiliency necessary to overcome adversity and the capacity to take advantage of opportunities that unexpectedly present themselves. "Central position" beyond the battlefield involves maintaining the balanced posture necessary to be ready for many different developments.

Francis Marion and a Leader's Use of Resources

"Great leaders don't blame the tools they are given. They work to sharpen them."

SIMON SINEK

Situational Awareness and Perception

James Kouzes and Barry Posner admonish leaders to "keep their antennae up, no matter where they are" and to make "idea gathering" an intentional part of their routine. They encourage leaders to open their internal meetings to "outsiders," to sample the organization's work as an anonymous consumer, and to solicit input from stakeholders.[1] The goal is to have the awareness and understanding of the situation necessary to determine how things relate to one another and to make decisions.[2]

Such awareness can also be gained by the "management by wandering around" (MBWA) technique advocated by Tom Peters and successfully used by Hewlett Packard in the 1980s. Management by wandering around involves "making the rounds" in order to improve connectivity and communication in the organization. Leaders see for themselves what is happening throughout the organization and, in the process, get firsthand information from informal channels, have an opportunity to share their vision and communicate their perspective through immediate and on-the-spot feedback, and are able to forge a bond with subordinates. The subordinates get access to the leader and are able to directly voice their concerns, ask questions about rumors, and make suggestions.

Within the military, commanders practice a form of MBWA through "battlefield circulation." While the staff is controlling the battle from the headquarters, commanders travel throughout the battlespace to gather their own information and form their own conclusions. They meet with subordinates, check on the progress of actions and orders, and get a perspective that cannot be obtained from a remote location. Otherwise, as Lieutenant General E. M. Flanagan wonders, how a leader "can know and lead and be responsible for his outfit from the desk in his office escapes me."[3]

Francis Marion and Battlefield Intelligence

In addition to his own personal knowledge of the local area, Marion maintained his situational awareness through a vast network of spies, patrols, scouts, other Patriot units, and friendly members of the local population.[4] These, Robert Bass reports, were "always on the qui vive" so that Marion "was never caught napping."[5] There is no shortage of examples of Marion's efforts to collect intelligence. A few illustrations follow:

When Major Micajah Ganey mobilized his militia in the Little Pee Dee River area in an attempt to surprise Marion, Marion's patrols reported the Loyalist muster and allowed Marion to instead surprise Ganey. Then Marion used information from the prisoners he had captured to ambush Captain Jesse Barefield at Blue Savannah.

Marion's defeat of Colonel John Coming Ball at Black Mingo Creek was made possible by reports from Captain Henry Mouzon, Lieutenant John Scott, and other volunteer militiamen that Ball was encamped at Shepherd's Ferry. Mouzon was an especially valuable asset to Marion. A highly skilled civil engineer and surveyor, Mouzon had made a map of South Carolina that was published in 1775, and his keen eye for terrain served Marion well.

Rather than sitting idle while he was rebuilding his force at his bivouac site at Port's Ferry, Marion sent out small patrols throughout the region to gather intelligence. One of these patrols returned to camp with reports of a recent Tory muster and that the enemy was presently encamped at an old muster field with lax security. Understanding the time sensitivity of the patrol's intelligence, Marion immediately moved forward and defeated the Tories at Tearcoat Swamp.

Marion showed this ability to respond quickly to intelligence reports when he received word from Captain Zachary Cantey about the location of Lieutenant Colonel John Watson's camp. Marion had been marching from Snow's Island to link up with Thomas Sumter, but, acting on Cantey's report, Marion diverted his force and set up an ambush at Wiboo Swamp.

In addition to his own patrols and reconnaissance, Marion's situational awareness was facilitated by his higher headquarters. It was General Nathanael Greene, for example, who informed Marion of the locations of Lieutenant Colonel John Watson and Lord Francis Rawdon in May 1781. That same month, Greene's aide-de-camp, Major Nathaniel Pendleton, informed Marion that the British had left Camden. Marion also received reports from parallel commands such as those from Brigadier General Thomas Sumter in June 1781 that the British were near Ninety Six.

A final way that Marion maintained situational awareness was by reports from friendly members of the local population. An example of this support is Mary Richardson who warned Marion of Banastre Tarleton's plan to ambush him near her plantation. Thanks to this information, Marion reversed his direction of march and avoided Tarleton's trap. When Tarleton learned that his plan had been frustrated and gave chase to Marion, Marion used local guides to evade Tarleton's pursuit through the trackless swamps.[6]

One explanation for Marion's remarkable situational awareness was the fact that he drew on so many different sources. He used his own military assets, as well as those above and lateral to him. He also used the local citizenry to keep him informed. Most importantly, Marion was able to turn this situational awareness in to action by processing the information in a timely manner and taking advantage of the opportunities it presented.

Capacity to Manage, Decide, and Set Priorities

While leadership and management are two distinct processes, there is a considerable amount of overlap between the two. Peter Northouse notes that "when leaders are involved in planning, organizing, staffing, and controlling, they are involved in management."[7] It is by operating in such spheres that leaders are able to ensure the "execution" which

Larry Bassidy and Ram Charan describe as "a systematic way of exposing reality and acting on it."[8] The details of management give a leader the comprehensive understanding of the organization that allows them to set realistic goals.[9] Bassidy and Charan argue that "leaders who excel at execution immerse themselves in the substance of execution and even some of the key details."[10] This situational awareness allows them to operate from the sense of reality that comes from truly knowing their people and their business.[11] Armed with that information, they can focus the organization on a very few clear priorities, and make the decisions necessary to ensure execution.

This is not to say that the process is an easy one. Bassidy and Charan highlight that many organizations "are filled with people who dance around decisions without ever making them. Some leaders simply do not have the emotional fortitude to confront the tough ones." What is required is decisiveness: "the ability to make difficult decisions swiftly and well, and act on them."[12] And while management and leadership may overlap in many areas, this is where the leader begins to step to the fore.

Francis Marion and the Judicious Use of Resources

A leader's most precious resources are almost always his human ones, and that was certainly true for Marion. Marion had to carefully preserve not just his men's lives, but also their time and morale. Consequently, he developed tactics that were very much dependent on intelligence, avoided decisive engagement, had a low risk of casualties, and had a pronounced chance of success. Locked in a war of attrition, Marion had to sustain his ability to harass and disrupt the British while safeguarding his force's ability to continue to survive and fight.[13] Scott Aiken credits this "extremely judicious expenditure of resources" for strengthening the faith Marion's men had in his leadership and military abilities, and for the success of the partisan campaign.[14]

The engagement at Tearcoat Swamp on October 26, 1780, is illustrative of the standard tactics Marion used to achieve low-cost results. While rebuilding his force at his bivouac site at Port's Ferry, Marion sent out small patrols throughout the region to gather intelligence. One of these patrols returned to camp on October 24 with reports of a recent Tory muster. After gathering in Camden to receive muskets, ammunition, saddles, and other supplies, some 80 Tories had marched to Tearcoat Swamp, between the Black River and the High Hills of the Santee River. Marion's patrol reported the Tories were now carelessly encamped at an old muster field with lax security. It was an inviting target for Marion who saw a chance to weaken the morale of the new Tory recruits before they "should become confirmed in the principles they had unwillingly adopted."[15]

Marion understood the time sensitivity of the patrol's intelligence, and he moved forward from his camp to Kingstree the same day he received the report. He had with him 150 men, but withheld from them his plans in order to persevere security. While he was moving, he initiated a deception campaign by spreading rumors that the partisans were headed to McCallum's Ferry to attack Tories there.[16]

Marion left Kingstree the morning of October 25 and approached Tearcoat Creek after darkness had fallen. He dispatched scouts who confirmed the Tories were camped in a large field just off of a road. While the position was protected in the rear by the swamp, the Tories had done little to enhance this natural strength. The scouts observed men playing cards around three large campfires and others who were asleep.[17]

Marion rested his men until midnight and then moved them into position early on October 26. On the signal of a pistol shot, the partisans attacked simultaneously from three directions. Two smaller groups attacked the Tory left and right flanks, and Marion led the largest group at the Tory front. The surprised Tories offered almost no resistance. Marion's men killed six Tories, wounded 14, and captured 23, while themselves losing only two horses. The Patriots also captured 80 horses, 80 muskets, ammunition, food, bridles, saddles, and personal baggage, which Marion used to arm and equip his men. The Patriots then withdrew back to Kingstree, having successfully established their influence near the High Hills.[18]

Leaders like Marion are tasked to "effectively accomplish the mission while conserving resources." Of the many resources they control, leaders prioritize human lives above material resources.[19] Marion understood this. As Lieutenant Colonel Henry Lee observed, Marion "risked the lives of his troops only when necessary."[20] At Tearcoat Swamp, Marion demonstrated his ability to reach out and strike British and Tory outposts and units and then disappear back into the swamps before he could be caught, accomplishing the mission and conserving resources.[21]

Organization

Bob Johansen asserts that "leaders are what they can organize."[22] Bill Creech adds that organization "more than anything determines the overall health and vitality of the system." "How you choose to organize can either make you or break you," he continues, because organization either "serves or squashes the human spirit."[23] As leaders consider how to organize, they have available basic models of hierarchal, flat, and self-organizing structures.

The wire diagram for a hierarchal organization is shaped roughly like a pyramid. There is one person at the top of the organization and beneath them are multiple other entities that each have their own leader. Leaders at any given level control the entity and the people below them. Coordination among lateral organizations is affected by the level that mutually controls them.

The hierarchical approach to organization has strengths and weaknesses. The centralized authority helps promote standardization and compliance. On the other hand, it tends to limit creativity and initiative. The presence of multiple entities facilitates specialization and focus in certain areas of expertise. It may also lead to bureaucratic in-fighting and discourage cooperation. The vertical structure maximizes the leader's ability to control the flow of information. While this control may help keep the organization "on message," it also can slow decision making and disadvantage subordinates.

The exact structure for a hierarchical organization is dependent on the idea of "span of control" or the number of subordinates a single leader can effectively be responsible for. For the first 60 years of the 20th century, most organizations were structured around military models with a span of control of six. In the 1960s, however, many organizations began experimenting with flatter, less hierarchical models. Spans of control in such organizations widened to between 15 and 20.[24]

The wire diagram for a flat organization is much more horizontal than for a hierarchical one. There are fewer levels of management between the highest individual and the rank and file members, resulting in a much more streamlined organization. Like the hierarchical approach, the flat model also has strengths and weaknesses.

All the members of the organization enjoy greater responsibility in a flat organization which increases the potential for individual productivity. However, the paucity of intermediate levels of management can make it difficult to coordinate and synchronize those individual efforts. Decision making and initiative are accelerated, but standardization can suffer. Flat organizations tend to contain more generalists, making specialized, in-depth knowledge more difficult to achieve.

As an alternative to traditionally managed organizations, Margaret Wheatley champions "self-organization." Organization, she argues, is a naturally occurring phenomenon, and, if left to their own devices, individuals will naturally create "systems of relationships where all members of the system benefit from their connections." By developing a shared understanding of what is important, what behavior is acceptable, what actions are required, what channels of communication and networks are helpful, and how work will get done, members of a self-organized system realize that "the system can do for itself most of what leaders have felt necessary to do to the systems they control."[25]

While emphasizing the need for "highly localized change activity," Wheatley is not advocating an organization that "spins off wildly in all directions."[26] She acknowledges the important role of the leader "to foster experimentation, to help create connections across the organization, to feed the system with rich information from multiple sources—all while helping everyone stay clear on what we agreed we wanted to accomplish and who we wanted to be."[27] While this self-proclaimed "Warrior for the Human Spirit" may represent the outer reaches of the organization continuum, she provides very practical advice that "if the organization can stay in a continuous conversation about who it is and who it is becoming, then leaders do not have to undertake the impossible task of trying to hold it all together."[28]

Francis Marion and Fort Watson

Current United States Army doctrine suggests that attackers of fixed and fortified enemy positions organize their force into assault, support, and breach elements. The support element suppresses enemy fire around the point of attack. The breach element reduces any obstacles and creates a lane through which the assault element can pass. The assault element destroys the enemy on the other side of the obstacles.[29] At Fort Watson, Marion displayed an instinctive understanding of this organization.

After the surrender of Charleston on May 12, 1780, the British army quickly occupied a chain of strategic posts in South Carolina and Georgia that included heavily garrisoned forts at Georgetown, Camden, Ninety Six and Augusta, with supporting posts at Forts Motte, Granby, Watson and Orangeburg.[30] The ensuing "War of the Posts" reached Fort Watson in April 1781. Upon arrival, Marion and Lieutenant Colonel Henry Lee immediately surrounded Fort Watson and when the British refused to surrender, the Patriots built "Maham's Tower" to help overcome the terrain advantage held by the British. On April 23, the eighth day of the siege, Marion launched his attack.

The Patriot support element was comprised of riflemen from Captain William McCottry's company. McCottry was a wise choice for this assignment. He was himself an expert marksman, and his company became known as "McCottry's Rifles" in honor of their skills.[31]

From their crow's nest position in Maham's Tower, McCottry's men rained a shower of bullets down on Fort Watson that drove the defenders to seek cover and rendered them unable to return effective fire. With the enemy so occupied, the breach element, organized in to two parties, one led by Robert Lee of Lee's Legion and the other a group of militia led by Ensign Baker Johnson, advanced. Edward McCrady reports that "such was the effect of the riflemen upon the top of the tower, having complete command of every part of the fort, that the besieged found it impossible to resist the lodgement effected by the attacking party."[32] Under such protection, Lee and Johnson's men quickly reduced the three abatis and began hacking away at the logs forming the wall of the stockade.[33]

Behind the breach element was the assault element composed of Lee's infantrymen and led by Captain Patrick Carnes. "Helmets down and bayonets fixed," Carnes's men stood "ready to charge through the opening and storm the fort."[34] Such exertions proved unnecessary. Before an assault could be launched, Fort Watson's commander Lieutenant James McKay was forced to surrender after his men refused to fight.

Marion's organization for success at Fort Watson reflected a firm understanding not just of the mission's requirements, but of the strengths of his men. For the support force he drew on the expert marksmen from his militia. For the assault force he drew on the disciplined and well-equipped Continentals of Lee's Legion. For the breach force, he had elements of each. Jim Collins likens an organization to a bus, and the leader's task is to get "the right people in the right seats."[35] At Fort Watson, Marion followed Collins's organizational prescription.

Delegative Leadership

If the organization has exceptionally motivated and expert subordinates, the leader might consider the delegative leadership technique. In this situation, the subordinates have so much initiative and capability that the leader can largely just tell them what needs to be done and trust them to complete the task without the degree of personal leader involvement required with other techniques. However, leaders must remember that while they may delegate authority, they cannot delegate responsibility. Thus, even in the delegative technique, the leader remains responsible for the final outcome.

The delegative leadership technique also lends itself to situations that can be compartmentalized into separate actions by different individuals or different teams. Using a "divide and conquer approach," the leader breaks the big task down into smaller sections and assigns each to a subordinate. The leader then focuses their energy on monitoring progress and ensuring synchronization.

Francis Marion and the Postell Brothers at Manigault's Ferry and Keithfield Plantation

Delegative leadership requires willing and able subordinates, and Marion had two in the persons of brothers James and John Postell. According to William Dobein James, to these two brothers, "nothing appeared difficult."[36] The trust Marion had in the Postells and other detachment commanders allowed him to decentralize operations and use delegative leadership. A good example can be seen in the twin engagements at Manigault's Ferry and Keithfield Plantation in January 1781.

On January 17, the tide of the war was turning in the Americans' favor with the defeat of the British army at the battle of Cowpens. The final outcome, however, was still undecided, and Lord Charles Cornwallis continued to seek a decisive victory in open battle. Nathanael Greene was under no such pressure, and merely had to ensure the survival of his army and the sustainment of Patriot morale. With time on his side, Greene could afford to fully develop his plans before acting. While he plotted his army's next move, Greene could use Marion to keep up the logistical pressure on the British.[37]

The American success at Cowpens left Marion feeling fairly safe from any immediate British attacks. He turned to the Postell brothers to take advantage of this opportunity, sending each with a few dozen horsemen south of the Santee River to do what damage they could along the road from Nelson's Ferry to Charleston.

John Postell headed first for Thomson's Plantation, but found that whatever stores were once there had been removed several days earlier. As he left Thomson's, however, Postell received intelligence of a quantity of rum, salt, sugar, flour, pork, and British uniforms at Manigault's Ferry, about five miles above Nelson's.[38] He struck the British redoubt there, levelling the position and destroying supplies. Postell's task was made easier by the fact that all but four of the enemy's guard force had left the position in response to his brother John's attack on Keithfield Plantation, near Moncks Corner. At Keithfield, John destroyed the enemy depot, burning 14 wagons full of clothing and 20 barrels of rum, killing two British and wounding two more, and taking 26 prisoners without losing a man.[39]

Marion reported the good news to Greene who replied on February 11, "give my particular thanks to Major and Captain Postell, for the spirit and address with which they executed your orders over the Santee."[40] Leaders wishing to use delegative leadership need trusted subordinates such as the Postells who will execute orders with "spirit and address." Such trust is easier to come by if there is a pre-existing relationship. For Marion and James Postell, for example, that relationship was reinforced by the time spent together as mess mates.[41] By delegating freedom of action to trusted men like the Postells, Marion was able to enlarge his area of operations and multiply his results.

Francis Marion and Leadership's Demand for Stamina and Resiliency

> "Fatigue makes cowards of us all."
>
> GEORGE PATTON

Physical Vitality and Stamina

Leadership is certainly not for the faint of heart, and physical vitality and stamina are needed to live what Joseph Badaracco describes as the "managerial life":

> Every day brings another over-full schedule, with scores of messages needing answers, big and little projects requiring shoves forward, tough conversations, and crises of all sizes. Most days end with a pile of work left undone. Most of these tasks require energy, care, attention to nuance, and some creativity—because people usually come through a manager's door with problems rather than solutions. And this stream of tasks continues for months and years.[1]

Badaracco concludes that leadership oftentimes resembles more of "a long, hard slog and not a stirring adventure."[2] It is, note James Kouzes and Barry Posner, more often found "in the daily moments" than in majestic and awe-inspiring sweeping gestures.[3] At times, it can seem like "an unending stream of problems and challenges."[4] But caring leaders don't simply endure these adversities with a grudging stoicism. They embrace them in the belief that they make their lives deeper and fuller.[5] To do so requires physical vitality and stamina.

Francis Marion in the Field

At the beginning of his partisan campaign in 1780, Marion was 48 years old. He was about five feet, two inches tall, weighed 110 pounds, and had been knock-kneed from birth.[6] "Wiry, tough, and physically hard," Marion lived with his men in their austere camps, sharing with them the long nights, meager diet, chance of disease, and exposure to the elements.[7] In fact, while he allowed his men to come and go based on their personal situations, Marion remained on the campaign trail continuously for most of two years. He led his partisans in 22 documented engagements and battles; a feat of endurance Scott Aiken concludes "a man of insufficient physical fitness and stamina could not have accomplished," especially under 18th-century conditions.[8] This physical vitality and stamina allowed Marion to conduct the long and rapid movements necessary to seemingly appear out of nowhere and catch his adversaries by surprise. An excellent example is the movement Marion conducted before the battle of Parker's Ferry.

In August 1781, Colonel William Harden, commanding the militia south of the Edisto River, was paralyzed by a swarm of increased British activity south of Charleston. Bearing down on Harden were Hessian Lieutenant Colonel Ernst Leopold von Borck and Loyalist Major Thomas Fraser with a force of 600 British, Hessian, and Loyalist troops to reinforce the already sizeable Tory presence in the area. In response to Harden's plea for help, Nathanael Greene instructed Marion, "if it is practical I wish you to give support to Col. Harden. You know the Colonel's force, your own and the enemy's, and will do as you think proper."[9] After sending Major George Cooper and a unit of mounted militia into the area of Moncks Corner and Dorchester to serve as a diversion, Marion slipped south with 200 selected men. Using obscure roads and trails and moving largely at night to avoid detection, Marion traversed a circuitous route of over 100 miles to link up with Harden near Round O in Colleton County on August 22.[10]

Marion continued on to Horse Shoe, reaching there the evening of August 26 and receiving 230 reinforcements which brought his total strength to over 400. He then marched across the great swamp at the head of the Ashepoo River and camped at Middleton Plantation, within five miles of Fraser's command. On August 29, Fraser moved his camp to Isaac Hayne's plantation, now just three miles from Marion. Convinced that the British would cross the Edisto at Parker's Ferry when returning to Charleston, Marion set up an ambush along the Parker's Ferry road at an intersection with the main causeway. There he learned that some 100 Tories under a "Colonel Cunningham" were waiting to join Fraser at the ferry.[11]

Marion was between two enemy forces. Nevertheless, he concealed the majority of his men behind an abatis in the heavily wooded swamp 40 yards from the Parker's Ferry Road. A second line of 80 men was placed to the right rear, with orders to march forward when the first line fired. A third mounted detachment was placed farther behind the second line and ordered to ride up and attack the British rear when the opportunity presented.[12]

Marion's plan was for the British to march into and through the ambush before the Patriots sprang the trap. By delaying initiation, the main body of the British column would have been on the road, two or four abreast, parallel to Marion's entire front line. Caught in column along a road, with an abatis between them and the enemy, the British would have sustained a brutal defeat. Unfortunately for Marion, a scouting party of Cunningham's men came down the road at dusk and spotted some of the Patriots on the left flank of Marion's front line. According to William Dobein James, the British had discerned Marion's position by spotting a white feather worn by one of the Patriots.[13] Cunningham's men fired and then fell back to the ferry and Marion sent a few of his horsemen after them. In the meantime, the sound of the fire alerted the British, and Fraser's dragoons were ordered forward. Riding fast, they entered Marion's kill zone and were devastated by the first volley. Unable to turn around along the narrow causeway, they had no choice but to push forward through the ambush, running the gauntlet.[14]

Meanwhile, the remaining British forces of infantry and artillery arrived and began to deploy in the confused darkness. They took further casualties including all of their artillerymen. Marion was still on the verge of a solid victory but then one of Marion's men yelled that the British were flanking on the right. The front line fell back into the second and third lines, and Marion attempted to rally them, but by that time the British had also fallen back and the battle was soon over. Marion held his ground for a few hours then retreated, his men out of ammunition and exhausted by the events of the last few days.

Parker's Ferry was a brief action with the initial volleys being the most violent and effective.[15] Marion reported that he inflicted 18 British killed and some 80 wounded, while suffering just one fatality and three wounded among his own men. He remained in the area until August 31, and on September 1, left Round O and conducted a 32-mile nighttime movement to Saint Stephen's Parish where he began preparations for his next mission, the September 8 battle of Eutaw Springs.[16]

Marion's tactical planning at Parker's Ferry is exemplary in many ways including his use of deception, intelligence, mastery of the terrain, and synchronization of different elements of the ambush. What made the actual engagement possible, however, was Marion's ability to conduct the arduous movement to reach Harden in the first place. It is for that reason that Scott Aiken singles out this particular engagement as illustrative of Marion's superior physical fitness.[17]

Leading by Example

Leaders are role models by nature, and the example they set can be either positive or negative. In leading by example, leaders not only show their subordinates "what right looks like," they reaffirm their commitment to the organization's values by demonstrating that their words match their deeds and aligning actions and values.[18] This includes making sure the leader's calendar, meeting agendas, budget, and other ways he spends his time and resources reflect what he says is important.[19]

Good leadership by example elicits something from the follower and helps him understand something about himself.[20] To that extent, leadership experts such as James Kouzes, Barry Posner, and Stephen Covey connect leading by example with "finding one's voice." This means that the leader finds their voice, and then helps others find theirs.[21] The leader communicates their voice not just in a single, formal announcement, but by repeatedly expressing phrases, stories, and examples of the environment and behavior the leader values. They ask for feedback from others on how their actions affect them, and also ask people questions that keep them constantly focused on the most important values and priorities.[22]

Leading by example goes beyond merely doing what is supposed to be done. Everyone should be doing that. Leading by example is a way that leaders influence others by using themselves to elicit a desired behavior response.

Francis Marion and Shared Hardships

One of the most famous legends surrounding Marion's shared hardships is the story of the sweet potato dinner. As Pastor Weems reports it, a British officer from Georgetown was conducted into Marion's secret camp to arrange for an exchange of prisoners. The officer was led to Marion, and the details of the exchange were soon settled. The visitor then prepared to leave, but Marion insisted, "Oh no! It is now about our time of dining; and I hope, sir, you will give us the pleasure of your company to dinner."

Looking around, the guest "could see no sign of a pot, pan, Dutch oven, or any other cooking utensil that could raise the spirits of a hungry man." Instead, there was only one of Marion's men tending to a heap of sweet potatoes roasting over some embers. On Marion's command, the partisan cook gathered some potatoes from the pile, blew and brushed off the ashes, and delivered them to Marion and his guest on a large piece of pine bark. As the soldier placed the meal between the two enemies, Marion said, "I fear, sir, our dinner will not prove so palatable to you as I could wish; but it is the best we have."

Midway through the meal the British officer broke into a laugh at the circumstances and marveled to Marion at the difference between their two camps. To the Briton's further surprise, Marion confessed that he and his men often subsisted on much less than what was now before them. When the visitor expressed his amazement that Marion could stand such conditions, Weems credits Marion with a poetic discourse on liberty, the heart, and freedom.

When the British officer returned to Georgetown, he reported his experience to Lieutenant Colonel John Watson, who noted that the man looked quite serious. "I have cause, sir, to look serious," said the officer. "I have seen an American general and his officers, without pay, and almost without clothes, living on roots and drinking water; and all for liberty! What chance have we against such men!" Weems adds that "the young officer was so struck with Marion's sentiments, that he never rested until he threw up his commission, and retired from the service."[23]

Perseverance

Angela Duckworth is a professor of psychology at the University of Pennsylvania. In her 2016 book, *Grit: The Power of Passion and Perseverance*, she reports that based on a 12-year study of military leaders, West Point cadets, and United States Army Special Forces soldiers, the greatest determinant of success is not natural talent or IQ, but a combination of passion and perseverance she calls "grit." According to Duckworth, a person of grit has "a passion to accomplish a particular top-level goal *and* the perseverance to follow though."[24]

Duckworth's perseverance takes many forms. One is "in the daily discipline of trying to do things better than we did yesterday." This form of discipline is what allows people to stick with a task and practice it over and over again until mastery is achieved. Duckworth also identifies hope as "a rising-to-the-occasion kind of perseverance." Hope, she writes, is necessary "from the very beginning to the very end" and what keeps us moving onward no matter how many times we get knocked down.[25]

Duckworth is quick to point out that perseverance does not equate to unimaginative obstinance. Lower-level goals can be abandoned if they can be exchanged for others that are more feasible or when a different means to the same end appears that is more efficient or otherwise somehow superior. It is for higher-level goals that Duckworth says "it makes more sense to be stubborn." That is where perseverance is essential and uncompromising.[26]

Francis Marion and Georgetown

On April 1, 1780, the British established a siege of Charleston. On May 12, Major General Benjamin Lincoln and the American garrison surrendered. Five days later British columns pushed out from Charleston to establish outposts from which to control South Carolina. Garrisons were placed on the coasts at Beaufort and Georgetown, and inland at Cheraw, Camden, Hanging Rock, and Ninety Six.

Georgetown, captured by Captain John Plumer Ardesoife of the Royal Navy without opposition on July 1, was a particularly strategic location. Although not as impressive as Charleston County's population of approximately 66,000, Georgetown County's 22,000 residents made it the second largest population center in the state.[27] As the easternmost position of the British outposts, it served as a depot of military supplies for the inland forts and for the British army when it advanced into the South Carolina interior. It also was an advantageous location to logistically support British designs on North Carolina and to serve as an escape route if the expedition failed. When Lord Charles Cornwallis began his march to North Carolina in April 1781, Lieutenant Colonel Nisbet Balfour stockpiled provisions at Georgetown in case of such an eventuality.[28]

Liberating Georgetown from the British would unleash a host of advantages for the Patriots. With Charleston too heavily defended to recapture, freeing Georgetown from British control would help sustain popular support for the Patriot cause in South Carolina. As a trading and transportation hub, renewed access to Georgetown would spur South Carolina's economy. Finally, Georgetown's large stock of stores could be put to immediate use by Nathanael Greene's army.[29]

Marion's preference was to attack soft targets such as British supply trains, but, because of Georgetown's importance, he staged four attacks against it. The first was launched from Grimes Plantation, about 60 miles away, in the early morning of October 8, 1780. While an advance party of some 30 horsemen led by Peter Horry distracted the British, Marion circled around and entered Georgetown without opposition. When he reached the enemy redoubt manned by 70 Tories commanded by Colonel James Cassells, Marion demanded their surrender. Cassells refused, and Marion knew he lacked the strength to force the issue. Instead, he paraded his men through town, collecting six horses and some baggage, and capturing and then paroling some Loyalist-leaning citizens. Before

British reinforcements could arrive, Marion withdrew to the swamps along the Little Pee Dee River.[30]

Marion tried again on November 15, attacking from his camp behind White Bay Swamp about two miles north of Georgetown. He sent Horry toward the Black River and the road to Georgetown, and he sent Captain John Melton to investigate a report that some British were camped at William Alston's plantation and to check out the Sampit Road leading in to town. Both these groups made enemy contact before reaching the town, and the disruption to the attack and the loss of surprise thwarted Marion's plans. In an especially painful personal blow to Marion, his nephew Gabriel was captured and executed by the British. Marion then led his men into camp at Shepherd's Ferry on the Black Mingo Creek.[31]

Marion's third attempt on January 25, 1781, began with much promise. Armed with excellent intelligence of the British defenses and reinforced by Lieutenant Colonel Henry Lee's Legion, Marion and Lee struck fast. The Patriots succeeded in capturing the British garrison's commander, Lieutenant Colonel George Campbell, but Loyalist soldiers inside the redoubt and in the barracks outside it mounted a formidable defense. Without artillery, the Patriots could not overcome the stronghold, and Marion and Lee called for a withdrawal to Murray's Ferry.[32]

By the time of Marion's fourth attack, the strength of the Georgetown garrison had been reduced to approximately 100 British troops. Marion arrived with his brigade in the vicinity of the town on May 28, 1781, and the men began to entrench themselves on the landward side of the British defenses. Seeing the impressive size of the Patriot force, the British abandoned the garrison at 9:00pm, boarded some vessels anchored in Winyah Bay, and withdrew down the bay toward the sandbar at the entrance of the harbor.[33]

In capturing Georgetown, Marion reflected the perseverance that leaders are willing to devote to obtain significant ends. He not only made repeated attempts, but also massed his forces and was willing to use positional warfare rather than his usual partisan tactics against such an important target. In finally gaining the prize, Marion certainly expended maximum effort.

Resiliency

Studies show that when faced with serious adversity, people generally fall into three categories: "those who were permanently dispirited by the event, those who got their life back to normal, and those who used the experience as a defining event that made them stronger."[34] Resiliency is what allows people to be in this third category. It is the elasticity, durability, and adaptability that make it possible to recover quickly from change, hardship, or misfortune, and to interpret setbacks as temporary and local. But resiliency is more than just "toughing it out." Resilient people show an openness to learning that allows them to grow from disappointment as well as success.[35]

Francis Marion and Snow's Island

The importance of Snow's Island has been described earlier in the vignette "Francis Marion and the Commons at Snow Island." It is understandable then that when Lieutenant Colonel Welbore Doyle managed to locate Marion's camp and destroy it in March 1781, the loss would be felt hard by both Marion and the community. In spite of this setback, the Patriots showed great resiliency.

Doyle's raid came as part of a two-pronged British attempt to bring Marion to bay. While Doyle led his force of British regulars and Loyalists along the Lynches River, a second force led by Lieutenant Colonel John W. T. Watson advanced along the Santee River. Doyle and Watson figured this deliberate and methodical approach might have better success in locating Marion than Lieutenant Colonel Banastre Tarleton's more impulsive one had enjoyed. If they were able to find Marion, the two columns were close enough together that they could render mutual support.[36]

Marion knew of the British movements and tracked their progress by a screen of scouts and spies. He took up positions at the few causeways that restricted the British march through the swamps and made the enemy fight dearly for each passage. For several weeks the two sides skirmished at places like Mount Hope Swamp, the Lower Bridge of the Black River, and Sampit Bridge. Marion's rearguard action traded space for time, but still the British kept up their pursuit.[37]

Lieutenant Colonel Hugh Ervin, who had supervised the construction of the redoubt at Dunham's Bluff, was defending Snow's Island with a small force, most of whom were sick or wounded or were serving as guards for the prisoners held in the Bull Pen. When word reached Ervin of Doyle's approach, he positioned the scant men he had along Clarke's Creek. Fearing the worst, Ervin also began dumping supplies into Lynches River to avoid their capture.[38]

Led by Tory guides, Doyle followed a series of horse trails that led him to the boat landing on Clarke's Creek. With Marion still a day's march away in his bivouac on the Sampit, Doyle pressed his advantage. Spreading his 300-man regiment along the bank of the stream, he outflanked Ervin's meager force and pounded them with enfilading fire. Ervin's men were driven back from the creek, suffering seven men killed. Doyle's force moved across the creek and quickly set to destroying everything they could. The British then withdrew without any losses and set up a camp on the north side of Witherspoon's Ferry.[39]

Marion was still on the Sampit when he learned of the disaster, and he hurried toward Snow's Island. As he passed through Williamsburg, many of his men could not resist leaving the ranks to visit their homes and families. By the time Marion went into bivouac at Indiantown, he was left with only 70 men.[40]

Marion must have been heart-broken, and the morale of his small band was plummeting, but rather than succumbing to inertia, Marion rallied. He delivered a stirring speech to his men. Even allowing for Parson Weems's liberties, Marion's words are a clarion call:

> Yesterday I commanded 200 men; men whom I gloried in, and who I fondly thought, would have followed me through my dangers for my country. And, now, when their country most needs their services, they all nearly all gone! And even those of you who remain, are, if report be true, quite out of heart; and talk, that you and your families must be ruined if you resist any longer! But, my friends, if we shall be ruined for bravely resisting our tyrants, what will be done to us if we tamely lie down and submit to them …. For my own part I look upon such a state of things as a thousand times worse than death. And God is my judge this day, that if I could die a thousand deaths, most gladly would I die them all, rather than live to see my dear country in such a state of degradation and wretchedness.[41]

The effect of Marion's speech was transformative, with Weems declaring the men "made up our minds to fight by his side to a glorious death." Reveling in the change, Marion taunted, "Well, now colonel Doyle, look sharp, for you shall presently feel the edge of our swords."[42]

Marion's men were soon in hot pursuit, and received word that Doyle was foraging at the Whig plantations south of the Lynches. The Patriot advance guard caught up with Doyle at Witherspoon's Ferry on April 3, and a brisk exchange left several British killed or wounded. Now knowing Marion was on his heels, Doyle hastened his retreat toward Camden.[43]

The Patriot recovery from the defeat at Snow's Island exemplifies resiliency in a variety of physical, psychological, tactical, and strategic ways. Although Doyle had destroyed Marion's supply base, Marion's forces quickly recovered from the loss and forced the British to flee to safety.[44] The capture of Fort Watson on April 23 helped replace much of what was lost, and Scott Aiken concludes that "at the end of this tactical episode, Marion's loss of supplies at Snow['s] Island was more than offset by Doyle's personnel losses."[45] Marion also quickly found alternatives to Snow's Island. He established a number of smaller bases at places like Peyre's Plantation, Cantey's Plantation, Black Mingo, and Wadboo Plantation that served him well throughout the rest of the campaign.[46] Most importantly, in spite of the Watson-Doyle effort, the Pee Dee region remained strongly in support of the Patriot cause.[47]

Francis Marion and Growth as a Leader

"When you stop growing, you start dying."

WILLIAM BURROUGHS

Seeking and Responding to Feedback

As important as introspection is to building one's self-awareness, David Brooks notes that the effort cannot be a solitary one. "Individual will, reason, compassion, and character," he argues, "are not strong enough to consistently defeat selfishness, pride, greed, and self-deception." "Everyone needs redemptive help from outside," he continues, "… to tell us when we are wrong, to advise us on how to do right, and to encourage, support, arouse, cooperate, and inspire us along the way."[1] Thus leaders can build their self-awareness based on the feedback of others.

Individuals enter into a new situation with a certain frame of reference that allows them to begin processing the information around them. While this experience provides a useful starting point, leaders must guard against the "confirmation bias" that occurs when they seek and interpret new information in ways that confirm preexisting beliefs. Feedback helps leaders avoid this limitation.

Leaders make an initial plan based on available information and assumptions supported by past experience and frame of reference. They then must expose the plan to reality in the form of feedback. As they gather additional information, they must see if it confirms or denies the assumptions they have made. They must consult with others to see if the plan makes sense to them and to see if there are different and better ideas. Finally, they must be aware of the fact that situations change. What may have been true at one point in time, may no longer be the case. Plans must be adjusted to reflect the current situation.

At the end of the day, the purpose of leadership is to accomplish a task. Feedback is what lets the leader know whether he is getting closer to or further away from that outcome.[2] Feedback can come in many forms, including from the environment, from other people, and from outcomes, and leaders must purposefully and aggressively seek it.

Francis Marion and the Third Battle for Georgetown

The strategic importance of Georgetown led Marion to launch four attacks against it. His third effort is particularly illustrative of the role of feedback. This feedback came in the form of reconnaissance, consultation with others, and the unfolding situation. It represents a cycle of feedback that Marion both initiated and responded to.

Marion began the cycle by sending Peter Horry on a reconnaissance in force down the Black River Ferry Road toward Georgetown on December 28, 1780. Based on Horry's and other intelligence, Marion reported to Nathanael Greene that the British had reinforced their Georgetown garrison to a strength of 300 men, including 20 who were well mounted, three nine-pound cannon, and two galleys in the Sampit River. Greene responded to this feedback by likewise reinforcing Marion, sending him Lieutenant Colonel Henry Lee and his legion of 300 Continental cavalry and infantry on January 20, 1781. Prior to Lee's arrival, Marion had a force of only some 90 men.[3]

The odds thus evened, Marion and Lee began thinking offensively. They realized, however, that because an attack on Georgetown would involve a significant commitment of Patriot combat power, it would be wise to consult Greene. While Greene fully understood the risks involved, the idea's potential gains appealed to him. He consented to the operation, while cautioning his subordinates to "get good intelligence before you attempt anything."[4]

In the modern military vernacular, such a feedback exchange between one level of command and another is called a "commander's dialogue." During this discussion, the subordinate commander tells his higher commander his understanding of the mission, the tasks he considers necessary to complete that mission, and any significant issues such as time or resources available that impact mission accomplishment. The purpose of the dialogue is for the subordinate commander to get feedback in the form of the guidance, support, and expectations needed for developing the plan.[5] In this case, Marion and Lee gained valuable insights into what Greene considered the risks and rewards of the operation, and, most importantly, his directive to optimize intelligence.

Given Marion's predilection for intelligence, Greene's admonition was probably more reinforcing than novel, but either way Marion acted on it. He and Lee dispatched additional reconnaissance to inform their plan of attack, and these patrols determined that the cavalry troop that had recently reinforced Georgetown had since departed, weakening the position. Based on all their sources, Marion and Lee estimated that the British now had about 200 men defending Georgetown. Moreover, the British had positioned their defenses on the garrison's landward side, leaving the approach by water open. To take advantage of this situation, Marion and Lee devised a plan to use boats to transport the legion's infantry downriver from Snow's Island while their cavalry and mounted partisans and militia would advance overland.[6]

During the actual attack, the Patriot force travelling by river arrived before the overland force and, fearing delay might lead to the enemy discovering their presence, attacked early. The attackers enjoyed such surprise that they captured Lieutenant Colonel George Campbell, the garrison commander, while he was still in his bed. The Patriots were unable, however, to capitalize elsewhere, and the British defenders oc-cupied twin positions in their barracks and in their redoubt that would allow them to catch the attackers in a deadly crossfire. When Marion and Lee arrived with the overland column, they quickly assessed this vulnerability. Such feedback from the unfolding situation allows adaptive leaders to respond appropriately to reality rather than to preconceived assumptions. Realizing that success was now unlikely, Marion and Lee ordered a withdrawal to Murray's Landing.[7]

Forecasting

Bob Johansen argues that as leaders contemplate growth in their organi-zation, they should consider what he calls "the sweet spot for forecasting" that occurs about 10 years into the future. This mark allows leaders to focus on emerging patterns rather than "the noise of the present." It also gives organizations an edge over competitors focused on the nearer term, but is not so far into the future that it seems unbelievable or irrelevant. With this 10-year forecast in hand, Johansen believes organizations can develop the future leadership capacities they will need.[8]

Francis Marion and the Marion–Ganey Truce

On June 17, 1781, after the British had evacuated Georgetown, Loyalist Major Micajah Ganey and Patriot Lieutenant Colonel Peter Horry signed a truce. With that agreement set to expire and uprisings in northeast South Carolina persisting, North Carolina Governor Alexander Martin and South Carolina Governor John Matthews agreed to dispatch Marion to settle the matter. That Martin would place 250 North Carolina troops under Marion's command for this purpose was a strong testimony to Marion's value and reputation.[9]

From near Snow's Island on June 2, Marion wrote Ganey that he was coming to discuss a treaty designed to "prevent the effusion of blood and distress of the women and children."[10] A rendezvous point was agreed to and as Marion approached the location, he positioned his men to isolate it on three sides. The Loyalists had just seized a boatload of rice on Black Lake and were transporting it up the lake in canoes, and they were engaged by Colonel John Baxter of Marion's command. A brief exchange ensued, but the Loyalists were little interested in fighting, and Ganey soon sent out a white flag.[11] Although Marion's men protested that it was beneath his dignity to consort with "a leader of banditti," Marion invited Ganey to cross the Pee Dee River and meet at Burch's Mill.[12] The initial negotiations, however, were a failure. Ganey was unwilling to renew the terms he had previously concluded with Horry, and the first meeting of the commissioners was so troubled that they nearly came to blows.[13]

Marion renewed his offer to Ganey to talk, and the two met again at Burch's Mill on June 8. This time the efforts were successful, and more than 500 of Ganey's men laid down their arms. The treaty specified that the Loyalists would cease hostilities, return all plundered property, and swear allegiance to the United States and South Carolina while renouncing their former loyalty to the Crown. In return, they were given full pardons and allowed to keep their personal property. Those who refused were given, with their families, safe passage to the British lines in Charleston.[14]

The generous terms offered by Marion reflected the same forecasting for the post-war order that he had shown in his restraint at Blue Savannah. Marion understood that if the country was to be united and happy after the war, forgiveness would be required.[15] He warned his men against exacting any "private satisfaction" against "reformed" Loyalists and instead "recommended as Christians to forgive and forget all injuries which have been committed by such who have been led away by our enemies."[16]

The fruits of Marion's magnanimity are dramatically illustrated by the behavior of Ganey. Not too long after signing the treaty, this erstwhile enemy went so far as to resign his British commission, and he and some of his men obtained amnesty by enlisting for six months in the South Carolina militia. In that capacity, they were part of Marion's force that defeated a few die-hard Loyalists at Wadboo Plantation in September 1782.[17]

New Leaders

Mentoring is "a future-oriented developmental activity focused on growing in the profession."[18] In this relationship, a more experienced leader—or mentor—provides advice and guidance to a more junior protégé. Mentoring benefits not just the protégé, but it helps the organization grow as well. It helps the organization attract new talent and enhances organizational commitment among protégés. When mentors help protégés develop a deeper understanding of the organization's direction and dynamics, organizational capacity increases. Because of the benefits it provides the organization, many organizations consider mentoring a key competency for their leaders.[19]

Whether through mentoring or some other process, leaders have a responsibility to create more leaders.[20] Many organizations become very good on the strength of a single leader who achieves results through personal discipline and sheer force of will. However, when that leader departs, the reason for the organization's success departs as well. There is no sustained growth.[21]

For this reason, some organizations go so far as to consider "training your replacement" to be a "moral obligation."[22] A leader who models the "I'm training my replacement" approach does so with a sense of commitment to and respect for the future health of the organization. Because the replacement will be there after the leader leaves, the leader values the replacement because they want them to do well at a position that the leader presumably considers important, since it is what they are currently doing. Leaders should resolve to leave the organization better than they found it, and developing a new generation ready to take the reins is a key part of a vibrant and growing organization.

Francis Marion and Failing to Achieve Level 5 Leadership

In January 1782, Marion was elected to the State Senate by the voters of St. John's Berkeley Parish. On January 11, he set out to Jacksonborough to take his legislative seat, leaving Peter Horry in command of his brigade. Almost from the moment he arrived in Jacksonborough, Marion began receiving frantic messages from Horry that Marion must return to the field.[23]

Horry faced several problems. Of course, Marion was missed. To add to that, there was general war-weariness and desertions were high and morale was low. Horry himself was sick, unsure of himself, and unable to maintain discipline. Worst of all, however, was the old quarrel between Horry and Hezekiah Maham over rank. It was all too much for Horry, and he asked to be relieved.[24]

Marion told Horry, "as soon as they can spare me I will return," but for the time being there was really little Marion could do. His presence was vital to the Senate's ability to maintain a quorum. In fact, the body had had to adjourn twice in February due to insufficient numbers. Still, Marion confided to Horry that "I assure you I am tired of legislating and wish myself with you."[25]

With Maham even unwilling to follow Marion's orders to accept Horry's authority, the squabble reached Nathanael Greene who on January 16 wrote Marion that "I think Col. Horry has clearly the right of out ranking Col. Maham."[26] Still Maham refused to relent, writing Horry that "I had my Regiment three months in the field on duty before you had yours … and shall not obey any order that you may be pleased to send."[27]

Rather than serve under Horry, Maham turned his dragoons over to Captain John Caraway Smith and rode to Jacksonborough to take his seat in the General Assembly. Horry too was finished. He turned the brigade over to Colonel Adam McDonald and retired to his plantation on the Santee River.[28]

In the midst of this drama, a new threat to the Patriot cause was rising in the form of Colonel Benjamin Thompson. Previously contenting himself with primarily seizing cattle, Thompson had crossed the Cooper River on February 23 with 200 horsemen, 500 infantry, and two field pieces. Such a force would be able to do much damage to Marion's disorganized brigade.[29]

Word of this new danger reached Marion in Jacksonborough, and both he and Maham left on February 24 to rally the brigade.[30] Horry remained ill at his plantation.[31] Thompson struck a clearly unprepared Marion at Tidyman's Plantation not far from Wambaw Creek on February 25. The British inflicted heavy losses on Marion's men and Thompson continued on to Charleston with his herd of cattle.[32]

Both Horry and Maham tried to blame Marion for the defeat. Horry faulted Marion for being with the legislature rather than the brigade while Maham claimed Marion had issued confusing orders.[33] With Georgetown open again as an active port, Marion dispatched Horry there to serve as commandant. Horry and Maham's depleted units were combined into one legion, and Maham was appointed commander. Horry reacted petulantly to the decision, writing his old friend Marion, "I am sensible to whom I am indebted for being turned out of Service and Mayham Continued." Ultimately, he turned his post at Georgetown over to Captain William Allston and rode home. Maham did not last long either. He fell ill and returned to his home in St. Stephen's Parish where he was captured by a Tory raid on May 16 and then paroled.[34] Neither man was with Marion when he disbanded his militia at Wadboo in December.

Whether Marion's charismatic leadership style was ill equipped to "train a replacement" or whether neither Horry nor Maham was up to the task can be debated. Either way, the result was that when Marion left the brigade, disorganization and inefficiency followed. Jim Collins contrasts Level 5 "great" leaders who set up their successors for even greater success in the next generation with Level 4 "good" leaders whose organization's success is dependent on their own presence and declines after they depart.[35] Marion and his brigade appear to have risen only to Level 4.

After-Action Reviews

Leaders also help their organization sustain its growth by ensuring continuity of operations. Many activities that an organization performs are cyclic or recurring in nature. Examples include municipal elections, academic semesters, and scheduled maintenance. Complex operations such as these are exhausting, and harried leaders must resist the temptation of moving from one major event to the next without capturing the lessons learned in order to foster continuous improvement.

As this introspection is performed, many great leaders like General George Marshall emphasize the need to "fix the problem, not the blame."[36] Likewise, General Dwight Eisenhower succinctly posited that "leadership consists of nothing but taking responsibility for everything that goes wrong and giving your subordinates credit for everything that goes well."[37] When things do go wrong, leaders must capture what can be learned from the experience. This growth can only happen when there is an environment that allows people to openly talk about what went wrong as well as what went right.[38] It is by learning to "conduct autopsies without blame," that Jim Collins notes leaders begin the process of "creating a climate where the truth is heard" and understanding and learning can occur.[39]

One way that leaders can avoid the recrimination and unproductive hand-wringing that often frustrates any real improvement is the After-Action Review (AAR) process. After-Action Reviews are usually conducted as soon as possible after an event in order to capture lessons learned and foster an environment of continuous improvement. "In-stride AARs" can also be conducted at appropriate times, rather than just at the end of the event, to allow subordinates and leaders to take immediate corrective actions.

Organizations use AARs to apply observations, insights, and lessons to future events to improve not only task proficiency, but also the quality of the event. The written copy of the AAR is one of many items leaders should include in the "continuity" or "pass down" books designed to promote individual and organizational growth by sustaining momentum.

The basic format for an AAR is:

- What was supposed to happen?
- What actually happened and why?
- How do we sustain good performance and improve less than optimal performance?

After-Action Reviews include a facilitator, event participants, and other observers. The facilitator can be the leader of the organization that conducted the action or someone from outside the organization or action. Either way, the facilitator guides the participants through the AAR process to identify strengths to be sustained and weaknesses that need to improve.

An AAR is distinct from a "critique" which usually "only gives one viewpoint and frequently provides little opportunity for discussion of events by participants."[40] Instead, AARs are part of an open learning environment where facilitators, participants, and observers freely discuss successes and honest mistakes. The best AAR results in participants identifying problems themselves and taking ownership of the actions they develop to solve them.

Francis Marion and Black Mingo Creek

After the engagements at Great Savannah and Blue Savannah in August and September 1780, Marion dispersed his men and withdrew to the Great White Marsh in North Carolina in order to avoid the converging forces of Major James Wemyss and Major Micajah Ganey. Wemyss took advantage of Marion's absence and wreaked havoc in the Williamsburg

District. Colonel John Coming Ball also brought his force into the district and set up a position at a tavern called Red House from which he could control traffic on the Post Road and be ready to move to either Indiantown or Kingstree if needed. He also prepared defensive positions along the banks of Black Mingo Creek to control traffic on it.[41]

Major John James kept Marion abreast of these and other developments in the Williamsburg District, and on September 24, Marion left the Great White Marsh and travelled three days until he crossed Lynches River where he received the latest intelligence about Ball. The report was that British security was lax. Marion immediately initiated a 12-mile night movement toward Black Mingo Creek.[42]

Shortly before midnight, the Patriots were crossing Willtown Bridge, about a mile upstream from Red House. Although the riders approached under the cover of a very dark night, a British sentry heard the clamor of their horses' hooves as they crossed the loose planks of the bridge. He fired a shot that alerted the rest of Ball's men.[43]

With surprise lost, Marion ordered an immediate attack. He divided his force, ordering Captain Thomas Waties and a force of infantry to launch a demonstration to the front of the tavern, a dismounted force under Major Hugh Horry to attack from the right, and a mounted force to attack from the left.[44]

Marion had expected Ball to fight from the protection of Red House. Instead, the British had used the advance warning to deploy in battle formation in a field to the west of the tavern. As Horry's men advanced through the field, the British delivered a devastating fire. After the initial shock, Horry's men rallied and continued forward while Captain Waties and his men found the British right flank and attacked there. Receiving pressure from two sides, the British broke ranks and fled to the safety of the Black Mingo Swamp. From there they continued their retreat to Georgetown.[45]

In just 15 minutes, Marion had routed the British, killing at least three and wounding or capturing 13 more. It was a clear Patriot victory, but Parson Weems lamented that "the surprise and destruction of the tories would have been complete, had it not been for the alarm given by our horses' feet in passing Black Mingo Bridge, near which they were encamped." As a result, Weems reports that "Marion never afterwards suffered us to cross a bridge in the night, until we had first spread our blankets on it, to prevent noise."[46]

It should be noted that John Oller believes Marion had employed such a precaution in engagements prior to Black Mingo, and that Weems tells the tale as he did in order to "make a better story."[47] Perhaps Oller is correct, but the point remains the same. Whether at Black Mingo or elsewhere, Marion at some point learned the hard way that rickety planks create noise, and he implemented a countermeasure. Furthermore, Marion continued to glean lessons for future use. A month later, Marion achieved "one of his greater successes in the general region of the Santee River" with a victory at Tearcoat Swamp.[48] There, "using tactics proved at Black Mingo," Marion again divided his men into three groups and routed a British force commanded by Lieutenant Colonel Samuel Tynes.[49] Whether in failure or success, Marion conducted After-Action Reviews and continued to adjust and improve his tactics.

Life-time Growth as a Leader

Growth as a leader requires the "learning agility" that Bob Eichinger, Mike Lombardo, and Dave Ulrich define as "the ability to reflect on experience and then engage in new behaviors based on those reflections." In order to do so, a leader must have "self-confidence to examine oneself, self-awareness to seek feedback and suggestions, and self-discipline to engage in new behaviors."[50] As leaders pursue this process, they undergo "development," which Nevitt Sandford defined as "the organization of increasing complexity." As leaders develop, they are able to integrate and act on many different experiences and influences.[51] Such development is continuous and open-ended.

In spite of F. Scott Fitzgerald's assertion that "There are no second acts in American lives,"[52] a cursory search of today's booksellers suggests there is great interest (and success) in the undertaking. In *Second Acts: Presidential Lives And Legacies After The White House*, Mark Updegrove explores the post-office lives of nine presidents. In *Second-Act Careers*, Nancy Collamer describes "50+ Ways to Profit from Your Passions

During Semi-Retirement." In *The Big Shift: Navigating the New Stage Beyond Midlife*, Marc Freedman offers advice to avoid mid-life crisis and enjoy mid-life opportunity. In *The Encore Career Handbook*, Marci Alboher describes "How to Make a Living and a Difference in the Second Half of Life." Whether due to increased longevity, economic necessity, or greater opportunity, there seems to be much current interest in not just growth within one career field, but growth from one successful career to another.

Psychoanalyst Erik H. Erikson outlined three stages of adult development. The first stage is intimacy and lasts from about age 21 to age 35. It is the most spontaneously creative period, and the young adult channels their energies into launching a career and starting a family. The second stage is generativity and lasts from age 35 to age 55. During this stage, the adult lays the foundations for the next generation and devotes much energy to reevaluation. It is a time of mid-life transition. The third stage is integrity and begins at age 55. It is a time when a person ties together their life experience and comes to terms with their life.[53] If, as Robert Chalmers asserts, development is "good change,"[54] each of Erikson's stages should be an improvement upon its predecessor.

Francis Marion as State Senator

In January 1782, when he was about 50 years old, Marion was elected to the State Senate by the voters of St. John's Berkeley Parish, but this was not his first experience with politics. Before the war he had been elected as a delegate to South Carolina's first Provincial Congress. When first elected to the legislature, Marion had to divide his energies to that body and his brigade. It was a difficult task, made more so by the failure of Peter Horry and Hezekiah Maham to cooperate in his absence. Marion served in the Senate from 1782 to 1786 and from December 1791 to May 1794. He also continued to serve in the militia until 1794.[55]

Like George Washington, Marion was a "moderate Federalist." John Oller assesses that Marion's "postwar state Senate career bears few marks of distinction," and it is indeed difficult to find specific instances of his legislative activity. He attended the South Carolina state convention that ratified the US Constitution in 1788, but for some unknown reason was absent from the final vote. Oller surmises that as a Federalist, Marion would have likely favored ratification, in contrast to states' rights advocates such as Thomas Sumter who voted against it.[56]

Parson Weems reports Marion as a staunch advocate of free schools, decrying any reluctance to allocate the necessary funds as "penny wit and pound foolishness." Weems goes as far as to credit Marion with blaming the war on an uneducated population, claiming that "had the people been enlightened, they would have been united."[57] As elsewhere, such grandiose rhetoric is likely a product of Weems's literary embellishment, but other aspects of Marion's character do suggest that he placed a high value on education. In his will written around 1773, Marion specified that his "Enfrenchised slave Peggy … shall be learned to Read and Wright to be paid out of my Estate." Likewise, he ordered that his nephew and godson William "be Educated, at charge of my Estate till he arrives to the age of twenty one years."[58] In spite of these sentiments, however, there is no extant record of Marion's involvement in any legislative discussions concerning free education.[59]

Marion did use his position in the Senate to advance his advocacy of post-war peace, reconciliation, and property rights. He staunchly supported Tories who applied for deliverance from the penalties of the Confiscation Acts and compellingly spoke on behalf of Tories requesting pardons. Marion was of the opinion that there was now a need for constructive work to be done in the development of South Carolina, and Tories could make a valuable contribution to that cause. He unsuccessfully protested against the bill that would protect officers such as Thomas Sumter from litigation resulting from their confiscation of private property to pay their troops.[60]

Perhaps the best assessment of Marion as a senator is Hugh Rankin's assertion that "he remained obstinately faithful to his ideals."[61] In doing so, Marion led his constituents by example and provided a consistency that helped ease the transition from war to peace. Rather than exploiting his military reputation for personal gain, Marion used his new position to continue to serve.

PART THREE

Summary

Conclusions about Leadership During the Lowcountry Campaign

This study of Francis Marion has attempted to review his leadership in terms of eight broad categories:

- a leader's frame of reference
- the responsibility of leadership
- the interpersonal component of leadership
- communicating as a leader
- a leader's need to solve problems
- a leader's use of resources
- leadership's demand for stamina and resiliency
- growth as a leader

In all of these areas, Marion demonstrated positive attributes that helped him be successful as a leader.

Marion built a useful frame of reference as a leader while fighting the Cherokees. During this experience he learned much about the British who would be his enemies during the American Revolution, as well as meeting and working with many men he would serve alongside in the Patriot cause. More importantly, Marion was exposed to both the nature of irregular warfare and the character of the militia. These experiences shaped his approach to fighting in the American Revolution. Marion also proved adept at leading through all four of Bolman and Deal's frames. When dealing with Continental soldiers, Marion made use of the structural frame. When dealing with militia and partisans, Marion relied on the human resource frame. When negotiating the distribution of finite resources with Greene, Marion followed the political frame. Perhaps most notably, to his men and the Patriot cause, Marion personified the symbolic frame. A frame of reference gives a leader a starting point for future actions. It uses experience to empower, rather than limit. Marion's frame of reference clearly gave him the perspective and perception to process new experiences.

Marion fully embraced the responsibility of leadership. Whether in volunteering to be a militia leader or continuing to serve as a state senator, he actively sought leadership opportunities and then approached them with holistic accountability. In the instance of the Marion–Ganey truce and elsewhere, he understood the big picture and his role in it. Throughout it all, perhaps most notably regarding Sumter's Law, Marion remained true to his principles.

Marion demonstrated a wide variety of interpersonal skills as a leader. He could manage difficult personalities such as the conniving lieutenant at Fort Johnson. He led with empathy and understanding in meeting the needs unique to partisan soldiers. He effectively chose his physical positions to both set the example and to maintain personal freedom of action. He understood that he was not operating in a vacuum and established a mutually beneficial relationship with the community at Snow's Island. He cooperated with his peers, even ones like Henry Lee with whom he also had differences. He was aware of the strengths and limitations of his followers and made good use of Maxwell's "law of the niche" when handling militia.

Marion communicated effectively as a leader, especially in his understanding of his audience. His orders to experienced subordinates like Peter Horry clearly established expectations without imposing undue limitations and allowed Horry to use his initiative. When addressing his men, Marion used charismatic rhetoric to motivate and inspire them, such as in the challenge to McLeroth near Halfway Swamp. On the other hand, Marion withheld information about the disaster at Camden from his men until he thought they could handle it.

Marion certainly had his share of problems to solve as a leader, and he was very much up to this challenge. His disciplined initiative at

Great Savannah, pragmaticism at Fort Motte, and nuanced assertiveness with his tactic of retreat all demonstrated his balanced approach to problem-solving. His support of Maham's innovation at Fort Watson and Marion's use of interior lines showed his creativity and flexibility.

As a partisan, Marion made judicious use of his few tangible resources and optimized his intangible ones. He led so as to conserve his manpower but expanded his span of control by delegation. He made excellent use of the abundant local intelligence available to him. He organized for success.

Marion was the epitome of stamina and resiliency as a leader. He withstood the rigors of grueling service in the field under extremely spartan conditions. His great reserves of endurance allowed him to lead by example in sharing hardships with his men. He persevered in pursuing difficult objectives such as at Georgetown and showed great resiliency in recovering from the loss of Snow's Island.

Finally, Marion understood leadership's relation to growth. He incorporated feedback into his decision making at Georgetown. He acted in the present with an eye to the future during his truce negotiations with Ganey. He learned lessons about security from his experiences at Black Mingo Creek. He personally grew from partisan leader to state senator. Marion was less successful in training subordinates like Horry and Maham to replace him as brigade commander, but he mitigated this weakness by his characteristic personal exertion.

In all these areas, Marion seemed to be a natural and intuitive leader. Marion the man and Marion the leader appear inseparable. He had a predisposition that facilitated being a leader, and his leadership style was largely the natural extension of his personal character. Few of us are so naturally situated, but by studying Marion we can learn much from his approach to leadership.

Epilogue

The introduction to this book began with a quotation from Henry St. John, 1st Viscount Bolingbroke that "history is philosophy teaching by examples." One must be careful of the exemplars he chooses, however, and many of our once-sacrosanct heroes have not borne up well to the critical revision of presentism: the idea of applying present values to past events. Francis Marion has thus far largely escaped such scrutiny, but his turn may someday come.

Marion was, of course, "a man of his times." He fought the indigenous Cherokee and he owned slaves. For some, such facts are enough to remove Marion from any favorable consideration. Perhaps, but in his analysis of Marion, James Pinkerton argues that "the applying of contemporary labels to historical figures is ... a dubious exercise."[1] Suffice it to say that circumspection and discernment are required. If we abandon presentism entirely, we call into question the idea that there are certain universal truths. If we ruthlessly apply it, however, we edge toward a moral arrogance that ignores the reality of environmental factors. In the middle ground is Anthony DeLellis's observation that "it is possible for people to respect someone who displays some values that are important to them but fails to display others."[2] In this spirit, Marion seems a worthy candidate for St. John's theory.

If not by today's standards, certainly by his era's, Marion was humane. He limited violence, safeguarded property, treated prisoners fairly, prohibited plunder, and helped forge a peaceful post-war society. These aspects of Marion's character are highlighted in several of this book's vignettes. One similar piece of Marion's story that eluded coverage in a vignette was his relationship with his slave Oscar. Slavery was, is, and always will be an evil, and Marion seems to have not understood that truth, but recorded here is a bit of what little we know of Marion and Oscar, provided for the reader to draw what conclusions he may.

Sometime between 1815 and 1825, South Carolina artist John Blake White painted "General Marion Inviting a British Officer to Share His Meal," which depicts the famous "sweet potato dinner" between Marion and a British officer in Marion's camp after the pair discussed some prisoner exchange details. The oil-on-canvas painting includes Marion, the British officer, and a Black man cooking the potatoes. In 1899, White's son donated the painting to the US Senate, where it has hung since.

The Black man in White's painting went unnamed, however, until Tina Jones embarked on genealogical research of the Marion branch of her family. She found a relative, Oscar, who was among the slaves that labored on the Marion plantation, and, in studying White's painting, concluded that Oscar was the man cooking the potatoes. Jones presented her research to the Office of the Senate Curator, which cares for the Senate's collection of 160 paintings and sculptures, and on December 15, 2006, a ceremony was held which featured a proclamation signed by President George W. Bush that expressed the thanks of a "grateful nation" and recognized Oscar Marion's "devoted and selfless consecration to the service of our country in the Armed Forces of the United States."[3]

Oscar was born to June and Chloe, slaves on Marion's father's Goatfield Plantation. June was Marion's plantation manager and obviously held in high regard. In his will written around 1773, Marion specified that he would "enfranchise and make free my faithful Negroe man Named June" and give him "twenty pounds [sterling] per annum as long as he lives."[4] Oscar, often called "Buddy," was also special to Marion and became his childhood companion.[5] Writing in 1938 with all the unfortunate paternalism of the era, William Boddie declares that "Marion and Buddy grew into the closest and most intimate of friends and no more loyal and faithful slave-servant-friend than Buddy ever glorified the Negro race in America." Boddie continues to describe Buddy as "unusually keen-sensed, intelligent, and strong."[6]

From those beginnings, Oscar stayed at Marion's side through thick and thin. While many other members of Marion's band came and went,

Oscar was with Marion for the seven long years of the Revolution. He hid out with Marion, moving from location to location along the Santee River when Marion was eluding the British after injuring his leg escaping from the party on Tradd Street before the British captured Charleston.[7] He fought in the siege of Savannah in 1779, the siege of Charleston in 1780, and the battle of Eutaw Springs in 1781.[8] In addition to White's painting, Oscar is prominently at Marion's side in several other works of art. In "Marion Crossing the Peede [Pee Dee]," William Tylee Ranney depicts Oscar rowing as Marion's men travel the river. In "Francis Marion (1732–95)," Alonzo Chappel renders Oscar as a soldier in full uniform, mounted on a horse and armed with a rifle.[9] While historians have no way of knowing the degree to which Oscar exercised free will in accompanying Marion on these and other adventures, Sean Busick, a professor of American history at Athens State University in Alabama, surmises that "it is safe to assume that had [Oscar] wanted to run away to the British he could have easily done so."[10]

While history is silent on how Marion may have treated his other slaves, John Oller asserts that "by all evidence, his core family group— June, Chloe, Buddy, Phoebe, and Peggy—were well cared for."[11] For whatever reason, however, Marion did not emancipate Oscar as he did June, and Oscar appears to have remained with Marion during Marion's retirement life at Pond Bluff.[12] Jones could find no evidence of Oscar ever marrying or having a family.[13]

Returning to presentism, James Pinkerton reminds us that "Marion, after all, lived and died in the 18th century. So, we can never know what he, or any other historical figure, might have thought had he lived in a different era ..." But Pinkerton goes one step further and adds "... just as we can never know what we would be thinking if we lived in a different era."[14] And it is because we don't know that, as we evaluate Marion, we should remember the admonition of Supreme Court Associate Justice Felix Frankfurter that "the indispensable judicial requisite is intellectual humility."[15]

Some Reminders of the Lowcountry Campaign

The landscape of today hardly resembles the lowcountry of Francis Marion. The greater Charleston urban metropolis extends from the peninsula up the neck to Moncks Corner. Marion's plantation home at Pond Bluff is now under Lake Marion. Thousands of acres of the countryside northeast of Charleston have been logged of its stately longleaf pines and replaced with quick-growing slash pine in the Francis Marion National Forest. Although much of the Pee Dee River basin remains rural and undeveloped, years of cotton growing in the upcountry of North and South Carolina has eroded the soils and deposited them downstream along the lower Pee Dee and Little Pee Dee rivers. The rivers themselves have changed their meandering stream beds; one of this book's authors has even seen a new oxbow lake develop along the Pee Dee just north of Snow's Island in the course of his lifetime. All these changes make it difficult to envision the South Carolina landscape at the time of Francis Marion. Nevertheless, there are still more than a few reminders of Marion and his brigade, and because of Marion's popularity, there have been considerable efforts to keep his memory alive.

One such effort occurred in 2005 when the South Carolina state legislature created the Francis Marion Trail Commission (FMTC), expressly with the mission of developing a heritage tourism trail focused on the life and campaigns of Marion. The FMTC sponsored several archaeological projects to verify the location of the many sites associated with Marion's partisan career and faithfully placed interpretive markers at many locations.[1]

While the FMTC is currently inactive, its efforts are being continued through other initiatives such as The Liberty Trail, a project of the American Battlefield Trust, the South Carolina Battleground Preservation Trust, and other partners, which aims to preserve and interpret the most significant of the over 200 battles and skirmishes of the American Revolution that occurred in South Carolina. In 2021, ground was broken at Fort Fairlawn, Camden, Waxhaws and Hanging Rock. These sites, along with Eutaw Springs, will be battlefield parks in the first phase of The Liberty Trail. Many Liberty Trail sites will of course be associated with Marion.

While The Liberty Trail is under construction, the interested observer can benefit from the many historical markers already emplaced by the South Carolina Department of Archives and History. Historical markers and interpretative panels such as these provide a convenient basis of a tour throughout the lowcountry to follow the exploits of Marion and his men. An overview of such a tour follows, but it should also be noted that many of the locations are on private lands. The information provided here should not be interpreted as an invitation to trespass!

In and around Charleston

Charleston is an obvious place to start any tour of Marion's story. At 106 Tradd Street, a visitor can see a house built around 1772 by Colonel John Stuart, who was the king's superintendent of Indian affairs. Stuart was a Loyalist, and the property was confiscated by the Patriots during the war. Tradition has it that this is the house where Marion, a teetotaler, injured his ankle while jumping out of the window to escape an all-night drinking party. The property is privately owned.

The Miles Brewton House, home of Miles and Mary Brewton, was built between 1765 and 1769, and still stands at 27 King Street. The home was inherited by Miles's sister, Rebecca Motte, after the Brewtons were lost at sea in 1775. When Charleston fell, Rebecca moved to Brewton's plantation on the Congaree River and built a new mansion, which was fortified by the British and called Fort Motte. The Miles Brewton house was used as a headquarters by the British. It is also privately owned. Fort Motte, where Marion and Henry Lee lay siege in 1781, is located on private property in Calhoun County, at the east end of Lang Syne Road, off of US 601. The Daughters of the American Revolution has placed a stone marker on the spot.

At the entrance to Charleston Harbor is Fort Moultrie National Historical Park on Sullivan's Island. This is the site where Patriots turned back a British naval attack against Fort Sullivan (renamed Fort Moultrie after the battle) on June 28, 1776. Marion commanded the left battery in that action. Although no standing structures related to the American Revolution still exist, the park service has interpretive exhibits related to the history of the various forts that have occupied the site from the Revolution to the 20th century, and the modified 1809 fort can be toured. The park is located at 1214 Middle Street.

West, across the harbor on James Island, once stood Fort Johnson. In that spot today is the South Carolina Marine Resources Center which includes the Hollings Marine Laboratory, an eight-acre facility owned by the National Oceanic and Atmospheric Administration. Fort Johnson's old powder magazine built in 1765 still stands. Marion and his light infantry were part of an attack against the fort in September of 1775, although Marion's men did not arrive until after the fort was taken. After the war, in 1784, the South Carolina legislature voted Marion commandant of the fort as a reward for his services.[2] This post, however, required him to live at the fort and eventually he resigned. The Marine Resources Center is located at the western end of Fort Johnson Road.

Throughout the Lowcountry

Travel south out of Charleston for about 36 miles on US Highway 17 and, immediately after crossing the Edisto River, on the right (north) side of the road is the site of the ruins of the village of Jacksonborough. Jacksonborough was where the South Carolina General Assembly met in January 1782, with Marion attending as a Senator. Part of the village is an archaeological site within the Edisto Nature Trail system.

Continue south on US 17 to State Route 64, turn north, and continue to the intersection with State Road S-15-40 about two miles west of Jacksonboro (as the town has been known since 1892). Turn right (north) and continue up the road to Padge H S Line Road, then left on Cemetery Road to the tomb of Isaac Hayne, who was hung by the British in 1781 after being accused of breaking his parole. Patriots throughout the southern colonies responded with indignation to the hanging. Hayne Hall is located off State Road 64 on Sparks Lane.

A mile further north on State Road S-15-40 is the intersection with the Parker's Ferry Road. Turn right (north), pass the ruins of the 19th-century Pon Pon Chapel, and continue up the road about seven miles to the intersection of the Parker's Ferry Road and Round O Road. Here is the site of Marion's ambush of a British detachment at the battle of Parker's Ferry. The heavily wooded battlefield has been purchased by the South Carolina Battleground Trust (SCBT) for preservation. Visitors should be aware that it is protected property. Also, note that Parker's Ferry Road is a dirt road and although maintained, it is best to have four-wheel drive available, especially after rains. A mile up the road is the actual ferry site and a Confederate Civil War fortification. This location is also under the protection of the SCBT.

Continue south on US 17 for about 32 miles from Jacksonboro and turn right (north) on to Old Sheldon Church Road. One mile up the road are the ruins of Old Sheldon Church. Built in the late 1740s, the church was burned by the British in 1779. Marion and a detachment of Continentals camped at a plantation in the vicinity after the failed attack on Savannah, Georgia. This camp has never been investigated by archaeologists but has been heavily collected by relic hunters.

Return to Charleston and proceed to Moncks Corner. The area is heavily developed; however, there is still one standing reminder of the age of Marion. Off Rembert C. Dennis Boulevard (US 52 bypass), behind a development of family housing, is a well-preserved British-built redoubt at what was once Fairlawn Plantation. It is one of two fortifications of the American Revolution still standing in South Carolina, the other being at Ninety Six National Historic Site. Lieutenant Colonel Hezekiah Maham attacked Fairlawn Plantation, and the British in the fort did not defend the plantation house, which was burned. The redoubt is protected by the SCBT and permission to access it should be obtained through them. Plans are being made to incorporate the redoubt into the Old Santee Canal Park and the Berkeley County Museum, which is located at the park. A historical marker placed by the FMTC at the park commemorates the redoubt and another commemorates the Patriot attack against the British at the plantation house. The museum has several exhibits focusing on the American Revolution in Berkeley County.

Across the Cooper River, east of Moncks Corner, are several sites associated with the Dog Days campaign of the hot summer of 1781, when Marion, under the command of Thomas Sumter, chased a British foraging party. Less than a mile south of US 52, on Highway 402, is Biggin Church. The location was a campground for Peter Horry, and in the summer of 1781, the British burned the church. A skirmish took place nearby between Horry and a British detachment under Major Thomas Fraser. The existing remains are of a later church, but are a beautiful ruin and cemetery well worth seeing.

Continuing south on Highway 402 is Wadboo Bridge, the site where two British vessels and the bridge were burned by Hezekiah Maham. Turning east on Rectory Hill Road, in about a quarter of a mile is Wadboo Barony. There Marion defeated a British party of dragoons under Fraser who attacked Marion's men within an avenue of cedars in August 1782. It was also where Marion's brigade camped and where he said farewell to his troops in December 1782. The property is privately owned, but an interpretive panel for the barony, placed by the FMTC, is located back at the Wadboo Bridge.

Returning to Highway 402, continue south to Huger and turn right on Cainhoy Road. At a bridge over a branch of the Cooper River is the site of the Quinby Bridge action and just to the north is where the battle of Quinby or Shubrick's Plantation was fought. There Sumter attacked the British under Lieutenant Colonel James Coates and ordered Marion to make a reckless attack in support of another detachment against well-fixed British soldiers in and around the slave quarters. Marion took heavy casualties and refused to work with Sumter again. The plantation is privately owned. An interpretive panel, placed by the FMTC, is located on the east side of the bridge.

Santee Country

Return to Moncks Corner and drive north on US 52 to State Highway 45. Turn left (west) to the lower Santee River region, where there are many sites associated with Marion. The grave of Hezekiah Maham, a commander in Marion's brigade, is located along Highway 45 about two miles west of Pineville. Continue about three and a half miles west of Pineville and turn right (north) on General Francis Marion Avenue. Marion's tomb is on the west side at the end of the road. This is also the site of Belle Isle Plantation, which was owned by Marion's brother, Gabriel. West of Belle Isle was Marion's Pond Bluff Plantation, which is now under Lake Marion.

Continue west on Highway 45, turn right (west) on State Highway 6, and continue about six miles to the Eutaw Springs battlefield. Marion was in command of the front line in this major engagement in September 1781. There is a small park with monuments and historical panels at the intersection of Highway 6 and State Road S-38-137. Most of the battlefield has been destroyed by development, especially to the west of the park.

From Eutaw Springs drive northwest along Highway 6 to I-95. Go north on I-95, across Lake Marion and exit right onto US 301, just at the end of the bridge. This road leads to the Santee National Wildlife Refuge. Turn left (north) into the refuge on Fort Watson Road and drive to the Indian Mound. On this mound the British built Fort Watson, which Marion and Lieutenant Colonel Henry Lee surrounded, besieged, and captured in April 1781. An interpretive panel, placed by the FMTC, is located at the entrance to the Wildlife Refuge.

The region east of Fort Watson, including Clarendon, Williamsburg, Georgetown, Horry, Florence, Marion, and Sumter counties, is where many Marion skirmishes with the British took place. There are few standing reminders of these encounters, except for historical markers, but The Swamp Fox Murals Society has resolved to not let the Marion story die. Extending from Fort Watson up I-95 to Manning, their efforts comprise the "Swamp Fox Murals Trail."

Thanks to this work, a number of murals depicting events in the life of Marion are scattered throughout Clarendon County. The Murals Society's website at https://clarendonmurals.com/. has maps and a cell phone app to locate and view the murals. Historical markers and interpretive panels in Clarendon County have been placed in the vicinity of such Marion skirmishes as Tearcoat Swamp (State Road 14-50, between I-95 and US 301), Wiboo Swamp (at the west end of Patriot Road, off State Road 260, about six miles south of Manning), and Halfway Swamp (on Old River Road, less than a mile south of Rimini).

Williamsburg County was a hotbed of Patriot fever during the American Revolution, and many of its citizens joined Marion's brigade. On Academy Street in Kingstree is an interpretive marker placed by the FMTC commemorating an event where Major John James of Marion's brigade completed a hit and run raid on a British detachment. Head northeast of Kingstree on SC 261 to Indiantown. About a half mile west is the Indiantown Presbyterian Church. The original church on this site was burned by the British as a "sedition shop." The current church dates to 1890; however, its cemetery contains the burial place of Major John James, a leader in Marion's brigade. An FMTC interpretive panel marks the church. Return through Kingstree to find a Bridges Campaign skirmish site at Lower Bridge on State Road 377, south of Salters.

The famous skirmish of Black Mingo has been archaeologically investigated by the FMTC and is located just south and west of Black Mingo Creek Bridge on State Road 41/51 about a mile north of Rhems.[3] An interpretive panel has been placed across the river at Mingo boat landing. A marker to the Black Mingo-Willtown Baptist Church is less than a quarter mile south of the battle site.

Marion County

Continue north on State Road 41/51 to Johnsonville where the road crosses Lynches Creek. At the bridge is a landing and park where an FMTC interpretive panel marks Witherspoon's Ferry, in the vicinity of where Marion took charge of the Williamsburg militia in August 1780 and began his career as a partisan leader. There is also a beautiful monument to Marion there.

Cross over the bridge and continue north about a mile to the intersection of State Road 21-99 where there is a historical marker for Port's Ferry. The ferry site is three miles northeast of the historical marker. Marion used the ferry numerous times to cross the Pee Dee River. It too was investigated by the FMTC, so the site is well documented, but on private land.[4]

Another site investigated by the FMTC is Burch's Ferry and mill site. This site is where Marion signed a peace treaty with Loyalists on June 8, 1782. The site is located along Old River Road, which runs from Kingsburg, north of Johnsonville, 14 miles to Mill Branch Road. Turn right (east) on Mill Branch and proceed about a mile to the end of the dirt road. There is an interpretive panel there marking the location of the ferry. The mill was located to the south on Mill Branch Creek and is on private land.

Return to Johnsonville and about two and a half miles to the east is Snow's Island, where Marion had his main camp and depot from at least November 1780 to March 1781.[5] Many of Marion's soldiers and supporters lived on Snow's Island and in the surrounding region. Snow's Island today is on private land. Although there is no access, the island can be seen by driving across the Pee Dee River on US 378, and turning right (west) on Dunham's Bluff Road. At the end of the road, about a mile and a quarter from the intersection, is Dunham's Bluff. There is a public boat landing there, and Snow's Island is visible across the Pee Dee River. In the woods east of the bluff line are the remnants of a small redoubt Marion's men built. The interpretive markers once there, unfortunately, have been stolen.

Dunham's Bluff and the land to the east and south down the peninsula between the Pee Dee River and the Little Pee Dee is a vast forested region that was called Britton's Neck during the American Revolution. This land is now owned and managed by the South Carolina Department of Natural Resources. Much of the land was once owned by families who supported Marion during the war. Turn east off US 378 on to State

Road 41, and about eight miles up the road is the approximate site of the skirmish at Blue Savannah. Although thought to be just south of the intersection of State Road 41 and US 501, archaeological investigations have not located the exact battlefield.

Georgetown

Georgetown was occupied by the British during much of the war after the fall of Charleston. There are no visible signs of Marion's four attacks against the British in the town; however, there are several historic markers commemorating events of the American Revolution. The first is along US 17, on a spit of land dividing the Pee Dee River and the Waccamaw River, just east of Georgetown. This marker commemorates Marion's attack on January 24, 1781. The second notes the capture and killing of Lieutenant Gabriel Marion, Marion's nephew, by the British that same month. It is located on White's Bridge Road, at its intersection with Alternate US 17. There was once another marker at the intersection of US 701 with Anthuan Maybank Drive commemorating Sergeant McDonald, one of Marion's sharpshooters, who bayoneted British Major Ganey in a skirmish, but that marker no longer stands. Another historical marker commemorates the battle at Sampit Bridge where Marion attacked Colonel John Watson in the last action of the Bridges Campaign. It is also along Alternate US 17, about six miles west of Georgetown, near the modern bridge across the Sampit River. Georgetown also commemorates the contributions of Marion at Francis Marion Park, on Front Street, next to the South Carolina Maritime Museum.

It is probable that more places in the United States have been named after Francis Marion than any other soldier of the American Revolution with the exception of George Washington. Especially in South Carolina, the place names, sites, markers, and memorials testify to Marion's enduring impact on the heart and soul of the state. They serve as poignant reminders of the contributions and sacrifices made by Marion and those like him that helped win America its independence.

Bibliography

ADRP 3–0, *Operations*. Washington, DC: Headquarters, Department of the Army, 2017.

ADRP 5–0, *The Operations Process*. Washington, DC: Headquarters, Department of the Army, 2010.

ADRP 6–22, *Army Leadership*. Washington, DC: Headquarters, Department of the Army, 2012.

ADRP 7–0, *Training Units and Developing Leaders*. Washington, DC: Headquarters, Department of the Army, 2012.

Aiken, Scott. *The Swamp Fox: Lessons in Leadership from the Partisan Campaigns of Francis Marion*. Annapolis, MD: Naval Institute Press, 2012.

Andrew, Rod. *The Life and Times of General Andrew Pickens*. Chapel Hill: The University of North Carolina Press, 2017.

Babits, Lawrence. *A Devil of a Whipping: The Battle of Cowpens*. Chapel Hill: The University of North Carolina Press, 1998.

Badaracco, Joseph. *Questions of Character: Illuminating the Heart of Leadership Through Literature*. Boston, MA: Harvard Business Review Press, 2006.

Bass, Robert. *Gamecock: The Life and Campaigns of General Thomas Sumter*. Orangeburg, SC: Sandlapper Publishing Co, 2000, original 1961.

——. *Swamp Fox: The Life and Campaigns of General Francis Marion*. Orangeburg, SC: Sandlapper Publishing Co, 1972, original 1959.

——. *The Green Dragoon: The Lives of Banastre Tarleton and Mary Robinson*. Orangeburg, SC: Sandlapper Publishing, Inc., 1973.

Bassidy, Larry and Ram Charan. *Execution: The Discipline of Getting Things Done*. New York: Crown Business, 2002.

Billias, George Athan, editor. *George Washington's Opponents: British Generals in the American Revolution*. New York: William Morrow and Company, Inc., 1969.

Birnbaum, Robert. *How Colleges Work*. San Francisco, CA: Jossey-Bass, 1988.

Boddie, William. *Traditions of the Swamp Fox: William Willis Boddie's Francis Marion*. Spartanburg, SC: The Reprint Company for the Williamsburgh Historical Society, 2000.

Bolman, Lee and Terrence Deal. *Reframing Organizations: Artistry, Choice, and Leadership*. San Francisco, CA: Jossey-Bass, 2013.

——. *How Great Leaders Think: The Art of Reframing*. San Francisco, CA: Jossey-Bass, 2014.

Borick, Carl P. *A Gallant Defense: The Siege of Charleston, 1780*. Columbia: University of South Carolina Press, 2003.

Broadwater, Robert P. "Gates, Horatio," In, *American Generals of the Revolutionary War: A Biographical Dictionary*. Jefferson, NC: McFarland & Company, 2007.

Brooks, David. *The Road to Character*. New York: Random House, 2015.

Browning, Henry. *Accountability: Taking Ownership of Your Responsibility*. Greensboro, NC: Center for Creative Leadership, 2012.

Buchanan, John. *The Road to Charleston: Nathanael Greene and the American Revolution*. Charlottesville: University of Virginia Press, 2019.

——. *The Road to Guilford Courthouse: The American Revolution in the Carolinas*. New York: John Wiley & Sons, 1997.

Bryant, William Cullen. "Song of Marion's Men," *Historic Poems and Ballads*. Ed. Rupert S. Holland. Philadelphia, PA: George W. Jacobs & Co., 1912.

Cadet Leader Development Program AY 2017–2018. Charleston, SC: The Citadel, 2017.

Cann, Marvin. "War in the Backcounty: The Siege of Ninety Six, May 22–June 19, 1781." *The South Carolina Historical Magazine*, no. 1 (January 1971): 1–14.

Caruana, Adrian. *Grasshoppers and Butterflies: The Light 3 Pounders of Pattison and Townshend*. Alexandria Bay, New York: Museum Restoration Service, 1979.

——. *The Light 6-Pdr, Battalion Gun of 1776*. Alexandria Bay, New York: Museum Restoration Service, 1977.

Chambers, Robert. *Ideas for Development*. New York: Routledge, 2005.

Citadel Training Manual. Charleston, SC: The Citadel, 2014.

Cohen, William. *The Stuff of Heroes: The Eight Universal Laws of Leadership*. Atlanta, GA: Longstreet, 1998.

Cole, Ryan. *Light-Horse Harry Lee: The Rise and Fall of a Revolutionary Hero—The Tragic Life of Robert E. Lee's Father*. New York: Simon and Schuster, 2019.

Collins, Jim. *Good to Great*. New York: Harper Business, 2001.

Conger, Jay. *The Charismatic Leader: Behind the Mystique of Exceptional Leadership*. San Francisco, CA: Jossey-Bass, 1989.

Conrad, Dennis M. Roger N. Parks, Martha J. King eds. *The Papers of Nathanael Greene, Volume IX*. Chapel Hill: The University of North Carolina Press, 1997.

Conrad, Dennis M., Roger N. Parks, Martha J. King, and Richard K. Showman, eds. *The Papers of Nathanael Greene, Volume VIII*. Chapel Hill: The University of North Carolina Press, 1995.

Covey, Stephen. *The 7 Habits of Highly Effective People*. New York: Simon and Schuster, 1989.

——. *The 8th Habit*. New York: Free Press, 2004.

Crawford, Amy. "The Swamp Fox," Smithsonian Magazine, (June 30, 2007), https://www.smithsonianmag.com/history/the-swamp-fox-157330429/.

Creech, Bill. *The Five Pillars of TQM*. New York: Truman Talley Books/Plume, 1995.

DeLellis, Anthony. "Clarifying the Concept of Respect: Implications for Leadership." *The Journal of Leadership Studies*, no. 2 (2000): 35–49.

Dictionary of National Biography. London: Elder Smith & Company, 1891.

Donnithorne, Larry. *The West Point Way of Leadership*. New York: Doubleday, 1993.

Dougherty, Kevin. *Military Decision-making Processes: Case Studies Involving the Preparation, Commitment, Application, and Withdrawal of Force*. Jefferson, NC: McFarland, 2013.

Draper, Lyman C. *Kings Mountain and Its Heroes: History of the Battle of Kings Mountain*. Johnson City, Tennessee: The Overmountain Press, 1881, Reprint 1996.

Duckworth, Angela. *Grit: The Power of Passion and Perseverance*. New York: Scribner, 2016.

Dunkerly, Robert and Eric K. Williams. *Old Ninety Six: A History and Guide*. Charleston, SC: The History Press, 2006.

Edgar, Walter. *Partisans and Redcoats: The Southern Conflict That Turned the Tide of the American Revolution*. New York: William Morrow, 2001.

Economist, The. "Span of Control," Nov 9, 2009, available http://www.economist.com/node/14301444. Accessed, January 18, 2022.

Encyclopedia of the American Revolution, 2 vols. New York: Thomson Gale, 2006.

Evans, Nancy, et al. *Student Development in College*. San Francisco, CA: Jossey-Bass, 2010.

Fens, Elizabeth. *Pox Americana: The Great Smallpox Epidemic of 1775–82*. New York: Hill and Wang, 2001.

Fishman, Ethan. *The Prudential Presidency: An Aristotelian Approach to Presidential Leadership*. New York: Praeger, 2000.

Flanagan, E. M. "Hands-on Leadership." *Army* (April 1992): 54–55.

FM 3-34.2, *Combined-Arms Breaching Operations*. Washington, DC: Headquarters, Department of the Army, 2002.

FM 6-22, *Army Leadership*. Washington, DC: Department of the Army, 2006.

FM 100-5, *Operations*. Washington, DC: Headquarters, Department of the Army, 1993.

FMFRP 12-18, *Mao Tse-tung on Guerrilla Warfare*. Washington, DC: Headquarters, United States Marine Corps, 1989.

Foner, Philip. *Blacks in the American Revolution*. Westport, CT: Greenwood Press, 1976.

Fraser, Jr., Walter, Jr. *Patriots, Pistols, and Petticoats: "Poor Sinful Charles Town" during the American Revolution*. Columbia: The University of South Carolina Press, 1993, original 1945.

Frierson, John. "Discipline by the Lash: The Order Book of General Francis Marion," *Carologue*, no. 4 (Winter 1999): 8–13.

Gardner, John. *On Leadership*. New York: Free Press, 1990.

George, Bill. "Authentic Leadership." In, eds. J. Timothy McMahon. *Leadership Classics*. Long Grove, IL: Waveland Press, 2010.

Gibbes, R. W. *Documentary History of the American Revolution, Volume 1*. Columbia, SC: Banner Steam-Power Press, 1853.

Goldsmith, Marshall. *What Got You Here Won't Get You There: How Successful People Become Even More Successful.* New York: Hyperion, 2007.

Golway, Terry. *Washington's General: Nathanael Greene and the Triumph of the American Revolution.* New York: Henry Holt and Company, 2005.

Gooding, James. *An Introduction to British Artillery, in North America.* Alexandria Bay, New York: Museum Restoration Service, 1988.

Gordon, John. *South Carolina and the American Revolution.* Columbia: The University of South Carolina Press, 2003.

Gregorie, Anne King. *Thomas Sumter.* Columbia, SC: The R. L. Bryan Company, 1931.

Greene, Jerome. *Historic Resource and Historic Structure Report, Ninety Six, A Historical Narrative.* Denver, CO: Denver Service Center, National Park Service, 1979.

Guignard Family Papers. Columbia, SC: The South Carolinania Library, ca. 1812.

Halpern, Belle Linda and Kathy Lubar. *Leadership Presence.* New York: Gotham Books, 2003.

Hamilton, T. M. *Colonial Frontier Guns.* Union City, TN: Pioneer Press, 1987.

Hart, E. Wayne. *Seven Keys to Successful Mentoring.* Greensboro, NC: Center for Creative Leadership, 2009.

Haw, James. "Every Thing here Depends on Opinion: Nathanael Greene and Public Support in the Southern Campaign of the American Revolution." *The South Carolina Historical Magazine*, no. 3 (July 2008): 212–231.

Heracleous, Loizos and Laura Alexa Klaering. "Charismatic Leadership and Rhetorical Competence: An Analysis of Steve Jobs's Rhetoric." *Group & Organization Management,* no. 2 (2014): 131–161.

Hickman, Kennedy. "Leaders of the American Revolution." ThoughtCo, Aug. 26, 2020, thoughtco.com/people-of-the-american-revolution-2360663. Accessed, 1/18/2022.

Horry, Peter. Marginal notes made in Horry and Weems, *The Life of General Francis Marion.*

Horry, Peter, and Parson M. L. Weems. *The Life of General Francis Marion: A Celebrated Partisan Officer, in the Revolutionary War, against the British and Tories in South Carolina and Georgia.* Philadelphia, PA: J. P. Lippincott, 1854. Reprint, Winston-Salem, NC: John F. Blair, 2000.

House, Robert. "A 1976 Theory of Charismatic Leadership," In, J. Timothy McMahon editor, *Leadership Classics,* Long Grove, IL: Waveland Press, 2010.

Hunter, James. *The Servant.* New York: Crown Business, 1998.

James, William Dobein. *A Sketch of the Life of Brigadier General Francis Marion.* Charleston, SC: Gould and Riley, 1821. Reprint Marietta, GA: Continental Book Company, 1948.

Johansen, Bob. *Leaders Make the Future: Ten New Leadership Skills for an Uncertain World.* Oakland, CA: Berrett-Koehler Publishers, 2009.

Jones, Tina. "Patriot Slave." *The American Legion* (October 28, 2011), https://www.legion.org/magazine/1562/patriot-slave, accessed 4 January 2021.

Keegan, John. *The Mask of Command*. New York: Elisabeth Sifton Books, 1987.

Kouzes, James and Barry Posner. *The Leadership Challenge*. San Francisco, CA: Jossey-Bass, 2012.

Lancaster, Bruce. "Heroic Huguenot." Review of The Swamp Fox. *Saturday Review* (January 31, 1959): 32–33.

Lee, Robert E, editor. *The Revolutionary War Memoirs of General Henry Lee*. New York: DeCapo Press, 1998, original 1812.

Legg, James B., Steven D. Smith, and Tamara S. Wilson. *Understanding Camden: The Revolutionary War Battle of Camden As Revealed Through Historical, Archaeological, and Private Collections Analysis*. Columbia: South Carolina Institute of Archaeology and Anthropology, 2005.

Lepage, Jean-Denis G. G. *Vauban and the French Military Under Louis XIV: An Illustrated History of Fortifications and Sieges*. Jefferson, NC: McFarland & Company, 2009.

Levinson, Harry. "A Second Career: The Possible Dream," Harvard Business Review (May 1983). Available https://hbr.org/1983/05/a-second-career-the-possible-dream. Accessed January 18, 2022.

Lipscomb, Terry. *Battles, Skirmishes, and Actions Which Took Place In South Carolina During the American Revolution*. Columbia: South Carolina Department of Archives and History, c.1991.

MacKenzie, Roderick. *Strictures on Lt. Col. Tarleton's History of the Campaigns of 1780 and 1781, in the Southern Provinces of North America*. London: R. Faulder, 1787.

Massey, Gregory and Jim Piecuch. *General Nathanael Greene and the American Revolution in the South*. Columbia: University of South Carolina Press, 2012.

Mattern, David. *Benjamin Lincoln and the American Revolution*. Columbia: University of South Carolina Press, 1998.

Maxwell, John. *The 17 Indisputable Laws of Teamwork*. Nashville, TN: Thomas Nelson, Inc, 2001.

——. *The 360° Leader*. Nashville, TN: Nelson Business, 2005.

McCrady, Edward. *The History of South Carolina in the Revolution, 1780–1783*, Volume 4. New York: MacMillan, 1902.

McMahon, Timothy, ed. *Leadership Classics*. Long Grove, IL: Waveland Press, Inc, 2010.

Middlekauff, Robert. *The Glorious Cause: The American Revolution, 1763–1789*. New York: Oxford University Press, 1982.

Montes, Sue Anne Pressley. "Post Revolutionary Recognition." The Washington Post, (December 16, 2006). Available https://www.washingtonpost.com/wp-dyn/content/article/2006/12/15/AR2006121502097.html.

Morgan, Michael. "Digging to Victory." *America's Civil War*, July 2003.

"Museum Around the Corner: A Painting's Story," Georgetown *Times*, (August 20, 2020). https://www.postandcourier.com/georgetown/community/museum-around-the-corner-a-paintings-story/article_6574fb59-dfd8-54a2-be03-2e6309f17983.html.

Neeley, Alfred. "Mr. Justice Frankfurter's Iconography of Judging." *Kentucky Law Journal*, no. 2 (1993): 535–573.

Neumann, George C. *Battle Weapons of the American Revolution*. Texarkana, Texas: Scurlock Publishing Company, 1998.

Northouse, Peter. *Leadership Theory and Practice*. Thousand Oaks, CA: Sage Publications, 2004.

O'Kelley, Patrick. *Unwaried Patience and Fortitude: Francis Marion's Orderly Book*. Conshohocken, PA: Infinity Publishing, 2006.

Oller, John. *The Swamp Fox: How Francis Marion Saved the American Revolution*. New York: Da Capo Press, 2016.

O'Shaughnessey, Andrew Jackson. *The Men Who Lost America: British Leadership, the American Revolution and the Fate of the Empire*. New Haven, CT: Yale University Press, 2013.

Piecuch, Jim. *Three Peoples, One King: Loyalists, Indians, and Slaves in the Revolutionary South, 1775–1782*. Columbia: University of South Carolina Press, 2008.

Pinkerton, James. "Francis Marion, The Real Patriot." *The American Conservative* (September 5, 2018). https://www.theamericanconservative.com/articles/francis-marion-the-real-patriot/.

Pulley, Mary Lynn and Michael Wakefield. *Building Resiliency: How to Thrive in Times of Change*. Greensboro, NC: Center for Creative Leadership, 2001.

Puryear, Edgar. *Nineteen Stars: A Study in Military Character and Leadership*. Novato, CA: Presidio, 1971.

———. *American Generalship: Character is Everything; The Art of Command*. Novato, CA: Presidio, 2000.

Quarles, Benjamin. *The Negro in the American Revolution*. Chapel Hill: The University of North Carolina Press, 1996.

Rankin, Hugh. *Francis Marion: The Swamp Fox*. New York: Thomas Y. Crowell, 1973.

———. *The North Carolina Continentals*. Chapel Hill: The University of North Carolina Press, 1971.

———. "Charles Lord Cornwallis: Study in Frustration." In, George Athan Billias, editor, *George Washington's Opponents: British Generals in the American Revolution*. New York: William Morrow and Company, Inc., 1969.

Rosebush, Michael. "Applying the Academy Training Philosophy." Colorado Springs, CO: United States Air Force Academy, 1985.

Rosenthal, Jack. "A Terrible Thing to Waste," *The New York Times Magazine*, (July 30, 2009). Available https://www.nytimes.com/2009/08/02/magazine/02FOB-onlanguage-t.html.

Roy, Rob and Chris Lawson. *The Navy SEAL Art of War: Leadership Lessons from the World's Most Elite Fighting Force*. New York: Crown Business, 2015.

Royster, Charles. "Introduction." In Lee, Robert E., editor, *The Revolutionary War Memoirs of General Henry Lee*. New York: De Capo Press, 1998.

Saberton, Ian, editor. *The Cornwallis Papers: The Campaigns of 1780 and 1781 in The Southern Theatre of the American Revolution.* The Naval & Military Press Ltd. East Sussex, UK: 2010.

Scotti, Anthony. *Brutal Virtue: The Myth and Reality of Banastre Tarleton.* Bowie, MD: Heritage Books, Inc., 2002.

Scheer, George F. and Hugh F. Rankin. *Rebels and Redcoats: The American Revolution Through the Eyes of Those Who Fought and Lived It.* New York: The World Publishing Company, 1957.

Schelhammer, Michael. "10 Fateful Hits and Misses." Online *Journal of the American Revolution*, September 19, 2013, https://allthingsliberty.com/2013/09/10-fateful-hits-misses/, accessed November 17, 2020.

Scoggins, Michael. C. *The Day It Rained Militia: Huck's Defeat and the Revolution in the South Carolina Backcountry, May–July 1780.* Charleston, SC: The History Press, 2005.

Sherman, William. *Calendar and Record of the Revolutionary War in the South, 1780–1781.* 10th edition. Seattle, WA: Gun Jones Publishing, 2018.

Simms, William Gilmore. *The Life of Francis Marion: The "Swamp Fox."* New York: G. F. Cooledge & Brother, 1844.

Smith, Steven. *Francis Marion and the Snow's Island Community: Myth, History, and Archaeology.* Asheville, NC: United Writers Press, Inc., 2021.

——. *Archaeological Evaluation of Wadboo Plantation, 38BK464.* Columbia: South Carolina Institute of Archaeology and Anthropology, 2008.

——. "The Search for Francis Marion's Snow Island Camp" University of South Carolina Scholar Commons 12-93, https://scholarcommons.sc.edu/cgi/viewcontent.cgi?article=1174&context=sciaa_staffpub. Accessed January 18, 2022.

Smith, Steven and James Legg. *Running the Gauntlet: Locating the Battle of Parkers Ferry, South Carolina August 30, 1781.* Columbia: South Carolina Institute of Archaeology and Anthropology, 2019.

Smith, Steven, James B. Legg, and Tamara S. Wilson. *The Archaeology of the Camden Battlefield: History, Private Collections, and Field Investigations.* Columbia: South Carolina Institute of Archaeology and Anthropology, 2008.

Smith, Steven; James B. Legg; Tamara S. Wilson; and Jonathan Leader. *'Obstinate and Strong': The History and Archaeology of the Siege of Fort Motte.* Columbia: South Carolina Institute of Archaeology and Anthropology, 2007.

Spring, Mathew. *With Zeal and Bayonets Only: The British Army in North America, 1775–1783.* Norman: University of Oklahoma Press, 2008.

Stephenson, Michael. *Patriot Battles: How the War of Independence Was Fought.* New York: Harper Perennial, 2007.

Talbert, Roy. "So Fine a Beach: Peter Horry's Summer of 1812." *The Independent Republic Quarterly*, no. 1–4 (2004): 1–14.

TC 25-20, *A Leader's Guide to After-Action Reviews.* Washington, DC: Department of the Army, 1993.

The South Carolina Encyclopedia. Columbia: The University of South Carolina Press, 2006.

Van Dierendonck David and Inge Nuijten, "The Servant Leadership Survey: Development and Validation of a Multidimensional Measure." *Journal of Business Psychology*, no. 3, Sept 2011.

Waters, Andrew. *The Quaker and the Gamecock: Nathanael Greene, Thomas Sumter, and the Revolutionary War for the Soul of the South.* Philadelphia, PA: Casemate, 2019.

Weigley, Russell. *The American Way of War: A History of United States Military Strategy and Policy.* Bloomington: Indiana University Press, 1977.

Wilcox, William B. "Sir Henry Clinton: Paralysis of Command." In, George Athan Billias, editor, *George Washington's Opponents: British Generals in the American Revolution.* New York: William Morrow and Company, Inc., 1969.

——. Editor, *The American Rebellion: Sir Henry Clinton's Narrative of His Campaigns, 1775–1782, with and Appendix of Original Documents.* London: Oxford University Press, 1954.

Williams, Beryl and Samuel Epstein. *Francis Marion: Swamp Fox of the Revolution.* New York: Julian Messner, 1956.

Wilson, David. *The Southern Strategy: Britain's Conquest of South Carolina and Georgia, 1775–1780.* Columbia: University of South Carolina Press, 2005.

Notes

Foreword

1   *Cadet Leader Development Program AY 2017–2018* (Charleston, SC: The Citadel, 2017), 3.
2   The Citadel, "The Citadel Training Manual" (Charleston, SC: The Citadel, 2020), 5–6.
3   Peter Northouse, *Leadership Theory and Practice* (Thousand Oaks, CA: SAGE Publications, 2004), 50.
4   Ibid., 39–40.
5   James Kouzes and Barry Posner, *The Leadership Challenge* (San Francisco, CA: Jossey-Bass, 2012), 335.
6   John Gardner, *On Leadership* (New York: Free Press, 1990), 48–53.
7   FM 6–22, *Army Leadership* (Washington, DC: Headquarters, Department of the Army, 2006), 9–5.
8   Angela Duckworth, *Grit: The Power of Passion and Perseverance* (New York: Scribner, 2016), 7.
9   Robert Chambers, *Ideas for Development* (New York: Routledge, 2005), 185.
10 Peter Horry and Parson M. L. Weems, *The Life of General Francis Marion: A Celebrated Partisan Officer, in the Revolutionary War, against the British and Tories in South Carolina and Georgia* (Philadelphia, PA: J. P. Lippincott, 1854 Reprint, Winston-Salem, NC: John F. Blair, 2000), 34.
11 Robert E. Lee, editor, *The Revolutionary War Memoirs of General Henry Lee* (New York: DeCapo Press, 1998, original publication, 1812), 585.
12 William Dobein James, *A Sketch of the Life of Brigadier General Francis Marion: and A History of His Brigade* (Marietta, GA: Continental Book Company, 1948, original 1821), 46.
13 Ibid, 71.
14 Peter Horry, marginal notes made in Horry and Weems, *The Life of General Francis Marion* (Columbia, SC: The South Carolinania Library, ca. 1812), 109.
15 Ibid., preface.
16 John L. Frierson, "Discipline by the Lash: The Order Book of General Francis Marion," *Carologue*, no 4 (Winter 1999), 8–13.

Leadership During the American Revolution

1 ADRP 3–0, *Operations* (Washington, DC: Headquarters, Department of the Army, 2017), 5–1.

2 Ibid., 3–1.

3 Andrew Jackson O'Shaughnessey, *The Men Who Lost America: British Leadership, the American Revolution and the Fate of the Empire* (New Haven, CT: Yale University Press, 2013).

4 All quotes, O'Shaughnessey, 361.

5 Ibid., 353.

6 Ibid., 357.

7 Kennedy Hickman, "Leaders of the American Revolution." ThoughtCo, Aug. 26, 2020, thoughtco.com/people-of-the-american-revolution-2360663.

8 George F. Scheer and Hugh F. Rankin, *Rebels and Redcoats: The American Revolution Through the Eyes of Those Who Fought and Lived It* (New York: The World Publishing Company, 1957), 128.

9 Michael Stephenson, *Patriot Battles: How the War of Independence Was Fought* (New York: Harper Perennial, 2007), 63–4.

10 *Encyclopedia of the American Revolution,* 2nd ed, Vol. 1, s. v. "Communication, Time."

11 Mathew H. Spring, *With Zeal and Bayonets Only: The British Army in North America, 1775–1783* (Norman: University of Oklahoma Press, 2008), 44.

12 Steven D. Smith, *Francis Marion and the Snow's Island Community: Myth, History, and Archaeology* (Asheville, NC: United Writers Press, Inc., 2021), 131–3.

13 ADRP 3–0, 3–2.

14 Ibid., 3–3.

15 O'Shaughnessey, 7.

16 Spring, 44–5.

17 John Oller, *The Swamp Fox: How Francis Marion Saved the American Revolution* (New York: Da Capo Press, 2016), 79.

18 Scott Aiken, *The Swamp Fox: Lessons in Leadership from the Partisan Campaigns of Francis Marion* (Annapolis, MD: Naval Institute Press, 2012), 31.

19 Greene quoted in Oller, 104.

20 Walter J. Fraser, Jr., Patriots, *Pistols, and Petticoats: "Poor Sinful Charles Town" during the American Revolution* (Columbia: The University of South Carolina Press, 1993, original 1945), 134–44.

21 ADRP 3–0, 3–4.

22 George C. Neumann, *Battle Weapons of the American Revolution* (Texarkana, TX: Scurlock Publishing Company, 1998), 17.

23 James B. Legg, Steven D. Smith, and Tamara S. Wilson, *Understanding Camden: The Revolutionary War Battle of Camden As Revealed Through Historical, Archaeological, and Private Collections Analysis* (Columbia: South Carolina Institute of Archaeology and Anthropology, 2005), 97–105.

24 Neumann, 11–12.

25 Spring, 204.

26 Neumann, 212.

27 See T. M. Hamilton, *Colonial Frontier Guns* (Union City, TN: Pioneer Press, 1987), for a detailed discussion of trade guns.

28 Carronades were short barreled cannon, useful on ships, and had less range than cannon. They were rarely found on the Revolutionary War battlefield as they were only introduced into service in 1779; however, the British apparently brought one to Fort Motte, a British fort that Francis Marion and Colonel Henry Lee besieged in 1781. S. James Gooding, *An Introduction to British Artillery, in North America* (Alexandria Bay, NY: Museum Restoration Service, 1988), 3, 8; Steven D. Smith, James B. Legg, Tamara S. Wilson, and Jonathan Leader, *"Obstinate and Strong": The History and Archaeology of the Siege of Fort Motte* (Columbia: South Carolina Institute of Archaeology and Anthropology, 2007).

29 Gooding, 4–14.

30 Ibid., 46.

31 Adrian Caruana, *The Light 6-Pdr, Battalion Gun of 1776* (Alexandria Bay, NY: Museum Restoration Service, 1977); Adrian B. Caruana, *Grasshoppers and Butterflies: The Light 3 Pounders of Pattison and Townshend* (Alexandria Bay, NY: Museum Restoration Service, 1979).

32 Caruana, 1979, 21.

33 ADRP 3–0, 3–4.

34 O'Shaughnessey, 357.

35 Ibid., 12.

36 Stephenson, 107.

37 Ibid., 104.

38 Terry Golway, *Washington's General: Nathanael Greene and the Triumph of the American Revolution* (New York: Henry Holt and Company, 2005), 313.

39 Stephenson, 107–8.

40 Smith, 2021, 30–1.

41 Ibid., 281.

42 Stephenson, 106.

43 Spring, 32.

44 Stephenson, 39.

45 Ibid., 38.

46 Ibid., 23–4.

47 Ibid., 28.

48 Ibid., 85.

49 Ibid., 169.

50 Ibid., 169.

51 Ibid., 170.

52 Ibid., 162.

53 Elizabeth A. Fens, *Pox Americana: The Great Smallpox Epidemic of 1775–82* (New York: Hill and Wang, 2001), 27–8, 92.

54 Ibid., 125.

55 Ibid., 122.

56 ADRP 3–0, 3–5.

57 See R. W. Gibbes, *Documentary History of the American Revolution, Volume 1* (Columbia, SC: Banner Steam-Power Press, 1853), 32 as an example.

58 Jean-Denis G. G. Lepage, *Vauban and the French Military Under Louis XIV: An Illustrated History of Fortifications and Sieges.* (Jefferson, NC: McFarland & Company, 2009).

59 *Encyclopedia of the American Revolution,* 2nd ed, Vol 1, s. v. "Engineers."

60 ADRP- 3–0, 3–6, 7.

61 O'Shaughnessey, 354.

62 Balfour to Cornwallis, December 4, 1780, Ian Saberton, *The Cornwallis Papers, Volume III* (Uckfield, England: The Naval & Military Press, Ltd., 2010), 104.

The Key Players

1 William B. Wilcox, "Sir Henry Clinton: Paralysis of Command," In George Athan Billias, editor, *George Washington's Opponents: British Generals in the American Revolution* (New York: William Morrow and Company, Inc., 1969), 73–102; William B. Wilcox, editor, *The American Rebellion: Sir Henry Clinton's Narrative of His Campaigns, 1775–1782, with and Appendix of Original Documents* (London: Oxford University Press, 1954), xiii–xiv.

2 Wilcox 1969, 82–3.

3 Ibid., 86.

4 Wilcox 1969, 94; *Encyclopedia of the American Revolution,* 2nd ed, Vol 1, s. v. "Clinton, Henry."

5 John Buchanan, *The Road To Guilford Courthouse, The American Revolution in the Carolinas* (New York: John Willey & Sons, 1997), 73–5; *Encyclopedia of the American Revolution,* 2nd ed, Vol 1, s. v. "Cornwallis, Charles.", 271–5; Hugh F. Rankin, "Charles Lord Cornwallis: Study in Frustration," in George Athan Billias, editor, *George Washington's Opponents: British Generals in the American Revolution* (New York: William Morrow and Company, Inc., 1969), 193–232.

6 Buchanan 1997, 76.

7 Rankin, 196.

8 *Encyclopedia of the American Revolution*, 2nd ed., Vol 1, s. v. "Cornwallis, Charles."

9 Buchanan, John. *The Road to Charleston, Nathanael Greene and the American Revolution* (Charlottesville: University of Virginia Press, 2019), 64–65.

10 Rankin, 213–15.

11 *Encyclopedia of the American Revolution*, 2nd ed., Vol 1, s. v. "Cornwallis, Charles."

12 Ibid.

13 Ian Saberton, editor, *The Cornwallis Papers: The Campaigns of 1780 and 1781 in The Southern Theatre of the American Revolution, Volume III* (The Naval & Military Press Ltd. East Sussex, UK: 2010), 77, n31.

14 John Oller, *The Swamp Fox: How Francis Marion Saved the American Revolution* (New York: Da Capo Press, 2016), 96–9.

15 William Dobein James, *A Sketch of the Life of Brigadier General Francis Marion: and A History of His Brigade* (Marietta, GA: Continental Book Company, 1948, original 1821), 97; Oller, 99; Saberton, 77.

16 Sir Stephen Leslie, "Hastings, Francis Rawdon," in *Dictionary of National Biography*, Volume XXV (London: Elder Smith & Company, 1891), 117–22.

17 *Encyclopedia of the American Revolution*, 2nd ed., Vol 2, s. v. "Rawdon-Hasings Francis."

18 Anthony J. Scotti, Jr., *Brutal Virtue: The Myth and Reality of Banastre Tarleton* (Bowie, MD: Heritage Books, Inc., 2002), 17.

19 *Encyclopedia of the American Revolution*, 2nd ed., Vol 1, s. v. "Waxhaws, South Carolina."; Robert D. Bass, *The Green Dragoon: The Lives of Banastre Tarleton and Mary Robinson* (Orangeburg, SC: Sandlapper Publishing, Inc., 1973), 80–3.

20 *Dictionary of National Biography*, Volume LV, s. v. "Tarleton, Sir Banastre."

21 Ian Saberton, editor, *The Cornwallis Papers: The Campaigns of 1780 and 1781 in The Southern Theatre of the American Revolution, Volume II* (The Naval & Military Press Ltd. East Sussex, UK: 2010), 199–200, n39.

22 Steven D. Smith, *Francis Marion and the Snow's Island Community: Myth, History, and Archaeology* (Asheville, NC: United Writers Press, Inc., 2021), 128–35.

23 Saberton, 200.

24 Buchanan, 1997, 144; *Encyclopedia of the American Revolution,* 2nd ed., Vol 1, s. v. "Gates, Horatio."

25 Buchanan, 1997, 149.

26 Robert P. Broadwater, "Gates, Horatio," *American Generals of the Revolutionary War: A Biographical Dictionary* (Jefferson, NC: McFarland & Company, 2007), 44.

27 Buchanan, 1997, 151.

28 *Encyclopedia of the American Revolution*, 2nd ed, Vol 1, s. v. "Camden, Campaign."

29 Buchanan, 1997, 265.

30 Ibid., 270–1.

31 Golway, 241.

32 Ibid., 313.

33 See Hugh Rankin, *Francis Marion, The Swamp Fox* (New York: Thomas Y. Crowell Company, 1973), 179.

34 Roy Talbert "So Fine a Beach: Peter Horry's Summer of 1812," *The Independent Republic Quarterly*, 38, no. 1–4 (2004), 1–14.

35 Sourth Carolina Encyclopedia, s. v. "Horry, Peter "Museum Around the Corner: Horry of Georgetown," Georgetown *Times*, May 29, 2019. accessed

October 25, 2020. https://www.postandcourier.com/georgetown/community/museum-around-the-corner-horry-of-georgetown/article_163f5cba-80f6-5436-99f4-8d432d08e960.html; Talbert, *Beach*, 1–14.

36 *Encyclopedia of the American Revolution*, 2nd ed., Vol 1, s. v. "Lee, Henry."; Michael Schelhammer, "10 Fateful Hits and Misses," online *Journal of the American Revolution*, September 19, 2013, https://allthingsliberty.com/2013/09/10-fateful-hits-misses/. accessed November 17, 2020.

37 Robert E. Lee, editor, *The Revolutionary War Memoirs of General Henry Lee* (New York: De Capo Press, 1998), 223–5; Oller, 115–17.

38 Royster, xii.

39 Talbert, "So Fine a Beach," 2.

40 *South Carolina Encyclopedia*, s. v. "Maham, Hezekiah."

41 Ibid.

42 Robert Bass, *Swamp Fox, The Life and Campaigns of General Francis Marion* (New York: Henry Holt and Company, 1972, original 1959), 5; Rankin, 3.

43 James, 1821; Peter Horry and Parson M. L. Weems, *The Life of General Francis Marion: A Celebrated Partisan Officer, in the Revolutionary War, against the British and Tories in South Carolina and Georgia* (Philadelphia, PA: J. P. Lippincott, 1854) Reprint, Winston-Salem, NC: John F. Blair, 2000; William Gilmore Simms. *The Life of Francis Marion: The "Swamp Fox."* (New York: G. F. Cooledge & Brothers, 1844).

44 Rankin, 4–5.

45 Oller, 24–5.

46 Horry and Weems, 22–3; Oller, 26–8.

47 Bass, 22.

48 Ibid., 30.

49 Oller, 4–5.

50 Smith, 2021, 104.

51 Ibid., 103–16.

52 Bass, 126.

53 Smith, 2021, 126–35.

54 Bass, 206–8.

55 Ibid., 210.

56 Oller, 193.

57 Bass, 230.

58 Oller, 222–3.

59 Bass, 238–9.

60 Ibid., 243–5.

61 *The South Carolina Encyclopedia*, s. v. "Sumter, Thomas."

62 Anne King Gregorie, *Thomas Sumter* (Columbia, SC: R.L. Bryan Company, 1931), 29–31.

63 *South Carolina Encyclopedia*, s. v. "Sumter, Thomas."

64 Ibid.

65 Gregorie, 121–3.
66 Ibid., 148–9.
67 Ibid., 176–9.
68 *South Carolina Encyclopedia*, s. v. "Sumter, Thomas."

Campaign Overview

1 Robert Middlekauff, *The Glorious Cause: The American Revolution, 1763–1789* (New York: Oxford University Press, 1982), 434–5; Jim Piecuch, *Three Peoples, One King: Loyalists, Indians, and Slaves in the Revolutionary South, 1775–1782* (Columbia: University of South Carolina Press, 2008), 36–7.

2 Jerome A. Greene, *Historic Resource and Historic Structure Report, Ninety Six, A Historical Narrative* (Denver, CO: Denver Service Center, National Park Service, 1979), 66–75.

3 *Encyclopedia of the American Revolution,* 2nd ed, Vol 2, s. v. "Moore's Creek Bridge."; David K. Wilson, *The Southern Strategy: Britain's Conquest of South Carolina and Georgia, 1775–1780* (Columbia: University of South Carolina Press, 2005), 25–32.

4 Wilson, 40–58; *Encyclopedia of the American Revolution,* 2nd ed., Vol 1, s. v. "Charleston Expedition of Clinton in 1776."

5 Wilson, 68–9.

6 *Encyclopedia of the American Revolution,* 2nd ed., Vol 2, s. v. "Savannah, Georgia."; Wilson, 74–7.

7 David B. Mattern, *Benjamin Lincoln and the American Revolution* (Columbia: University of South Carolina Press, 1998), 58, 64; Piecuch, 139; Wilson, 84–8, 100–1.

8 Wilson, 91–8.

9 Mattern, 73–4; Wilson, 123–31.

10 *Encyclopedia of the American Revolution*, 2nd ed., Vol 1, s. v. "Savannah, Georgia."; Wilson, 133–92.

11 Carl P. Borick, *A Gallant Defense: The Siege of Charleston, 1780* (Columbia: University of South Carolina Press, 2003), 28; Wilson, 198–9.

12 Wilson, 207.

13 Borick 2003, 129; *Encyclopedia of the American Revolution,* 2nd ed., Vol 2, s. v. "Monck's Corner, South Carolina."

14 Borick 2003, 177–8.Wilson, 234–5.

15 Wilson, 258–61.

16 Borick 2003, 236–8.

17 Hugh F. Rankin, *The North Carolina Continentals* (Chapel Hill: The University of North Carolina Press, 1971), 239.

18 Terry W. Lipscomb, *Battles, Skirmishes, and Actions Which Took Place In South Carolina During the American Revolution* (Columbia: South Carolina Department of Archives and History, c1991), 4–5.

19 Walter Edgar, *Partisans and Redcoats: The Southern Conflict That Turned the Tide of the American Revolution* (Columbia: Harper Collins, 2001), 58–9, 81–5; Michael C. Scoggins, *The Day It Rained Militia: Huck's Defeat and the Revolution in the South Carolina Backcountry, May–July 1780* (Charleston, SC: The History Press, 2005).

20 Anne King Gregorie, *Thomas Sumter* (Columbia, SC: R. L. Bryan Company, 2000), 80, 90–3.

21 Steven D. Smith, James B. Legg, and Tamara S. Wilson, *The Archaeology of the Camden Battlefield: History, Private Collections, and Field Investigations* (Columbia: South Carolina Institute of Archaeology and Anthropology, 2008).

22 Steven D. Smith, *Francis Marion and the Snow's Island Community: Myth, History, and Archaeology* (Asheville, NC: United Writers Press, Inc., 2021).

23 Gregorie, 94–95, 100–3, 121–3.

24 John Buchanan, *The Road to Guilford Courthouse: The American Revolution in the Carolinas* (New York: John Wiley & Sons, 1997), 178–9.

25 Buchanan, 225–37. Lyman C. Draper, *Kings Mountain and Its Heroes: History of the Battle of Kings Mountain* (Johnson City, TN: The Overmountain Press, 1881, Reprint 1996).

26 Lawrence Babits, *A Devil of a Whipping: the Battle of Cowpens* (Chapel Hill: The University of North Carolina Press, 1998), 150.

27 William Thomas Sherman, *Calendar and Record of the Revolutionary War in the South, 1780–1781.* 10th edition (Seattle, WA: Gun Jones Publishing, 2018), 362.

28 Buchanan, 358.

29 Ibid., 360.

30 Rankin, 290.

31 *Encyclopedia of the American Revolution,* 2nd ed., Vol 1, s. v. "Guilford Court House."

32 Ibid; Buchanan, 380.

33 Rankin, 314–16.

34 Former American General Benedict Arnold had changed sides in August 1780 and now was a brigadier general in the British army.

35 *Encyclopedia of the American Revolution,* 2nd ed., Vol 2, s. v. "Southern Campaigns of Nathanael Greene."

36 Lipscomb, 6–8.

37 Smith, 2021, 126–32.

38 Gregorie, 136–43.

39 John Buchanan, *The Road to Charleston: Nathanael Greene and the American Revolution* (Charlottesville: University of Virginia Press, 2019), 74.

40 Smith, 2021, 146.

41 Buchanan 2019, 93–103; *Encyclopedia of the American Revolution,* 2nd ed., Vol 1, s. v. "Hobkirk's Hill."

42 Gregorie, 157–8.

43 Robert Dunkerly, Robert and Eric K. Williams, *Old Ninety Six: A History and Guide.* (Charleston: The History Press, 2006), 65–6.

44 Dunkerly and Williams, 65–66; Greene, 159; Roderick MacKenzie, *Strictures on Lt. Col. Tarleton's History of the Campaigns of 1780 and 1781, in the Southern Provinces of North America* (London: R. Faulder, 1787), 149, 155, 158.

45 John Oller, *The Swamp Fox: How Francis Marion Saved the American Revolution* (New York: Da Capo Press, 2016), 177.

46 Ibid., 199–201; Steven D. Smith and James Legg. *Running the Gauntlet: Locating the Battle of Parkers Ferry, South Carolina August 30, 1781* (Columbia: South Carolina Institute of Archaeology and Anthropology) 2019.

47 Buchanan 2019, 218–21.

48 Ibid., 230–3.

49 Ibid., 259.

50 *Encyclopedia of the American Revolution*, 2nd ed., Vol 2, s. v. "Southern Campaigns of Nathanael Green."

51 *Encyclopedia of the American Revolution,* 2nd ed., Vol 1, s. v. "Georgia Expedition of Wayne."

52 Oller, 222–3.

53 Buchanan 2019, 315–16.

54 Oller, 231–3; Steven D. Smith, *Archaeological Evaluation of Wadboo Plantation, 38BK464* (Columbia: South Carolina Institute of Archaeology and Anthropology, 2008).

55 Buchanan 2019, 327–328.

Francis Marion and a Leader's Frame of Reference

1 FM 6-22, *Army Leadership* (Washington, DC: Department of the Army, 2006), 12–10.

2 Bob Johansen, *Leaders Make the Future: Ten New Leadership Skills for an Uncertain World* (Oakland, CA: Berrett_Koehler Publishers, 2009), 161.

3 See Ibid., 5–6 for Johansen's "positive definition of VUCA" (volatility, uncertainty, complexity, and ambiguity).

4 John Oller, *The Swamp Fox: How Francis Marion Saved the American Revolution* (New York: Da Capo Press, 2016), 24.

5 Ibid., 24.

6 Ibid., 24–5.

7 Ibid., 25.

8 Ibid., 25.

9 Ibid., 26–7.

10 Ibid., 28.

11 Robert Bass, *Swamp Fox: The Life and Campaigns of Francis Marion* (Columbia, SC: Sandpiper Press, 1972), 9.

12 Ibid., 9.

13 Ibid., 5–17.

14 Lee Bolman and Terrence Deal, *Reframing Organizations: Artistry, Choice, and Leadership* (San Francisco, CA: Jossey-Bass, 2013), 5. Hereafter cited as Bolman and Deal, *Reframing*.

15 Lee Bolman and Terrence Deal, *How Great Leaders Think: The Art of Reframing*, (San Francisco, CA: Jossey-Bass, 2014), 19. Hereafter cited as Bolman and Deal, *Leaders* and Johansen, 15.

16 Bolman and Deal, *Leaders,* 19.

17 Bolman and Deal, *Reframing*, 15–16.

18 John Maxwell, *The 17 Indisputable Laws of Teamwork* (Nashville, TN: Thomas Nelson, Inc, 2001), 195. Hereafter cited as Maxwell, *Teamwork*.

19 Oller, 43.

20 John Gordon, *South Carolina and the American Revolution* (Columbia: The University of South Carolina Press, 2003), 5.

21 Oller, 44.

22 Ibid., 44.

23 Bass, 22.

24 Bolman and Deal, *Reframing*, 16.

25 Peter Horry and Parson M. L. Weems, *The Life of General Francis Marion: A Celebrated Partisan Officer, in the Revolutionary War, against the British and Tories in South Carolina and Georgia* (Philadelphia, PA: J. P. Lippincott, 1854 Reprint, Winston-Salem, NC: John F. Blair, 2000), 178.

26 William Willis Boddie. *Traditions of the Swamp Fox: William Willis Boddie's Francis Marion.* (Spartanburg, SC: The Reprint Company for the Williamsburgh Historical Society, 2000), 80.

27 Rankin, 58.

28 Scott Aiken, *The Swamp Fox: Lessons in Leadership from the Partisan Campaigns of Francis Marion* (Annapolis, MD: Naval Institute Press, 2012), 54.

29 Horry and Weems, 179.

30 Bolman and Deal, *Reframing*, 16.

31 James Haw, "Every thing here depends on opinion: Nathanael Greene and Public Support in the Southern Campaign of the American Revolution," *The South Carolina Historical Magazine* 109: 3 (July 2008), 222.

32 Robert Bass, *Gamecock: The Life and Campaigns of General Thomas Sumter* (Orangeburg, SC: Sandlapper Publishing Co, 2000), 166. Hereafter cited as Bass, *Sumter*.

33 Marion to Greene, 6 May 1781, *The Papers of Nathanael Greene*, Dennis M. Conrad, Roger N. Parks, Martha J. King, and Richard K. Showman, eds. (Chapel Hill: The University of North Carolina Press, 1995), 8: 214–16.

34 Andrew Waters. *The Quaker and the Gamecock: Nathanael Greene, Thomas Sumter, and the Revolutionary War for the Soul of the South* (Philadelphia, PA: Casemate, 2019), 109–10.

35 Ibid., 110.

36 Bolman and Deal, *Reframing*, 16–17.
37 Gordon, 93–4.
38 Ibid., 94–5.
39 Oller, 10.
40 Bass, 46–7; Rankin, 66–7.
41 Quoted in Aiken, 11–12.
42 Ibid., 13–15.
43 William Cullen Bryant, "Song of Marion's Men," *Historic Poems and Ballads.* Ed. Rupert S. Holland. (Philadelphia, PA: George W. Jacobs & Co., 1912), 182.

Francis Marion and the Responsibility of Leadership

1   John Gardner, *On Leadership* (New York: Free Press, 1990), 49.
2   Joseph Badaracco, *Questions of Character: Illuminating the Heart of Leadership Through Literature* (Boston, MA: Harvard Business Review Press, 2006), 102.
3   Ibid., 113.
4   Ibid., 102.
5   Hugh Rankin, *Francis Marion: The Swamp Fox* (New York: Thomas Y. Crowell, 1973), 46–8.
6   Ibid., 48–9.
7   Scott Aiken, *The Swamp Fox: Lessons in Leadership from the Partisan Campaigns of Francis Marion* (Annapolis, MD: Naval Institute Press, 2012), 61–2.
8   Rankin, 57.
9   Ibid., 49–50, 57.
10 John Oller, *The Swamp Fox: How Francis Marion Saved the American Revolution* (New York: Da Capo Press, 2016), 57.
11 Badarracco, 114.
12 Henry Browning, *Accountability: Taking Ownership of Your Responsibility* (Greensboro, NC: Center for Creative Leadership, 2012), 7.
13 Rankin, 58.
14 Aiken, 111.
15 Ibid., 112 and Robert Bass, *Swamp Fox: The Life and Campaigns of Francis Marion* (Columbia, SC: Sandpiper Press, 1972), 49.
16 Aiken, 112.
17 Ibid., 112; Bass, 50–1.
18 Aiken, 17; 113.
19 Bass, 51.
20 Gordon, 110.
21 Bass, 51.
22 John Gordon, *South Carolina and the American Revolution* (Columbia: The University of South Carolina Press, 2003), 125; Rankin, 136.
23 Gordon, 125–6.

24 Gregory Massey and Jim Piecuch. *General Nathanael Greene and the American Revolution in the South* (Columbia: University of South Carolina Press, 2012), 120.

25 Gordon, 126–7.

26 Bruce Lancaster, "Heroic Huguenot," Review of The Swamp Fox, *Saturday Review* (January 31, 1959): 33.

27 Aiken, 162.

28 Ibid., 28.

29 For a concise discussion of Mao's three phases, see FMFRP 12-18, *Mao Tse-tung on Guerrilla Warfare* (Washington, DC: Headquarters, United States Marine Corps, 1989), 21–2.

30 Bill George, "Authentic Leadership," in *Leadership Classics*, ed. J. Timothy McMahon (Long Grove, IL: Waveland Press, 2010), 580.

31 David van Dierendonck and Inge Nuijten, "The Servant Leadership Survey: Development and Validation of a Multidimensional Measure," *Journal of Business Psychology*, no. 3 (Sept 2011): 252–3.

32 Stephen Covey, *The 8th Habit* (New York: Free Press, 2004), 46–9.

33 *South Carolina Encyclopedia*, s. v. "African Americans in the Revolutionary War" and Andrew Waters, *The Quaker and the Gamecock: Nathanael Greene, Thomas Sumter, and the Revolutionary War for the Soul of the South* (Philadelphia, PA: Casemate, 2019), 68–9.

34 Philip Foner, *Blacks in the American Revolution* (Westport, CT: Greenwood Press, 1976), 65.

35 Rankin, 231–2.

36 Benjamin Quarles, *The Negro in the American Revolution* (Chapel Hill: The University of North Carolina Press, 1996), 103.

37 William Willis Boddie, *Traditions of the Swamp Fox: William Willis Boddie's Francis Marion* (Spartanburg, SC: The Reprint Company for the Williamsburgh Historical Society, 2000), xv.

38 Waters, 183.

39 Boddie, 264; Rankin, 268.

Francis Marion and the Interpersonal Component of Leadership

1 James Kouzes and Barry Posner, *The Leadership Challenge* (San Francisco, CA: Jossey-Bass, 2012), 30. Brower quoted in John Maxwell, *The 17 Indisputable Laws of Teamwork* (Nashville, TN: Thomas Nelson, Inc, 2001), 203. Hereafter cited as Maxwell, *Teamwork*.

2 John Oller, *The Swamp Fox: How Francis Marion Saved the American Revolution* (New York: Da Capo Press, 2016), 37.

3 Peter Horry and Parson M. L. Weems, *The Life of General Francis Marion: A Celebrated Partisan Officer, in the Revolutionary War, against the British and Tories in South Carolina*

and Georgia (Philadelphia, PA: J. P. Lippincott, 1854) Reprint, Winston-Salem, NC: John F. Blair, 2000, 25.

4 Ibid., 26.

5 Ibid., 26.

6 Ibid., 26–7.

7 Ibid., 27.

8 Ibid., 27.

9 Ibid., 28.

10 Marshall Goldsmith, *What Got You Here Won't Get You There: How Successful People Become Even More Successful* (New York: Hyperion, 2007), 207–8.

11 James Hunter, *The Servant: A Simple Story About the True Essence of Leadership* (Roseville, CA: Prima, 1998), 125.

12 William Cohen, *The Stuff of Heroes: The Eight Universal Laws of Leadership* (Atlanta, GA: Longstreet, 1998), 175–6.

13 Scott Aiken, *The Swamp Fox: Lessons in Leadership from the Partisan Campaigns of Francis Marion* (Annapolis, MD: Naval Institute Press, 2012), 6.

14 William Gilmore Simms, *The Life of Francis Marion: The "Swamp Fox"* (New York: G. F. Cooledge & Brother, 1844), 234.

15 Hugh Rankin, *Francis Marion: The Swamp Fox* (New York: Thomas Y. Crowell, 1973), 123.

16 Simms, 140.

17 Aiken, 114–17.

18 Simms, 140–1.

19 Aiken, 122.

20 Hunter, 125.

21 Belle Linda Halpern and Kathy Lubar, *Leadership Presence* (New York: Gotham Books, 2003), 8.

22 Ibid., 3.

23 John Keegan, *The Mask of Command* (New York: Elisabeth Sifton Books, 1987), 10–11.

24 Bass, 206–207; John Gordon, *South Carolina and the American Revolution* (Columbia, The University of South Carolina Press, 2003), 159–61; Oller, 168–9.

25 Gordon, 161; Oller, 173–4.

26 Oller, 174.

27 Bass, 207–8.

28 Anne King Gregorie, *Thomas Sumter* (Columbia, SC: The R. L. Bryan Company, 1931), "Footnote 83," 179.

29 Oller, 174.

30 Gregorie, 179.

31 "Francis Marion to Greene, July 19, 1781," *The Papers of Nathanael Greene*, Dennis M. Conrad, Roger N. Parks, Martha J. King, eds. (Chapel Hill: The University of North Carolina Press, 1997), 9: 47–8.

32 Quoted in Aiken, 46.

33 ADP 3-0, *Operations* (Washington, DC: Headquarters, Department of the Army, 2019), 1–6.

34 Bob Johansen, *Leaders Make the Future: Ten New Leadership Skills for an Uncertain World* (Oakland, CA: Berrett_Koehler Publishers, 2009), 89.

35 James Kouzes and Barry Posner, *The Leadership Challenge* (San Francisco, CA: Jossey-Bass, 2012), 57–8.

36 John Maxwell, *The 17 Indisputable Laws of Teamwork* (Nashville, TN: Thomas Nelson, Inc, 2001), 23–4. Hereafter cited as Maxwell, *Teamwork*.

37 Kouzes and Posner, 19.

38 Gordon, 82 and 104.

39 Ibid., 105.

40 Robert Bass, *Gamecock: The Life and Campaigns of General Thomas Sumter* (Orangeburg, SC: Sandlapper Publishing Co, 2000), 227 and 275.

41 Gordon, 107.

42 Johansen, 13.

43 Johansen, 135, 139–40, 143.

44 Simms, 168.

45 Oller, 104–5.

46 Aiken, 159; Steven D. Smith, "The Search for Francis Marion's Snow's Island Camp" University of South Carolina Scholar Commons 12–93, https://scholarcommons. sc.edu/cgi/viewcontent.cgi?article=1174&context=sciaa_staffpub. Accessed, January 18, 2022.

47 Aiken, 159; Steven D. Smith, *Francis Marion and the Snow's Island Community: Myth, History, and Archaeology* (Asheville, NC: United Writers Press, Inc., 2021), 105.

48 Oller, 106.

49 For a thorough discussion of Marion and his relationship with the Snow's Island community see, Smith, 2021.

50 Bass, 124–5; Oller, 107.

51 Oller, 107.

52 John Maxwell, *The 360° Leader* (Nashville, TN: Nelson Business, 2005), 159–60.

53 Ibid., 159–63.

54 Robert Birnbaum. *How Colleges Work* (San Francisco, CA: Jossey-Bass, 1988), 102.

55 Ibid., 102.

56 Ibid., 103.

57 Gregory Massey and Jim Piecuch. *General Nathanael Greene and the American Revolution in the South* (Columbia: The University of South Carolina Press, 2012), 20.

58 Ryan Cole, *Light-Horse Harry Lee: The Rise and Fall of a Revolutionary Hero—The Tragic Life of Robert E. Lee's Father* (New York: Simon and Schuster, 2019), 102.

59 Aiken, 188–9.

60 Rankin, 186.

61 Aiken, 167.

62 Rankin, 189.

63 Boddie, 189–90.
64 Oller, 150.
65 Aiken, 229–30.
66 Boddie, 199–200
67 Rankin, 206.
68 Maxwell, *Teamwork*, 33–4.
69 Ibid., 34–6.
70 Ibid., 218.
71 Ibid., 250.
72 Ibid., 169.
73 Ibid., 41.
74 Ibid., 33.
75 Oller, 192.
76 Ibid., 193.
77 Ibid., 193.
78 Rod Andrew, *The Life and Times of General Andrew Pickens* (Chapel Hill: The University of North Carolina Press, 2017), 147.
79 Gordon, 164–5.
80 Rankin, 243.
81 Ibid., 246.
82 Gordon, 165–6.

Francis Marion and Communicating as a Leader

1 John Maxwell, *The 17 Indisputable Laws of Teamwork* (Nashville, TN: Thomas Nelson, Inc, 2001), 202.
2 Stephen Covey, *The 7 Habits of Highly Effective People* (New York: Simon and Schuster, 1989), 194–5.
3 James Kouzes and Barry Posner, *The Leadership Challenge* (San Francisco, CA: Jossey-Bass, 2012), 281.
4 Michael Rosebush, "Applying the Academy Training Philosophy" (Colorado Springs, CO: United States Air Force Academy, 1985), np; Larry Donnithorne, *The West Point Way of Leadership* (NY: Doubleday, 1993), 159; William Cohen, *The Stuff of Heroes: The Eight Universal Laws of Leadership* (Atlanta, GA: Longstreet, 1998), 87.
5 Covey, 174.
6 Ibid. 224; Donnithorne, 28; Kouzes and Posner, 253.
7 Scott Aiken, *The Swamp Fox: Lessons in Leadership from the Partisan Campaigns of Francis Marion* (Annapolis, MD: Naval Institute Press, 2012), 85.
8 Robert Bass, *Swamp Fox: The Life and Campaigns of Francis Marion* (Columbia, SC: Sandpiper Press, 1972), 124 and 127; Hugh Rankin, *Francis Marion: The Swamp Fox* (New York: Thomas Y. Crowell, 1973), 4–5 and 147.

9   ADRP 5-0, *The Operations Process* (Washington, DC: Department of the Army, 2019), 2–19.

10 Ibid., 2–17.

11 John Oller, *The Swamp Fox: How Francis Marion Saved the American Revolution* (New York: Da Capo Press, 2016), 121.

12 The order was sent to Postell on December 30, 1780, from Marion's camp at Snow's Island and may be read in its entirety at Aiken, 93.

13 Aiken, 60.

14 *South Carolina Encyclopedia,* s. v. "Fishing Creek."

15 Bass, 42.

16 William Willis Boddie, *Traditions of the Swamp Fox: William Willis Boddie's Francis Marion* (Spartanburg, SC: Williamsburgh Historical Society, 2000), 87.

17 Aiken, 59.

18 Bass, 45.

19 Aiken, 59.

20 Ibid., 107.

21 Ibid., 109.

22 Robert House, "A 1976 Theory of Charismatic Leadership," in *Leadership Classics,* ed. J. Timothy McMahon (Long Grove, IL: Waveland Press, 2010), 252.

23 Ibid., 171.

24 Jay Conger, *The Charismatic Leader: Behind the Mystique of Exceptional Leadership* (San Francisco, CA: Jossey-Bass, 1989), 33.

25 Peter Northouse, *Leadership Theory and Practice* (Thousand Oaks, CA: SAGE Publications, 2004), 171–2.

26 Conger, 33.

27 Northouse, 172.

28 Ibid., 172.

29 Conger, 34.

30 Ibid., 109, 132–3.

31 Northouse, 172.

32 Conger, 31.

33 Loizos Heracleous and Laura Alexa Klaering, "Charismatic Leadership and Rhetorical Competence: An Analysis of Steve Jobs's Rhetoric," *Group & Organization Management,* no. 2 (2014): 135.

34 Ibid., 134.

35 Rankin, 130–2.

36 Ibid., 134.

37 Oller, 98.

38 ADRP 5–0, 2–23.

39 Ibid., 2–20.

40 Rankin, 58.

41 Aiken, 92.

42 Peter Horry and Parson M. L. Weems, *The Life of General Francis Marion: A Celebrated Partisan Officer, in the Revolutionary War, against the British and Tories in South Carolina and Georgia* (Philadelphia, PA: J. P. Lippincott, 1854) Reprint, Winston-Salem, NC: John F. Blair, 2000, 98–9.
43 ADRP 5–0, 2–20.

Francis Marion and a Leader's Need to Solve Problems

1 John Gardner, *On Leadership* (New York: Free Press, 1990), 49.
2 FM 100–5, *Army Leadership* (Washington, DC: Department of the Army, 1999), 2–12.
3 Bob Johansen, *Leaders Make the Future: Ten New Leadership Skills for an Uncertain World* (Oakland, CA: Berrett_Koehler Publishers, 2009), 55.
4 Scott Aiken, *The Swamp Fox: Lessons in Leadership from the Partisan Campaigns of Francis Marion* (Annapolis, MD: Naval Institute Press, 2012), 106–7.
5 Ibid., 108.
6 Ibid., 108–9.
7 Ibid., 110.
8 Ibid.,182. See also 160.
9 James Kouzes and Barry Posner, *The Leadership Challenge* (San Francisco, CA: Jossey-Bass, 2012), 209.
10 Johansen, 20.
11 Ibid., 29.
12 Gardner, 124–5.
13 Jack Rosenthal, "A Terrible Thing to Waste," *The New York Times Magazine*, July 30, 2009. Available https://www.nytimes.com/2009/08/02/magazine/02FOB-onlanguage-t.html.
14 John Oller, *The Swamp Fox: How Francis Marion Saved the American Revolution* (New York: Da Capo Press, 2016), 147.
15 Ibid., 145.
16 Ibid., 147.
17 Ibid., 146.
18 Robert Bass, *Swamp Fox: The Life and Campaigns of Francis Marion* (Columbia, SC: Sandpiper Press, 1972), 171.
19 Oller, 147.
20 Bass, 171; Oller, 147.
21 Oller, 149.
22 Bass, 177; Oller, 149–50;.
23 Oller, 150; Rankin, 189.
24 See "Digging to Victory" by Michael Morgan in the July 2003 edition of *America's Civil War* for information about the version of Maham's Tower at Vicksburg.

25 Ethan Fishman, *The Prudential Presidency: An Aristotelian Approach to Presidential Leadership* (New York: Praeger, 2000), 87.

26 Kevin Dougherty, *Military Decision-making Processes: Case Studies Involving the Preparation, Commitment, Application, and Withdrawal of Force* (Jefferson, NC: McFarland, 2013), 173–4.

27 Fishman, 87.

28 Joseph Badaracco, *Questions of Character: Illuminating the Heart of Leadership Through Literature* (Boston, MA: Harvard Business Review Press, 2006), 140.

29 Quoted in Stephen Covey, *The 8th Habit* (New York: Free Press, 2004), 81.

30 Roderick Mackenzie, *Strictures of Lt. Col. Tarleton's History of the Campaigns of 1780 and 1781* (London: 1787), 151–2.

31 Steven D. Smith, James B. Legg, Tamara S. Wilson, Jonathan Leader, *"Obstinate and Strong": The History and Archaeology of the Siege of Fort Motte* (Columbia: South Carolina Institute of Archaeology and Anthropology, 2007).

32 Aiken, 174; Bass, 193–5; William Willis Boddie, *Traditions of the Swamp Fox: William Willis Boddie's Francis Marion* (Spartanburg, SC: The Reprint Company for the Williamsburgh Historical Society, 2000), 196–9; John Gordon, *South Carolina and the American Revolution* (Columbia, The University of South Carolina Press, 2003), 152–3; Hugh Rankin, *Francis Marion: The Swamp Fox* (New York: Thomas Y. Crowell, 1973), 205–6.

33 Badaracco, 117.

34 Ibid., 170.

35 Gardner, 53.

36 Joint Pub 3–0, Operations (Washington, DC: Joint Chiefs of Staff, 2006), IV-19.

37 Aiken, 38.

38 Bass, 79–80.

39 Rankin, 111.

40 Ibid., 112–13.

41 Ibid., 113.

42 Aiken, 39.

43 Peter Northouse, *Leadership Theory and Practice* (Thousand Oaks, CA: SAGE Publications, 2004), 8.

44 Johansen, 20.

45 Northouse, 10.

46 Kouzes and Posner, 209.

47 Gardner, 53.

48 Northouse, 8.

49 Russell Weigley, *The American Way of War: A History of United States Military Strategy and Policy* (Bloomington: Indiana University Press, 1977), 81–3.

50 Gordon, 104–5.

51 Aiken, 89.

52 Aiken, 132–4.

53 Ibid., 164.

Francis Marion and a Leader's Use of Resources

1   James Kouzes and Barry Posner, *The Leadership Challenge* (San Francisco, CA: Jossey-Bass, 2012), 181.

2   FM 5-0, The Operations Process (Washington, DC: Headquarters, Department of the Army, 2010), 1–4.

3   E. M. Flanagan, "Hands-on Leadership," *Army* (April 1992): 54.

4   Scott Aiken, *The Swamp Fox: Lessons in Leadership from the Partisan Campaigns of Francis Marion* (Annapolis, MD: Naval Institute Press, 2012), 30.

5   Robert Bass, *Swamp Fox: The Life and Campaigns of Francis Marion* (Columbia, SC: Sandpiper Press, 1972), 49.

6   Aiken, 30–1.

7   Northouse, 10.

8   Larry Bassidy and Ram Charan, *Execution: The Discipline of Getting Things Done* (New York: Crown Business, 2002), 22.

9   Ibid., 43

10 Ibid., 28.

11 Ibid., 57.

12 Ibid., 123.

13 Aiken, 47.

14 Ibid., 16.

15 Ibid., 119.

16 Ibid., 119.

17 Ibid., 119.

18 Ibid., 120–1.

19 ADRP 6–0, 2–10.

20 Aiken, 45.

21 John Gordon, *South Carolina and the American Revolution* (Columbia: The University of South Carolina Press, 2003), 118.

22 Bob Johansen, *Leaders Make the Future: Ten New Leadership Skills for an Uncertain World* (Oakland, CA: Berrett_Koehler Publishers, 2009), 125.

23 Bill Creech, *The Five Pillars of TQM* (New York: Truman Talley Books/Plume, 1995), 11.

24 "Span of Control," *The Economist*, Nov 9, 2009, available http://www.economist.com/node/14301444.

25 Margaret Wheatley, "Goodbye, Command and Control," in *Leadership Classics*, ed. J. Timothy McMahon (Long Grove, IL: Waveland Press, 2010), 429.

26 Ibid., 431.

27 Ibid., 432.

28 Ibid., 431.

29 FM 3-34.2, *Combined-Arms Breaching Operations* (Washington, DC: Headquarters, Department of the Army, 2002), Chapter 1.

30 Marvin Cann, "War in the Backcounty: The Siege of Ninety Six, May 22-June 19, 1781," *The South Carolina Historical Magazine*, no. 1 (January 1971): 1.

31 John Oller, *The Swamp Fox: How Francis Marion Saved the American Revolution* (New York: Da Capo Press, 2016), 8.

32 Edward McCrady, *The History of South Carolina in the Revolution, 1780-1783*, Volume 4 (New York: MacMillan, 1902), 175.

33 Hugh Rankin, *Francis Marion: The Swamp Fox* (New York: Thomas Y. Crowell, 1973), 188–9.

34 Bass, 178.

35 Jim Collins, *Good to Great* (New York: Harper Business, 2001), 13.

36 William Dobein James, *A Sketch of the Life of Brigadier General Francis Marion: and A History of His Brigade* (Marietta, GA: Continental Book Company, 1948, original 1821), 15.

37 William Willis Boddie, *Traditions of the Swamp Fox: William Willis Boddie's Francis Marion* (Spartanburg, SC: The Reprint Company for the Williamsburgh Historical Society, 2000), 156; Rankin, 156–7.

38 Rankin, 159.

39 Aiken 32–3; Bass, 138–139; Rankin, 159.

40 Bass, 138–9.

41 Bass, 127.

Francis Marion and Leadership's Demand for Stamina and Resiliency

1   Joseph Badaracco, *Questions of Character: Illuminating the Heart of Leadership Through Literature* (Boston, MA: Harvard Business Review Press, 2006), 76.

2   Ibid., 70.

3   James Kouzes and Barry Posner, *The Leadership Challenge* (San Francisco, CA: Jossey-Bass, 2012), 342–3.

4   Badaracco, 70.

5   Ibid., 76, 82.

6   John Oller, *The Swamp Fox: How Francis Marion Saved the American Revolution* (New York: Da Capo Press, 2016), 3.

7   Scott Aiken, *The Swamp Fox: Lessons in Leadership from the Partisan Campaigns of Francis Marion* (Annapolis, MD: Naval Institute Press, 2012), 57.

8   Ibid., 49.

9   Robert Bass, *Swamp Fox: The Life and Campaigns of Francis Marion* (Columbia, SC: Sandpiper Press, 1972), 213–14.

10 Hugh Rankin, *Francis Marion: The Swamp Fox* (New York: Thomas Y. Crowell, 1973), 236.

11 Ibid., 237; Oller 182. Probably this was Robert Cunningham, a cousin of the infamous William "Bloody Bill" Cunningham.

12 Steven Smith and James Legg, *Running the Gauntlet: Locating the Battle of Parkers Ferry, South Carolina August 30, 1781* (Columbia: South Carolina Institute of Archaeology and Anthropology, 2019), 34.

13 Smith and Legg, 34.

14 Aiken, 139; Smith and Legg, 34. Marion states that the Loyalists ran the gauntlet, implying that he placed his men on both sides of the road. Smith and Legg's archaeological investigation clearly shows that Marion's men were only on one side of the road, which makes sense as a two-sided ambush would have had Marion's militia firing at each other less than 100 yards apart.

15 Smith and Legg, 41.

16 Aiken, 140.

17 Ibid., 49.

18 Kouzes and Posner, 17 and 74.

19 Ibid., 96.

20 Badaracco, 55.

21 Kouzes and Posner, 16; Stephen Covey, *The 8th Habit* (New York: Free Press, 2004), 5.

22 Kouzes and Posner, 96–7.

23 Horry and Weems, 141–4.

24 Angela Duckworth, *Grit: The Power of Passion and Perseverance* (New York, Scribner, 2016), 250.

25 Ibid., 91–2.

26 Ibid., 74.

27 Aiken, 177.

28 Aiken, 177–8.

29 Ibid., 178.

30 Rankin, 106–7.

31 Ibid., 117–20.

32 Aiken, 188–9.

33 Ibid., 191.

34 Jim Collins. *Good to Great* (New York: Harper Business, 2001), 82.

35 Mary Lynn Pulley and Michael Wakefield, *Building Resiliency: How to Thrive in Times of Change* (Greensboro, NC: Center for Creative Leadership, 2000), 7.

36 John Gordon, *South Carolina and the American Revolution* (Columbia: The University of South Carolina Press, 2003), 142.

37 Ibid., 142.

38 Rankin, 175.

39 Ibid., 176, Aiken, 135, and Bass, 156–7.

40 Bass, 158 and Aiken, 135.

41 Peter Horry and Parson M. L. Weems, *The Life of General Francis Marion: A Celebrated Partisan Officer, in the Revolutionary War, against the British and Tories in South Carolina and Georgia* (Philadelphia, PA: J. P. Lippincott, 1854) Reprint, Winston-Salem, NC: John F. Blair, 2000, 174–6.

42 Ibid., 176.
43 Aiken, 135–6.
44 Ibid., 136–7.
45 Ibid., 75.
46 Ibid., 161.
47 Gordon, 143.

Francis Marion and Growth as a Leader

1   David Brooks, *The Road to Character* (New York: Random House, 2015), 12–13.
2   James Kouzes and Barry Posner, *The Leadership Challenge* (San Francisco, CA: Jossey-Bass, 2012), 284.
3   Scott Aiken, *The Swamp Fox: Lessons in Leadership from the Partisan Campaigns of Francis Marion* (Annapolis, MD: Naval Institute Press, 2012, 187.
4   Aiken, 188; Hugh Rankin, *Francis Marion: The Swamp Fox* (New York: Thomas Y. Crowell, 1973), 153.
5   ADRP 7-0, *Training Units and Developing Leaders* (Washington, DC: Headquarters, Department of the Army, 2012), 3–4.
6   Aiken, 188; O'Kelley, Patrick. *Unwaried Patience and Fortitude: Francis Marion's Orderly Book* (Conshohocken, PA: Infinity Publishing, 2006), 508–510; Rankin, 153.
7   Aiken, 189.
8   Bob Johansen, *Leaders Make the Future: Ten New Leadership Skills for an Uncertain World* (Oakland, CA: Berrett_Koehler Publishers, 2009), 7.
9   John Oller, *The Swamp Fox: How Francis Marion Saved the American Revolution* (New York: Da Capo Press, 2016), 226.
10 Ibid., 226.
11 Aiken, 149–50.
12 Robert Bass, *Swamp Fox: The Life and Campaigns of Francis Marion* (Columbia, SC: Sandpiper Press, 1972), 236.
13 Aiken, 150.
14 Oller, 227.
15 Bass, 236.
16 Oller, 227.
17 Aiken, 150.
18 FM 6–22, *Army Leadership* (Washington, DC: Headquarters, Department of the Army, 2006), 8–11.
19 E. Wayne Hart, *Seven Keys to Successful Mentoring* (Greensboro, NC: Center for Creative Leadership, 2009), 9.
20 Edgar Puryear, *American Generalship: Character is Everything; The Art of Command* (Novato, CA: Presidio, 2000), 188.
21 Jim Collins. *Good to Great* (New York: Harper Business, 2001), 130.

22 Rob Roy and Chris Lawson, *Navy SEAL Art of War: Leadership Lessons from the World's Most Elite Fighting Force* (New York: Crown Business, 2015), 180.

23 Oller, 217.

24 Rankin, 267.

25 Oller, 218–19.

26 Bass, 225.

27 Ibid., 226.

28 Bass, 229.

29 Rankin, 271.

30 Bass, 230.

31 Ibid., 274.

32 Gordon, 172–5.

33 Rankin, 275.

34 Ibid., 277–8.

35 Collins, 130.

36 Edgar Puryear, *Nineteen Stars: A Study in Military Character and Leadership* (Novato, CA: Presidio, 1971), 285.

37 Ibid., 285.

38 Kouzes and Posner, 201.

39 Collins, 78.

40 TC 25–20, *A Leader's Guide to After- Action Reviews* (Washington, DC: Department of the Army, 1993), 1.

41 Aiken, 114–15.

42 Ibid., 115.

43 Ibid., 115.

44 Ibid., 116.

45 Ibid., 116.

46 Peter Horry and Parson M. L. Weems, *The Life of General Francis Marion: A Celebrated Partisan Officer, in the Revolutionary War, against the British and Tories in South Carolina and Georgia* (Philadelphia, PA: J. P. Lippincott, 1854) Reprint, Winston-Salem, NC: John F. Blair, 2000, 108.

47 Oller, 73.

48 John Gordon, *South Carolina and the American Revolution* (Columbia: The University of South Carolina Press, 2003), 117.

49 Bass, 76.

50 Quoted in Kouzes and Posner, 202.

51 Nancy Evans, et al, *Student Development in College* (San Francisco, CA: Jossey-Bass, 2010), 6.

52 Fitzgerald wrote this comment in his notes for his unfinished novel, *The Last Tycoon.*

53 Harry Levinson, "A second career: The possible dream," Harvard Business Review (May 1983). Available https://hbr.org/1983/05/a-second-career-the-possible-dream.

54 Robert Chambers, *Ideas for Development* (New York: Routledge, 2005), 185.

55 Oller, 242–3.

56 Ibid., 242–3.

57 Horry and Weems, 229.

58 Oller, 31.

59 Ibid., 243.

60 William Willis Boddie, *Traditions of the Swamp Fox: William Willis Boddie's Francis Marion* (Spartanburg, SC: The Reprint Company for the Williamsburgh Historical Society, 2000), 263–4; Rankin, 291–2.

61 Rankin, 291.

Epilogue

1 James Pinkerton, "Francis Marion, The Real Patriot," September 5, 2018, https://www.theamericanconservative.com/articles/francis-marion-the-real-patriot/.

2 Anthony DeLellis, "Clarifying the Concept of Respect: Implications for Leadership," *The Journal of Leadership Studies*, no. 2 (2000): 35–49.

3 Sue Anne Pressley Montes, "Post Revolutionary Recognition," The Washington *Post*, December 16, 2006. Available https://www.washingtonpost.com/wp-dyn/content/article/2006/12/15/AR2006121502097.html.

4 John Oller, *The Swamp Fox: How Francis Marion Saved the American Revolution* (New York: Da Capo Press, 2016), 31.

5 Ibid., 20.

6 William Willis Boddie, *Traditions of the Swamp Fox: William Willis Boddie's Francis Marion* (Williamsburgh, SC: Williamsburgh Historical Society, 2000. Reprint, Spartanburg, SC: The Reprint Company, 2000), 3.

7 Oller, 4.

8 "Museum around the corner: A painting's story," Georgetown *Times*, August 20, 2020. https://www.postandcourier.com/georgetown/community/museum-around-the-corner-a-paintings-story/article_6574fb59-dfd8-54a2-be03-2e6309f17983.html.

9 Tina Jones, "Patriot Slave," *The American Legion*, (October 28, 2011). https://www.legion.org/magazine/1562/patriot-slave.

10 Amy Crawford, "The Swamp Fox," *Smithsonian Magazine* (June 30, 2007). https://www.smithsonianmag.com/history/the-swamp-fox-157330429/.

11 Oller, 245.

12 Robert Bass, *Swamp Fox: The Life and Campaigns of Francis Marion* (Columbia, SC: Sandpiper Press, 1972), 243.

13 Montes.

14 Pinkerton.

15 Alfred Neeley, "Mr. Justice Frankfurter's Iconography of Judging," *Kentucky Law Journal*, no. 2 (1993): 559.

Some Reminders of the Lowcountry Campaign

1   Steven D. Smith, Tamara S. Wilson, and James B. Legg, *The Search for Francis Marion: Archaeological Survey of 15 Camps and Battlefields Associated With Francis Marion* (Columbia: South Carolina Institute of Archaeology and Anthropology, 2008).
2   John Oller, T*he Swamp Fox: How Francis Marion Saved the American Revolution* (New York: Da Capo Press, 2016), 36–7, 239–40.
3   Smith et. al. 2008, 39–46.
4   Ibid, 31–7.
5   Steven D. Smith, *Francis Marion and the Snow's Island Community: Myth, History, and Archaeology* (Asheville, NC: United Writers Press, Inc., 2021).

Index

Accountability, 99–101

After Action Reviews (AARs), 178–81

Arbuthnot, Marriot, 28

Arnold, Benedict, 28, 31, 39, 71

Attakullakalla, Chief, 86

Augusta, Georgia, 45, 46, 50, 58, 60, 61, 66, 72, 74, 75, 142, 157

Balfour, Nesbit, 23, 30, 166

Ball, John Coming, 151, 180

Barefield, James, 100–1, 151

Biggins Bridge, 35

Black Mingo Creek, South Carolina, 64, 110, 151, 167, 179–81, 189, 199

Blackstock's Plantation, 36, 52, 65

Blue Savannah, South Carolina, 64, 100–1, 110, 151, 175, 179, 201

Boddie, William. *see* Marion, Francis; problems with reliability of early biographies of

Brewton House, 194

Bridges Campaign, 37, 199, 201

British forces, general description of, 24

Britton's Neck, South Carolina, 49, 100, 200

Buford, Abraham, 36, 60, 98

Burgoyne, John, 22, 26, 27, 39

Camden, South Carolina, 8, 9, 22, 30, 31, 33, 34, 36, 37, 38, 39, 40, 41, 45, 49, 50, 60, 61, 63–4, 68, 71, 72, 73, 74, 75, 94, 102, 120, 122, 130–2, 133, 138, 141, 143, 145, 146, 148–9, 152, 154, 157, 166, 170, 188, 194

Campbell, Archibald, 57–8

Campbell, George, 167, 173

Central position, *see* interior lines

Charismatic rhetoric, 132–5, 188

Charleston, South Carolina, 10, 15, 20, 22, 27, 30, 33, 34, 35, 37, 39, 42, 43, 46, 48, 49, 50, 51, 52, 56, 57–61, 63, 66, 71, 74, 75, 76, 77, 78, 79, 80, 81, 86, 89, 91, 98, 99, 103, 105–7, 115–16, 131, 133, 136, 140, 143, 145, 148–9, 157, 159, 161, 162, 165–6, 175, 177, 192, 193, 194, 195, 201

Cherokee Indians, fighting against, 47–8, 51–52, 86–7, 90, 115, 128, 187

Clark, Elijah, 65, 72

Clinton, Henry, 6, 26–9, 30–2, 34, 35, 37, 56, 57, 60, 61, 91, 98, 116

Coates, John, 76, 112, 197

Combat power, 3–25

Commons, 116–18

Confiscation Act, 105, 183

Continentals, role of in American army, 23

Continuity, 178–9

Cornwallis, Charles Earl, 4, 6, 20, 23, 27, 28, 29–32, 35, 36, 37, 38, 40, 42, 45, 50, 61, 63–71, 73, 79, 94, 98, 100, 102, 128, 135, 136, 146, 159, 166

Cowpens, South Carolina, 8, 30, 31, 36, 42, 45, 49, 66–7, 70, 71, 72, 78, 116, 123, 135, 159
Cruger, John, 74–5
Culminating point, 145, 147
Cunningham, William, 24, 79

D'Estaing, Henri Hector, 59
de Kalb, Johann, 43, 91
delegative leadership, 158–9
development, 181–2
disciplined initiative, 137–9, 188–9
Dog Days Campaign, 112, 197
Dorchester, South Carolina, 53, 76, 79, 91, 107, 161
Doyle, Welbore Ellis, 140, 149, 168–70
Dunham's Bluff, 117, 169, 200

Ervin, Hugh, 169
Eutaw Springs, South Carolina, 42, 48, 50, 52, 77–9, 122–4, 163, 192, 194, 198
Expectations, 125–7, 132

Fairlawn Plantation, 47, 194, 196
Fanning, David, 24
Feedback, 129, 171–3, 181, 189
Ferguson, Patrick, 65
Fires, as an element of combat power, 3, 10–14
Fishing Creek, South Carolina, 36, 52, 65, 94, 130–1
Forecasting, 173–4
Fort Dorchester, 48
Fort Granby, 45, 53, 72–4, 75
Fort Johnson, 51, 60, 91, 106–7, 188, 195
Fort Motte, 22, 45, 50, 73–4, 75, 93, 121, 143–4, 189, 194–5
Fort Moultrie, see Fort Sullivan
Fort Sullivan, 22, 29, 35, 48, 56–7, 60, 195

Fort Watson, 37, 45, 46, 50, 53, 71, 72, 73, 74, 76, 120–1, 140–2, 143, 148–9, 156–8, 170, 189, 198–9
Frame of reference, 24, 85–7, 171, 187
France, becomes allies with American colonies, 27, 57
Francis Marion Trail Commission, 193–4, 197–200
Fraser, Thomas, 51, 81, 161–2, 197
French and Indian War, see Cherokee Indians, fighting against

Gage, Thomas, 26
Ganey, Micajah, 100, 110, 151, 174–5, 179, 189
Gates, Horatio, 5, 30, 38–40, 41, 43, 49, 63–4, 66, 73, 91, 94–5, 98–9, 100, 102, 130, 131, 135–6
Georgetown, South Carolina, 44–7, 49, 50, 64, 71, 72, 73, 75, 103, 105, 118, 120, 127, 148–9, 157, 164, 165–7, 172–4, 177, 180, 189, 201
Grant, James, 47–8, 87
Great Savannah, South Carolina, 52, 64, 95, 110, 138, 179, 189
Greene, Nathanael, 7, 8, 9, 10, 16, 20, 22, 23, 28, 30–1, 34, 37, 40–3, 45, 46, 49–50, 53, 66, 68, 70–81, 92–3, 102–3, 104–5, 112–13, 116, 119–21, 122–4, 128, 140–1, 152, 159, 161, 166, 172, 173, 188
Guilford Court House, North Carolina, 8, 28, 31, 36, 42, 45, 68, 70, 78, 116, 123–4

Halfway Swamp, South Carolina, 33, 110, 133, 188, 199
Hampton, Wade, 124
Hanging Rock, South Carolina, 36, 52, 63, 166, 194
Harden, William, 77, 161, 163
Hayne, Isaac, 162, 196

Hillsborough, North Carolina, 31, 40, 66, 68, 91, 98, 130

Hobkirk's Hill, South Carolina, 8, 34, 37, 42, 72, 73

Horry, Elias, 136

Horry, Hugh, 43, 138, 180

Horry, Peter, 43–5, 46–7, 51, 90, 105, 117, 119, 129, 131, 135–6, 138–9, 149, 166–7, 172–3, 174, 176–8, 182, 188, 189, 197

Howard, John, 80, 123

Howe, William, 26, 27, 30, 32

Huck, Christian, 61, 99

Huger, Isaac, 87, 115

Human resource frame, 88, 90–2, 187

Information, as an element of combat power, 3, 6–7

Information flow, 129–30

Intelligence, as an element of combat power, 3, 9–10, 24

Interior lines, 148–9, 189

Jacksonboro, South Carolina, *see* Jacksonborough, South Carolina

Jacksonborough, South Carolina, 43, 53, 176–7, 195–6

James, John, 100, 146, 180, 199

James, William Dobein, *see* Marion, Francis; problems with reliability of early biographies of

Jomini, Antione Henri de, 148

Keithfield Plantation, 158–9

Kettle Creek, Georgia, 58

King's Mountain, South Carolina, 9, 65

Kingstree, South Carolina, 33, 154, 180, 199

Kosciuszko, Thaddeus, 74

Laurens, John, 58, 81

"law of the niche," 121–2, 124, 188

Leadership
  as an element of combat power, 3
  assessment of British, 4
  assessment of Patriot, 5–6
  definition of, 3
  as opposed to management, 147, 153
  presence, 111.
Leading by example, 163

Lee, Charles, 39–40, 56

Lee, Henry, 6, 35, 37, 45–6, 47, 50, 53, 68, 71, 74, 75, 76, 78, 79, 80, 93, 112, 119–21, 124, 140–2, 143–4, 149, 154, 167, 172–3, 188, 195, 198

Lenud's Ferry, 35, 60, 136

Leslie, Alexander, 37, 81

Liberty Trail, 194

Lincoln, Benjamin, 57, 58, 59, 60, 63, 115, 165

Loyalists, role of in British strategic thinking, 7, 27, 28, 54, 56

Lyttelton, William, 47, 86

Maham, Hezekiah, 43–4, 46–7, 51, 112, 119, 120, 141–2, 176–8, 182, 189, 196, 197, 198

"Maham's Tower," 46, 74, 120, 140–2, 143, 157

Majoribanks, John, 78–9, 124

"Management By Wandering Around," 150–1

Manigault's Ferry, South Carolina, 158–9

Marion, Francis
  acquires nickname of "Swamp Fox," 94–6
  approach to leading militiamen, 109–11, 124, 139, 153, 188–9
  as State Senator, 43, 47, 50, 80, 176, 182–3, 188, 189, 195
  assumes command of Williamsburg and Britton's Neck militias, 40, 49, 64, 91, 99, 135, 200

attitude toward Loyalists, 174–5, 183
birth and boyhood of, 43, 47, 191
charismatic rhetoric of, 132–5,
    169–70, 188
communication style of, 128–9, 188
death of, 51
delegative leadership style of, 158–9,
    189
fighting Cherokees, 47–8, 86–7, 187
marriage of, 51
Mason Locke Weems's hagiography
    of, xvi, 44, 90
physical description of, 44, 161
post-American Revolution, 51
problems with reliability of early
    biographies of, 47
promotion to brigadier general of, 49
relationship with Henry Lee, 45, 50,
    71, 119–21, 188
relationship with Nathanael Greene,
    49, 52, 66, 73, 92–4, 102–3
relationship with Thomas Sumter, 53,
    64–5, 72, 76
respect for personal and property
    rights of, 53, 77, 104–5, 183
service in the Second South Carolina
    Regiment, 43, 48, 59, 89–90, 91
stamina of, 161–3, 189
story of the sweet potato dinner and,
    164–5, 191
Tradd Street affair of, 49, 192, 194
use of intelligence, 151–2, 189
use of retreat as a tactic, 100–1,
    145–7, 189
use of Snow's Island, 49, 116–18, 168
see also locations of specific battles
    and engagements for Marion's role
    in them.
Marion, Gabriel, 86, 167, 198, 201
Marion, Oscar, 190–2
Marion–Ganey Truce, 174–5, 188
Martin, Alexander, 174

Martin, Josiah, 56
Matthews, John, 105, 174
McCottry, William, 142, 157
McDonald, Adam, 51, 177
McKay, John, 140–2, 157
McLeroth, Robert, 32–3, 133–5, 188
Mentorship, 175–6
Militia, nature of, 8, 20, 23, 90–2
Mission command, as an element of
    combat power, 3, 7–8
Mission orders, 135
Moncks Corner, South Carolina, 34, 35,
    53, 60, 76, 81, 112, 115, 127–8, 159,
    161, 193, 196, 197, 198
Moore's Creek Bridge, 56, 58
Morgan, Daniel, 23, 30–1, 36, 39, 42,
    49–50, 66–8, 70, 103, 123, 124
Motte, Rebecca, 144, 194
Moultrie, William, 47–8, 56–8, 60, 87,
    106, 107
Movement and maneuver, as an element
    of combat power, 3, 8–9
Musgrove's Mill, South Carolina, 65,
    131

Nationalism, 24–5
Nelson's Ferry, South Carolina, 23, 52,
    78, 95, 100, 131, 132, 133, 138–9,
    140, 146, 159
Ninety Six, South Carolina, 22, 34, 42,
    43, 45, 46, 50, 53, 54, 56, 61, 66,
    72, 74, 75, 79, 103, 142, 152, 157,
    166, 196

Oconostota, Chief, 86
Orangeburg, South Carolina, 53, 73,
    157
Organization
    as an element of combat power, 22–4
    types of, 155–6

Parker, Peter, 27, 29, 56, 77

Parker's Ferry, South Carolina, 50, 161–3, 196

Partisan, nature of, (*see* militia)

Patronage system, 4, 38

Perseverance, 165

Phillips, William, 28, 31–2

Pickens, Andrew, 5, 6, 34, 42, 45, 58, 67, 71, 72, 75, 78–9, 80, 87, 104, 115–16, 122

Political frame, 88, 92–4, 188

Pond Bluff, South Carolina, 48, 192, 193, 198

Port's Ferry, South Carolina, 100, 110, 117, 151, 153, 200

Postell, James, 158–9

Postell, John, 127–9, 158–9

Pragmatism, 142–3, 189

Presentism, 190, 192

Prevost, Augustin, 58

Prevost, Mark, 58–9

Principles, 103–5

Protection, as an element of combat power, 3, 21–2

Purrysburg, South Carolina, 57–8

Quinby's Bridge, 47, 76, 112–13, 121, 197

Race to the Dan Campaign, 28, 31, 36, 42, 45, 68, 70, 71

Ramsey's Mill, South Carolina, 70

Ramsour's Mill, South Carolina, 61, 68

Rawdon, Francis Lord, 30–1, 33–5, 37, 68, 71–5, 78, 135, 143, 159

Rawdon-Hastings, Francis Lord, *see* Rawdon, Francis Lord

Resiliency, 161, 168, 170, 189

Rocky Mount, South Carolina, 52, 63

Round O, South Carolina, 80, 161, 163, 196

Rugeley's Mill, South Carolina, 39–40, 63, 73

Rutledge, John, 36, 49, 50, 53, 56, 65, 76, 98, 115

Savannah, Georgia, 10, 15, 22, 42, 43, 48–9, 57, 59, 72, 76, 80, 192, 196

"second acts," 181–2

Second South Carolina Regiment, 43, 59, 89–90

Servant leadership, 108–9, 111

Shelby, Isaac, 65

Shubrick's Plantation, 50, 53, 76, 112, 197

Simms, William Gilmore, *see* Marion, Francis; problems with reliability of early biographies of

Situational awareness, 150–2, 153

Small pox, 19–20, 141

Snow's Island, 6, 37, 44, 49, 72, 88, 116–18, 120, 140, 149, 151, 168–70, 173, 174, 188, 189, 193, 200

"Song of Marion's Men," 95–6

South Carolina, geography of, 54

Southern Campaign, general description of, 54–82

Span of control, 155, 189

Stamina, 160–2

Stewart, Alexander, 78, 79, 122

Structural frame, 88–90, 91, 187

Sullivan's Island, South Carolina, 43, 52, 56, 89, 195

Sumter, Thomas, 5, 6, 8, 33, 34, 36, 42, 50, 51–3, 63, 64–5, 66, 71, 72, 73, 75, 76, 80, 92, 94, 95, 99, 104–5, 112–13, 115–16, 120–1, 130–1, 138, 140, 147, 152, 183, 197

"Sumter's Law," 53, 77, 104–5

Sustainment, as an element of combat power, 3, 14–21, 24

"Swamp Fox," story of origin of name, 94–6

Swamp Fox Murals Trail, 198–9

Symbolic frame, 88, 94–6, 188

Tactic of retreat, 100–1, 145–7, 189

Tarleton, Banastre, 30, 35–7, 42, 45, 49, 52, 60–1, 63–5, 66–8, 94–5, 98–9, 100, 103, 123, 130–1, 145–7, 152, 168

Task and purpose, 128–9

Taylor, Thomas, 53, 76, 112–13

Tearcoat Swamp, South Carolina, 64, 110, 151, 153–4, 181, 199

Thompson, Benjamin, 80, 177

Tidyman's Plantation, 51, 80, 177

Tynes, Samuel, 181

Unity of effort/unity of command, 6, 113–14, 116, 119, 121, 126, 136

Vanderhorst, John, 134

Vauban, Sebastien Le Pestre de, 21–2

Videau, Mary Esther, 51

Wadboo Plantation, 51, 81, 127–8, 170, 175, 177, 197

Wambaw Bridge, 44, 47, 51

War of the Posts, 103, 157

Washington, George, 5, 7, 9, 17, 20, 27, 28, 30, 32, 38, 39, 40, 41, 44, 45, 63, 66, 102, 182, 201

Washington, William, 67, 78–9, 123–4

Watson, John, 37, 50, 70–2, 73, 140, 148–9, 152, 164, 168, 170, 201

Waxhaws, South Carolina, 36, 60, 98, 194

Weems, Mason Locke, 44, 47, 90–1, 107–8, 164, 169–70, 180–1, 183

Wemyss, James, 110, 179

Wiboo Swamp, South Carolina, 148, 152, 199

Williamsburg, South Carolina, 91, 94, 99, 110, 135, 169, 179–80, 198–9

Wilmington, North Carolina, 15, 28, 31, 42, 70–1, 73

Winnsboro, South Carolina, 50, 65, 66

Witherspoon's Ferry, 49, 117, 131, 149, 169–70, 199

Yorktown, Virginia, 28–9, 32, 36, 42, 79, 103, 131